With *Awakening the Witchblood*, King brin[g]
important elements for Witchcraft, namely th[e]
King works from the premise that the Witchblood is an inherent powe[r]
of all humanity due to the connection we all have with the source through
the fallen angels' intervention. Yes, the fallen angels, because *Awakening
the Witchblood* also considers the angelic origin of the Witchblood. King
perceives this blood as potentially ready to be awakened through practice
and mystical experience, placing the Witch as a practitioner of an art
midway between being born and being made. From this premise, King casts
new eyes on old sources, like Gardner, Leland, Valiente, and Cochrane,
and brings in the voices of Michael Howard and Andrew Chumbley to
aid in the new light he is casting upon Witchcraft, the "spiritual practice
that works with paradox and dialects," as he writes. In this journey, King
introduces us to the people of Elphame, the Grigoris, Aradia's legacy, and
the usual suspects of Moon, Grove, and Forest as he presents rituals to
summon and for the purpose of dedication, along with charms to bind,
curse, and cause. The power of herbs and the importance of trance and
sabbatic night flight is a fine and important red thread flowing through
Awakening the Witchblood in its ultimate quest: the pursuit of self and
integrity, the Great Work itself, as it was inscribed on the Pythonic temple
of Apollo in Delphi, "Know Thyself."

—Nicholaj de Mattos Frisvold,
author of *Craft of the Untamed*

As the saying goes, "blood is thicker than water" and Nathan King
shows that it is also deeper than the soul. He beckons you on a journey
to fathom timeless mysteries and bids you (as did the Oracle at Delphi)
to know your true self. King weaves details of modern Witch history
through the loom of ancient myth and various cultures to help you find
your power and unique place as a Witch.

—Sandra Kynes, author of *Star Magic* and
Llewellyn's Complete Book of Correspondences

As generations of new occult writers arise, I've noticed that many forget
about the importance of the past: of past beliefs, past writings, and
past understandings that gave birth to the occult vision of the present.
Nathan King's book *Awakening the Witchblood* was a pleasure to read
because King is in touch with the wisdom that has gone before him and

before all of us. The book puts King's own insights on display and shares many critical points of praxis, but most importantly, it takes the reader on a well-informed journey through the foundations of Witchcraft and magic—foundations that are critical to any true understanding. I felt that I was reading King's tribute to his own practice, but also a worthy tribute to the history that created him and so many others.

—Robin Artisson, author of *The Clovenstone Workings: A Manual of Early Modern Witchcraft*

An inspiring, authentic, unique, and invaluable book from a true master of the craft. *Awakening the Witchblood* is the perfect acquisition for each practitioner of magic and sorcery seeking to dive deeper into the traditional and majestic art of the Witch. Nathan King teaches with love and a profound dedication to making the reader understand the valuable information they have in their hands: traditions, practice, and magic from the hands of the most devout master of modern sorcery. *Awakening the Witchblood* will rapidly turn into one of the most important and well-thumbed books on the shelves of every Witch.

—Elhoim Leafar, author of *Dream Witchery*

There is Witchlore that few dare to talk about. Nathan King awakens the blood of the Witch so that we may transcend the spiritual and mythic realms to reconnect to our magic. In *Awakening the Witchblood,* we are taught the secrets of old-world witchery that will rekindle the hearthfires of the Witch and ignite our spirits once again.

—Chris Allaun, author of *The Black Book of Johnathan Knotbristle*

AWAKENING
THE
WITCHBLOOD

EMBODYING THE ARTE MAGICAL

ABOUT THE AUTHOR

Nathan King is a Michigan based Witch, Occultist, psychic and High Priest (Minos) of the Minoan Brotherhood Tradition. He spent a good deal of his magical life being trained in historic Salem, Massachusetts. He has been featured on SYFY and Travel Channel during his time in witch-city, and has worked with several shops and events within his field. Nathan is also a practitioner of Folkloric Witchcraft and carries a deep passion for spiritual contact and pagan spirituality as a living art form. Nathan is an active ritualist and workshop lecturer at several events throughout the Midwest as well as being a theater enthusiast and animal lover.

For more information about Nathan and his other magical work, visit his website at witch-path-readings.square.site.

NATHAN KING
AWAKENING
THE
WITCHBLOOD

EMBODYING THE ARTE MAGICAL

Chicago, Illinois

ISBN: 978-1-959883-22-7
Library of Congress Control Number on file.

Disclaimer: Crossed Crow Books, LLC does not participate in, endorse, or have any authority or responsibility concerning private business transactions between our authors and the public. Any internet references contained in this work were found to be valid during the time of publication, however, the publisher cannot guarantee that a specific reference will continue to be maintained. This book's material is not intended to diagnose, treat, cure, or prevent any disease, disorder, ailment, or any physical or psychological condition. The author, publisher, and its associates shall not be held liable for the reader's choices when approaching this book's material. The views and opinions expressed within this book are those of the author alone and do not necessarily reflect the views and opinions of the publisher.

Cover design by Wycke Malliway.

Published by:
Crossed Crow Books, LLC
6934 N Glenwood Ave, Suite C
Chicago, IL 60626
www.crossedcrowbooks.com

Printed in the United States of America.
IBI

CONTENTS

PART ONE

CHAPTER ONE
KNOWING OUR TRUTH; KNOW THYSELF • 5

CHAPTER TWO
DEFINING THE BLOOD • 15

CHAPTER THREE
SKULL AND BLOOD: ANCESTORS • 28

CHAPTER EIGHT
LUCIFER: THE BRINGER OF LIGHT • 98

PART TWO

CHAPTER NINE
RITUALS AND SPELLS OF THE WITCHBLOOD • 115

CHAPTER TEN
PREPARATIONS OF THE ARTE • 119

CHAPTER ELEVEN
INSTRUMENTS OF THE ARTE,
TOOLS OF THE TRADE • 134

INTRODUCTION

From vein to vein and cell to cell, power is stirring within you. This book has been a long time in the making. It started in a beaten-up notebook with a big pentacle printed on the cover and then turned into years of research, practice, and reflection. A fellow Witch, author, and brother of the Craft gave me a piece of advice that was the seed of inspiration for this work. His words were simple and infused with wisdom: "An author writes a book when they have something specific to say."

I find the most joy in being able to share and teach. I'm a firm believer that when you find the right people, there is a powerful connection to the unnamed path. It is a power that is shared and gained. I had been working and studying the myths and legends concerning the Witchblood for about five years before the Malliway brothers found me. There were too many connections or synchronicities for me not to be compelled to finally sit down, organize my research, and write. This work is an offering to the spirits of my covens, my hearth, and my traditions of Witchcraft. It is an offering to my Gods, my ancestors, and my priesthood.

As my first published work, I am thrilled to present this book. My wish for you, my dear reader, is that it will give you some answers and inspiration as you awaken the Witch within!

This book would not have been possible without the love and support of all these amazing people. I give you all my deepest gratitude! Rev. Jonathan Navi Sousa, Bennet Little, Thorn Mooney, Jason Mankey, Ivo Dominguez Jr., Blake Malliway, Wycke Malliway, Becca Fleming, Lee Anderson, Francesca Vitali, and Jack Chanek. To all my friends and family in Salem, MA, the members of *Eldridge Coven, Twa Corbies,* and *Temenos Thea Nychta!* You are all my most beloved of our Witchblood family. May the Gods preserve the Craft!

PART ONE

CHAPTER ONE

KNOWING OUR TRUTH; KNOW THYSELF

Imagine yourself under a canopy of stars, taking in the expansive pulse of the night sky. You're able to get a sense of the celestial reflections upon the Earth while feeling your place in the vastness of the universe. You may feel small, or you may feel completely elated, but either way, you pause. In this pause, we realize not only our place within the cosmos but just how much out there is unknown, how much is of the other. This is when we get our first brush with what Witches may call the "otherworld" of spirits, mystery, and magic. Now imagine yourself at the beginning of time, when humankind was just starting, at the very beginning of a great leap forward. You see a woman looking up at that same vast expanse. She is looking at the same Moon, and the same stars, and she is even thinking the same question that presented itself to you: simply "who am I?" It is in this question that the doors to wonder are opened.

It is our instinct to question everything around us. Starting in childhood, humans want to have the stability of certainty. However, we live in a world ruled by nature, and nature is anything but certain. The only certainty is change and the constant reassessment of how these changes sculpt our personal experiences. When we are reminded of the other, the uncertain, we are reminded of the powers of magic. Magic is the power and the mystery of change. It is in that reflective pause that nature and life around us can hold us at the circle's edge and grant us a challenge: to know the self.

By knowing the self and all its complications, you may know the outside world a little bit better. We are not as different from each other as we may think. This interconnectedness of all things, or the belief in a universal collective consciousness, is one of the Witch's most commonly held beliefs. You are here because you, like all creation, act as a living embodiment of the unfathomable, constantly creative, and destructive universe. There is unity and division brought on by the power of knowing the self, for creation and destruction are two sides to the same coin. One cannot exist without the other, just like we cannot live without the Sun and the Moon, life and death, and knowing and unknowing.

As you may have already noticed, Witchcraft is a spiritual practice that works with paradoxes and dialects. We work with *Mysteries* with a capital "M." These are the bigger questions asked of the human experience. Mysteries are hidden secrets of the universe yet to be unveiled, the bigger questions of life, death, and rebirth. The simple question "Who am I?" is the Mystery that brought me to the path of Witch-hood, along with the desire to know myself and what nature had embedded in me. For what is more human than the desire to know the self in all its complications? I'm reminded of the biblical creation myth where, through the natural impulse to know oneself, Eve bit into the forbidden fruit. She was offered consciousness through the Mother, the feminine principle of creation in biblical myth. To know the self is to know our deeper purpose, what we may call *the Great Work*.[1] These are questions we rationally will never be able to communicate fully because Mysteries are only granted by experience—and the understanding we may gain from the experience—if we are willing to reflect and walk between the worlds. This is a principle called *gnosis*.[2]

The most intense experiences are the ones that have shaped us to react and change when the environment around us shifts. All environments possess a *spirit of place*, and Witches tend to have a keen sense of intuition

---

1   "The Great Work" is a phrase used commonly in occult and magical spaces, popularized during the Victorian Age's occult resurgence and revival. It is believed to have been popularized with the works of Aleister Crowley's Order of Thelema but is also found in many Lodges and Orders of ceremonial magicians. This comes from the Latin phrase *magnum opus*, used in Hermetic philosophy since ancient times as a way of expressing the practitioner's Divinely influenced or true Will, plugging the individual into their purpose of this lifetime.

2   *Gnosis* comes from the Greek word meaning "knowledge." This refers to *personal knowledge*, or the inherently divine knowledge one attains through their own spiritual connection and experience.

when it comes to the environments and spirits surrounding betwixt and between them, for Witches exist in the liminal spaces. As wisdom keepers and seekers alike, we walk that fine line between what is truth and what is interpretation, yet we can accept both as perfectly valid interpretations and experiences. As Witches, we often weave stories to gain an understanding of ourselves as individuals. Artists, Witches, and storytellers have a unique aptitude for discovering the Mysteries of the Earth and the universes that exist beyond the self. This skill set of meaning-making and expressing an inner truth is so important to the magic that occurs in any ceremony. Although this willingness to experience the sacred can be vulnerable, it is an invaluable key to the Craft of the Wise. It is only through our heartfelt experiences that the potential for a magical Mystery can grant us access to the truth within. So, we come to the phrase "know thyself."

Humanity is always seeking truth. However, this begs the question of what truth really is and how we begin to seek it. For Witches, truth is the highest form of Mystery. It is the non-mutually exclusive acceptance of opposing ideas and experiences: reality and actuality; ego, nonego, and superego; and all of the ideas and experiences that exist in the gray areas between these concepts. Imagine looking out the window and seeing a tree. The reality you are experiencing is a tree outside your window but, in actuality, that tree has roots in the dirt traveling deep down and across the Earth's interior. These roots give the tree nutrients and life it needs to stand strong and tall. The reality of the tree includes the network of roots and mycelium not seen with the naked eye.

Simply put, reality is relative. This is where we may run into problems with our intellect or ego getting in the way of mystical experiences. If we rely only on what we can see, we miss the actualities of truth. Just because someone may not see something in the fullness of its existence does not mean it's not real. Encountering this is usually a shock. Sometimes it destroys the previous truth, and that feeling can be shattering. There must always be some form of destruction of what was to create the way for what is of our highest ideals and in line with our truth.

This idea of knowledge as a destructive force to make way for the higher good is best represented in The Tower card of the tarot. This card will often come up in a reading during times of instability for the querent, speaking to themes of lacking a foundation or losing control. This sense of falling from grace is most commonly brought on by the querent's own ego or hubris. However, there remains the possibility for personal renewal if the warning to stay humble and keep learning is taken. In the ancient world, hubris was acknowledged and performed as one of the central themes of classical Greek tragedies, with the theater originating in the cults of Dionysus.[3] Hubris can act as a catalyst for self-discovery into the Mysteries when it makes us question ourselves with self-compassion. This is part of the core process of *shadow work,* a practice of self-reflection that several Witches set aside as a holistic part of their practice. It can be uncomfortable when this questioning is brought on by our encounters with spirits and the unseen forces we have a working relationship with. For the hidden truths to be revealed, we need to walk that long and crooked path of Witchcraft, unsure where its turns and thorns may be.

Witches have always doubled as mystics by utilizing the large array of practices the Craft has for self-discovery, spirit contact, and the pursuit of understanding the world on both mundane and metaphysical levels. The struggle with these life-altering questions and perceptions is what fires up the forge within us. This force tempers and hits iron, turning it into the double-edged blade of personal truth. As the struggle of hubris and knowledge of self can cut, it still impacts our wisdom. The sword is our new sense of self that holds our highest ideals, experiences, and the virtues we take away from the fires of mystical experience. These spiritual contacts and methods of altering energy allow for the forging of new reality-altering experiences and a sense of gained control, intel, and connection to seeking the highest form of truth. There is a mystical experience in just seeking to engage in a lifestyle of magic itself.

Truth is very much related to the Witch's conceptualization of fate, or rather *The Fates* or the *Wyrd.* Fate is not just an embodiment of Ultimate Truth but is specifically viewed classically as a triple-formed or triple-faced aspect of the one and the many Great Goddess.[4] She is of the source, the Moon, the mythical void from which all light bursts

---

3   Per the dramatic and spiritual origins taking place at the festivals of Dionysus or *Dionysia,* featuring notable playwrights such as Euripides and Sophocles.

4   Not to be confused with the common philosophy of the Triple Goddess as a Maiden, Mother, and Crone. This idea is a modern invention of the folklorist Robert Graves and his work of *The White Goddess.* While it is a highly influential text and a wonderful work of inspired vision and folklore, this book should not be relied on for historical accuracy. Most Goddess forms traditionally do not fit this mold, despite the common belief.

forth in the darkness, and the creator of the universe. Her three faces are seen in the waxing, waning, and full moons. As a Mistress of Time and the daughter(s) of the night, she represents the fabric of all that was, is, and will be. The Greeks conceptualized her as the *Moirai,* each face of her making up a covenant of the Alpha and Omega that weave with us.

It must be remembered that we all make our fate; the choice is always our own. The Fates weave the threads that, by our words and actions, provide those strands of our *Moira.* This gives us a deeper symbolic connection to the astral cord or Witch's cord, as seen in several Witchcraft traditions and explored further in Chapter Eleven. The Goddess is the effect of all our causes, for she was there when the fabric of life was woven, and when, if ever, that tapestry of existence is ever finished, she will still be ever-present.

As a Witch, it is my firmly held belief that we work with Wyrd and she works *with* us, not against us. She simply gives us what we give her in this lifetime, as she knows the deepest Mysteries of not just our individual souls, but of the collective consciousness. Here lies another principle of magic: cause and effect. This goes for what is within the self and what actions will change the delicate interconnectedness of life. All that is taken must be given, and all that is given must also be taken. This is not karma or the law of three, but simply personal accountability. Sometimes the ripple catches up with us and sometimes it doesn't. If every Witch really got back what they sent out three times back, there probably wouldn't be many Witches left.

There is an ultimate power in self-awareness and the knowledge of our personhood. This sense of self-awareness and control is also our personal sovereignty as beings that are both human and Divine. We are sovereign in our decisions and interactions in our own magical circles, taking authority in our autonomy and our gnosis. This is not sovereignty over a land mass or power for power's sake, but over the land of our physical bodies and the skies of our breath. However, self-knowledge is nothing new. Self-knowledge will always remain a process to pay attention to and strive toward.

The phrase "know thyself" goes back to ancient Greek and Roman times. It is famously recorded as one of the many maxims utilized by the cults of Apollo, inscribed above the temple of Apollo in Delphi and the chambers of the Oracle of Delphi. It was made famous by the writings of such Greek philosophers as Socrates and Pausanias, as well as in Aeschylus's story of

Prometheus. It was then popularized again in the seventeenth century by the famed French philosopher Rene Descartes. These philosophers commented on the recorded antiquity of this phrase or echoed the same wisdom of self-knowledge as key to the pursuit of a sacred life. The phrase as a well-circulated maxim existed in Greece between 300–400 BCE but may bear even older origins.[5] Its legacy has carried throughout the Western world with much thanks to the Age of Enlightenment and rationalistic philosophy. The soul's search for self has never vanished and some very powerful words of wisdom have survived alongside it.

It is speculated that the phrase "know thyself" came from the Seven Sages of the priesthood of Apollo but its legendary origins are much more prophetic in essence.[6] There is a famous myth of Apollo splaying a great python at Delphi, so a temple was erected there in his honor. Legend holds that the name of Apollo's oracle or seer was "Pythia," relating to the same myth. "Know thyself" was spoken by the voice of Apollo himself through his High Priestess, whose job as an oracle was to ensure her trance could summon the God through her body as the physical medium. This utterance of Pythia has clearly made its way through the human consciousness. Credit to the Gods where credit may certainly be due.

Aristotle puts the phrase into a deeper context of personal self-knowledge, including ideas of knowing one's measure or limits, knowing what specific questions to ask the Pythoness, and having awareness of the things we do not know. As Aristotle said, "Knowing yourself is the beginning of all wisdom."[7] This rings especially true for Witches, for the word *Witch* originates from the Anglo-Saxon words *wicce* and *wicca*, both of which mean "wise person."

The pursuit of wisdom is, similarly, the pursuit of truth. It is in wisdom we can heal, counsel, and bear witness to the external changes once the internal foundation of awareness is cultivated by the practitioner. However, like the Craft, wisdom is an experiential process—an extremely delicate

5   Best, Kenneth and Mitchell S. Green. "Know Thyself: The Philosophy of Self-Knowledge." *UConn Today*, 7 Aug. 2018. today.uconn.edu/2018/08/know-thyself-philosophy-self-knowledge

6   Bates, Douglas C. "The Forgotten Delphic Maxim." *Medium*, 24 Mar. 2021. pyrrhonism.medium.com/the-forgotten-delphic-maxim-e4fb640cc4e5.

7   Aristotle and H. Rackham. *The Nicomachean Ethics*. Harvard University Press, 2003.

process where, through surrender and suffering, we find the sparks of wisdom. A friend once told me that to ask for wisdom is to ask for trouble, and in my experience, I hold this quote in kinship. As the old saying goes, "We must suffer to learn." It is the dramatic and tragic experiences that tend to stay with us. The memory of the sting acts as a warning so we don't repeat that same trouble. Wisdom comes with age and Witches have always held our elders and teachers in the highest regard, despite their flaws and failings. The age of wisdom is truly one of experience itself. Like any craft, some people are more naturally skilled while others take time to learn and cultivate their skills. Witches are not only born but also Witches are made.

Witches build upon prior experiences, reshaping and revisiting the basics, for that is where we truly begin and where we find ourselves to advance further, coming full circle. Advanced Witchcraft is in the deeper connection and personal gnosis of what we see, hear, and feel through all the senses; it is in the act of engaging with the basics in pursuit of absorbing them. The power in wisdom is not just for the betterment of ourselves but for the betterment of the world we live in. Once we start to do good for ourselves, we can do that much more for others; we can stand up for our ethics and principles as sovereigns, and the people around us are affected that much better.

Witches have always been creatures of influence depending on where that power has been directed. Part of magic is not only in the ability to create, but also to co-create a universe that is healthier and in the image we would want to see it. We work alongside the Gods and spirits, and they act in important, reciprocal personal relationships. They are our partners rather than those we bow to, although some still pray to and venerate these spirits as one of the many paths to building these relationships with the otherworld. Truly being on equal footing with the otherworld is an important facet of the Witch's worldview because that world directly overlaps with ours on another plane or experience of existence. Many refer to this building of spiritual relationships as maintaining a "right relationship." Being in a right relationship means honoring and following through with that awareness of ourselves, the land we live on, and the spiritual forces always surrounding us. If we ignore these internal signs or run from these callings, we no longer live in line with our truth, and then there is no longer a right relationship.

In Witchcraft, this awareness starts in the physical body, in what we feel and know in the currents of our blood. It is the blood that allows us to have a heart that beats and a mind that thinks. Witchcraft, unlike many mainstream religious or spiritual practices, is not an external practice of seeking or honoring the Divine. Witches know how to turn the mind internally and seek within. We honor and work the physical body because that is the plane of existence we are on. Earth is a physical embodiment of not just the Divine but of all power, as we will come to understand it. Witchcraft is entirely of the physical body because we are spiritual beings having the human experience. The human experience is visceral and embodied, and as beings inherently connected to the universe, we are embodied for a reason.

When we experience an emotion, we recognize it by the physical sensations that follow. When we are cut, we feel pain; when we are happy, we jump for joy on the dance floor; when we are depressed, we are exhausted and can barely move. All emotions and spiritual sensations are one of embodiment because we are vessels of not just the Gods, but of raw power. The untapped potential of the Witch lives in every cell of the human spirit. This power can be anything depending on how we use it and, most importantly, where we direct it. Magic is a process. When it is stirred up and given a "charge" or a direction, we feel this immediate release. For many, this is a very physical feeling, and I'm yet to meet a Witch who doesn't have this instinctual and indescribable feeling. Though sensitive people see or hear the psychic information that comes through, we all *feel* it through the senses.

The popular Occult phrase "as above, so below" became popularized by Éliphas Lévi.[8] This Hermetic law can also be phrased as "so within, is so without." This phrase alone—and both in tandem—lends our language to a reminder of the physical work we do as Witches and the internal process that must first take place. We all house a collection of spirits, Gods, and ancestors, and within the self is the spiritual temple of the Aeon where all those beings live. Working within the internal soul is where we feed not just spirits but, more importantly, the self.

Witchcraft holds a Mystery: Witches are the emanations and descendants of Divine beings that came to Earth. We will explore many of these myths, but they start in the self. The self is of the Gods and is made up of the same stars, dust, and clays of primordial creation. We must remember

---

8   Strube, Julian. "The 'Baphomet' of Eliphas Lévi: Its Meaning and Historical Context," *Correspondences*, vol. 4 2017, pp. 37–79.

to honor the self first and foremost. If we are unstable, our magic will be unstable. We are the foundations of manifestation, and it is only through the self's choice that magic is made manifest. We are not separate from what we hold within as divine vessels, but the journey of seeking within is the true power of the Witch as I've come to know it. Power is not just in self-knowledge, which will never be fully attained, but in the ability to experience the totality of what it means to be a human being.

The Gods experience humanity through and within us, for that is where they always have been. This is one way in which the Old Ones have never truly disappeared; they speak through us and see with our eyes when we embody Divinity. They have continued to inspire us as the catalysts of change. We are the instruments of their wishes and will upon the Earth because we are of the physical realm. We must know these things internally to execute them physically. For we are of the Gods, and the Gods are of us, as is the same for our ancestors, spirits, and any shade of the night. Returning to the Mystery of interconnectedness upon the loom of the Wyrd, she watches, weaves, listens, and waits for us to answer her call. This call is to make love, to celebrate life to its fullness, and to enjoy the ride of the wheel that continues to turn. It is to experience all there is to the human or "Fool's Journey." The wheel is many things, represented by the Wheel of Fortune in the tarot, the Wheel of the Year as we celebrate the sabbats, and the wheel of the zodiac in which we all have a sign we were born under.

Witches are the agents of change and the vessels that hold the Gods and spirits, and we have seen this change happen already. For example, Witchcraft was illegal in England until the year 1951,[9] and immediately following, Gerald Gardner publicly announced himself as a Witch and granted to the world a structure of practice we recognize today as modern Initiatory Wica.[10] Now, we have the means and the representation to live and thrive in most Westernized countries. We can trace a lot of

---

9   Valiente, Doreen. *The Rebirth of Witchcraft*. Robert Hale, 1989. See also *The Fraudulent Mediums Act 1951 (14 & 15 Geo. 6. c. 33)*.

10   Please note: *Wica* is a traditional initiatory tradition, not to be confused with *Wicca*, a broader form of Craft that is extremely different from the "ins" of Initiatory Wica after training and initiation. Common conceptions of Wicca (especially in the Witchcraft craze of the 90s) are not what I would consider Initiatory Wica, therefore, the spelling I use will reflect these distinctions.

our modern praxis from Gerald Gardner and his predecessors, but he's worth crediting as the catalyst of change to today's Pagan and Witchcraft practices. He is among many other Occultists who started the wave of change including, but not limited to, figures like Aleister Crowley, Doreen Valiente, and Cecil Williamson, along with anthropologists and folklorists such as Margaret Murray, Robert Graves, and Sir James Frazer. They were all like us: folks fascinated with the other, the world of spirits, and the hidden magic that was waiting for a movement.[11]

Magic works on the path of least resistance. Those able to simply answer the practice's call are the ones who embody the Old Ones. We are one of the fastest-growing religions and spiritualities today, and this sense of empowerment is a major draw. Power is not a dirty word but rather a means of change and freedom of expression. It's all in how we use it. Just like we use our muscles and our mind, this is a natural power (or even a supernatural power, because nature is super)!

The image of the Witch has changed throughout history, but the image of the Witch in union with an unseen force continues to evoke the memory of our Pagan ancestors. Witches have something about them that has always been appealing. The Witch evokes the sleeping God within all people, waiting and ready to awaken, still conjuring the feelings of empowerment that come with being in contact with the unseen and having control over one's life. For most, we have come a long way from the horrors of the Witch trials, but we still have more changes to make and more work to do. Magic evolves us and evolves the world as we desire to shape it. This evolution and healing occurs as a community, as individuals, covens, and as a worldwide network of wisdom keepers and magic makers, but this transformation starts within the self. It starts with the Witchblood.

---

11 For a more complete and cohesive history of Modern Witchcraft as it came into its current incarnation, I highly recommend *Triumph of the Moon* by Ronald Hutton.

CHAPTER TWO

DEFINING THE BLOOD

Witches are not just users of magic; we are a physical embodiment, reflection, and power of it. Have you ever felt different from the rest of the world? How many times have you been called "weird"? Did you feel like the black sheep (or goat) of your family? For many, there is an internal sensation of rocking, a restlessness as if the soul may leap out of the body. If you have experienced the impulse to cast a spell or send an evil eye towards a jerk, you've likely felt your blood *quicken*. This sensation is the Witchblood inside of you. We cannot deny that some people run from their intuition and assimilate into the rest of the world, mostly living unconsciously. Witches are set apart from the world because their magic and the expression of their craft come from their experiences on the fringes. The way many of us feel like outsiders may be described as *otherworldly*, and often, using my mother's euphemism for "psychic," *intuitive*.

Experiences with the supernatural can connect us to a lineage or a current of praxis that has existed long before our existence as individuals. Blood can be changed by mystical or initiatory experiences, especially when the practitioner uses the varied traditional rites of Witchcraft. This blood, now transformed by the nature of the rites, is then adopted into a wider cosmology of magical forces and family of fellow practitioners. Going past the idea of *who initiated who* in various Witchcraft traditions, several Mysteries of the Craft go back to an origin story. These creation stories are varied, including different mythos, symbols, or timelines to the point that some are nearly unrecognizable to each other, yet share a common theme. They connect us to the idea of spiritual intelligences who came to Earth and formed an intimate bond with humanity, passing on, both literally and figuratively, a covenant of raw Witch-fire or pure power.

The legends are of those numerous Gods and angels that passed on the divine light of the source that transformed us from primates to humanity. Some traditional sayings related to this idea of inheriting a lineage are termed as the "fire in the clay" or "breath of the old." Both sayings illustrate the spark of life from whence all things came and to where all things return: "from womb to tomb." Transformed by these interactions of profound spiritual experience, a Witch is born, a Witch is made, and the Witch lives today.

Witchblood is the blood that has been awakened or transformed by the active will of having spiritual and physical engagement with the powers of the otherworld. On a broader scale, Witchblood is what holds the magical memory of all humanity once the practice is learned, developed, and consistently engaged in some way to the practice of the Craft. These are the powers of psychic contact, sorcery, and interconnection with the source of creation. It is the blood that runs through the body of every Witch, granting them with a consciousness and a spiritual language.[12]

However, nobody wakes up one day and is suddenly a Witch. "Witch" is the title of a practitioner who engages with the Craft. Witchcraft itself is many things, but in its very name, it is an art form, a Craft, *the Arte Magickal.* Witchcraft is truly based on orthopraxy, not orthodoxy. What you *do* bestows the title of Witch upon you, acknowledged by the people or powers that are.

The Witch's Craft is many things and varies across time and cultures. It is my view that Witchcraft consists of practices derived from a multi-collection of Occult knowledge and techniques, historically and today. It involves relationships with spirits, ancestors, deities, divination, and psychic ability. Another key feature is the possession of secret knowledge and the knowledge of the landscape and the various beings that are within the land. This can be called *animism,* as the Witch is well acquainted with the personalities and varied qualities of the natural world. This includes the Green World (understanding the use of plants, trees, herbs), stones, animals, and cosmic or planetary forces.

---

12 This language of humanity is of *symbolism,* the same universal language that spirits speak. Symbolism is the profound manifestation of humanity and magic working together.

Witchcraft may also be attributed to phenomena such as mentally projecting one's spirit outward in dream or trance, conjuring and creating spells or spirits instructed with specific tasks to have specific outcomes in the Witch's favor. Most practitioners facing the bravery of magic dedicate their practice to helping others in their community and themselves. Magical abilities can be used for good or for ill, and often exist alongside businesses for monetary gain or monastic priesthoods. To this day, there is no definitive historical definition of the Craft, no one unique set of practices, or even an original practice all forms of the Craft can be traced to. However, spirit working and hidden knowledge are consistently seen across today's numerous Witchcraft practices. It is a Witch's power to actively engage in these types of skills and communications, often acting as a liminal walker between the spiritual and mundane world as the intermediary for healing, sorcery, and protection.

For Witches, the emphasis is placed on the "awakening" of the blood rather than the blood itself, as the awakening is a real psychological process of change that we go through. It is the change that occurs when an individual goes through a formal initiation, altering their life course. Awakening is a journey of processing, recording, and tapping into the spiritual frequency of the Craft, just as emotional and mental as it is spiritual. The blood having close contact with these powers or frequencies is said to transform, or, rather, awaken the spiritual bloodline of humanity with its pre-existing connection to the powers, Divinity, and hidden company of spirits. Blood is a universally honored fluid of life and death. Its essence contains the wisdom of those before and the potential of those descendants yet to come. In antiquity, blood was often connected with the imagery of sacrifice and, in Christianity, redemption. Blood was a representative of Divinity within the cults of Zagreus or Dionysus, as his blood was the juice of the grape fermented into the bounty of wine and thus, to the practitioner, a drink of the nectar of the Gods.[13] This wine made sacred helps alter the mind into a state of Divine ecstasy and epiphany of enlightenment, change, or oneness with the Gods. We can look at the blood as something symbolic or physical because magic works both ways, indeed.

---

13   Perry, Laura. *Labrys & Horns: An Introduction to Modern Minoan Paganism.* Potnia Press, 2020. See also Rosemarie Taylor-Perry. *The God Who Comes Dionysian Mysteries Revisited.* Algora Pub, 2003

Awakening is a transformation and, therefore, a lifelong process of both being *and* becoming one's true self, the self in totality as a spiritually alive human being. In awakening, something touches the Mysteries of love, life, death, and rebirth. The body becomes an instrument of power to continue creation and destruction in partnership with all that is within the self. The realization that magic and the call to love are the same is often a shared experience among those who have claimed their right as Witches. Awakening can take the form of initiation into a specific tradition, group, or family. In my opinion, this is the most reliable access point, but certainly not the only one. Any dedication to a set of established practices—and a consistent engagement in working with the Witch's worldviews—is just as valid. The Witch only initiates to allow the Gods to work through them, for it is these powers themselves that initiate. In this way, initiation is as much a physical rite as it is an act of declaration, introduction, and awakening of the Witch soul within. This exists on an interpersonal level and is not for the outsider to judge or discriminate against what makes a Witch. If the initiation of oneself or into a group truly takes hold, the practitioner and the world around them will likely respond the same to the change after the fact, as it will be evident to all that something has changed within the individual.

There is a large and often blended body of Witch-lore.[14] There are legends of fallen or lost civilizations and realms where otherworldly beings came from. According to these legends, they came into contact with humanity in the earliest days of advancement in skills and hunting. As strange as it may seem, this myth is found almost universally. There are numerous exchanges across cultures of angelic beings, fallen ones, and faery folk, beings that I describe as "spiritual intelligences." These powers of the otherworld were passed on by the intimate connection between spirit and huu, incarnating the process of initiation and transcendental experience with the spiritual world physically in the passing of the Mysteries. Traditionally, the lore of these exchanges has been a part of the origin story of a Witch's practice. These stories naturally have evolved over centuries of cultural exchange and time. However, the stories remain made up of the original wrappings of the time they were developed in. Here, we can start to peel back the layers to seek the hidden

---

14 Term borrowed from *Mastering Witchcraft: A Practical Guide for Witches, Warlocks, and Covens* by Paul Huson._

truths behind these beings, for all stories examined in this book have to be carefully considered. Teaching through the devices of narrative and symbolism has been used since the beginning of language to describe the indescribable. It is clear from these universally found stories that there is an inherent wisdom waiting to be unveiled. Just like we have evolved, so have our teaching mechanisms and allegorical traditions. Our understanding will always be shaped by the diversity of the exchange in storytelling and myth.

OF THE BLOOD

Some people are born more sensitive than others. As children develop skill sets, some skills come more naturally while other talents need more time to be developed. Some people have a proclivity toward creating visual art, while others are great at mathematics. We all have strengths and weaknesses, and it would be impossible to find someone who naturally possesses the knack for every skill. In this way, a psychic cannot be fully developed in all areas of psychic ability. For example, clairvoyance, mediumship, and scrying may be one developed psychic's set of gifts, while claircognizance and psychometry are not. This doesn't mean they can't all be developed; it just means we have certain levels of prowess in different areas.

Some skills, however, can be fostered. The same is true for a proclivity toward Witchcraft. Just like any craft, this is something that can be hard to develop in someone who naturally doesn't have a calling for it, as having a calling to the path of Witchdom is crucial to the Witch's journey. A *calling* is specifically any personal interest in the other world that offers a spark and foundation for the wandering Witch. Often, the Occult acts as a bridge to other forms of art and self-expression. Witchcraft truly is the craft of all crafts, as all acts of magic consist of a diverse set of art forms and trades along with the act of honoring the self and the sacred.

All humans descend from one Great Mother, known in science as "Mitochondrial Eve."[15] In our development as a species, *Homo sapiens* developed some crucial, othering traits. We developed language: the power of the word and the capacity to conceptualize and relay information

---

15 Rice University. "Mitochondrial Eve: Mother of all humans lived 200,000 years ago." *ScienceDaily*, 17 Aug. 2010. sciencedaily.com/releases/2010/08/100817122405.htm

faster through words and symbolism. It may feel quite basic for us in the twenty-first century, but it is very magical to bring the formless into form. One of the Witch's main jobs as a spirit worker is to use icons and symbols to bring the astral into the material world and, thus, into ourselves. Mitochondrial Eve may have been the first woman of magic. Beyond language, hunting, building, and toolmaking were also great evolutionary advancements for humanity, occurring due to our ancestors' mastering of fire and metals, which is vastly important to Witch-lore, deities, and more.[16]

It is easy to forget that we are animals just as much as we are humans, but it is this great leap in consciousness that allowed us to survive as humanity. This enchantment of growth, to me, is a force of magic. Like alchemists creating the substance of gold, there is a mystical link and correspondence to the development of the modern human condition. The gold still being refined, in this instance, is the human consciousness.

Blood is our life source. It fuels the brain and gives the nutrients and oxygen it needs so we can have thoughts and behaviors. Blood has always been considered sacred. It needs to be explicitly stated, however, that there is no such thing as a genetically "pure" or "complete" bloodline. It just doesn't exist. This is especially worth mentioning due to the recent rise in white supremacy and the horrific nature of some to exclude, hate, and spread nationalistic ideologies. It even festers in our Pagan communities with such groups misusing the symbols and folklore of the Northern mythos. They are simply hiding behind false beliefs, false history, and racial prejudice.

This idea of reclaiming false history in the name of purity and sacredness is anything but sacred. Nobody is superior to another in the circle of life—it's a circle, after all. Because of generations of breeding with one another, any genetic link with the original Witches of old and any deity or spirit has been spread throughout all humankind. It is our birthright to not only celebrate this but also to share and to take joy in the revelry of it. This idea of superiority, whether magical or biological, is absolute nonsense, especially when it excludes and suppresses the natural gift of all humanity, nor does your heritage immediately make you a natural authority figure or leader.

---

16 Tubal-Cain and Brigid, to name a few. The magical correspondence of blacksmiths and craftspeople are the surrogates of divine inspiration (*Awen* in Welsh) in what is created and brought into physical or verbal manifestations, including poetry and inspired speech.

Once awoken, we are all of the Witchblood. We all bear the quiet embers of the Witch-fire that, once something deeply affecting happens, allows us to come into our own blood, vocation, and power. We find our way to the World Tree and join our chosen family of Witches. We, who eternally dance around the Sabbatic fires of Witch-hood, as children of the Sun, Moon, and stars, bear the titles of a priesthood of Witchcraft workers. Within dream, trance, and ritual, we go to this liminal working space of the eternal flame that brings us into all the elements of the Arcane.

HEREDITARY WITCHCRAFT

If the gifts of the Witch are inherently in everyone, what does this say about those who claim immediate Witch-hood because of family ancestry? Granted, this does not invalidate the possibilities of those descended or brought up in Pagan and Witching families, as they most certainly exist. Witchcraft is a practice and one that is *orthopraxic*, meaning a "right practice." Therefore, Witchcraft is all about what you do and not what you believe, and certainly not where or from whom you are descended. Just because you may have ancestry—especially if you were brought up outside of that immediate region or culture—does not mean you know the immediate implications and feelings of what it means to be of that people. It may be part of your ethnic background and contribute to your genetic memory, but, in my opinion, this does not immediately make you a Hereditary Witch. Witchcraft is, however, yours to explore and connect with, as many Witches have reclaimed these traditions with deep study, research, and training from people and sources of those cultures. There is a connection that exists in contemporary incarnations of the Craft with these family-based traditions, and these families still mostly practice secrecy. However, a Witch walks the path alone first and foremost, for upon trusting the self, the Witch truly lives.

The Craft often reclaims its origins by reconstructing or revising the practices or beliefs found in the Craft's long history and reworks them into the modern practitioner's worldview. This is not to say that certain family traditions aren't rooted in practices of folk magic, rituals, and family mythologies that have been handed down from generation to generation, but these often can be traced back to Pagan roots. As creatures of our environment, what we are surrounded by and what our families encourage and discourage play a key role in our development. Free thinking was once considered the mark of a Witch. Even reading was considered an act that may unlock the secret door to conjuring Devils and raising hell. It is safe to assume that the Catholic Church knew that knowledge was power. During the Middle Ages, the Church could not afford to be challenged by the development of new ideas and free thinking or the remembrance of the old religion of Witching practices.

During my time living publicly as a Witch in Salem, Massachusetts, it was especially concerning when people would approach me to declare their title of "Hereditary Witch" without understanding the implications. Many make claims and falsify their ancestry to the Salem Witch trials, as if being related to any of the puritanical people murdered means they are of a superior heritage of Witches. This idea is disturbing, as it denotes a lack of understanding of puritanical history; the long, complex history of Witchcraft; and how its definition is constantly changing. To this day, many have a preconceived notion that Witchcraft can be defined as one thing or as a uniform set of practices throughout history. They may share traits and commonalities, but Witchcraft practices are varied, independent, and vastly different through a variety of cultural lenses.

Witch is a word, in and of itself, that has been reclaimed and is now accepted as something empowering and desirable. However, what Witch meant to the average layperson in sixteenth-century England was very different. According to most evidence from the Witch trials, and even what was recorded for most of the millennia, Witch was a label used to describe the evil workers of magic.[17] Despite this, laypeople knew that these "cunning people" could be employed to use their gnostic (and especially Christian) variations of folk healing and herbalism to counteract this evil. The cunning folk would never dream of calling themselves "Witches," but their tools and methods were almost the same. There is commonality but not complete universality in Witchcraft. It will never be fully understood or defined. Therefore, it operates as several practices, art forms, religions, lifestyles, and political movements.

Witchcraft is extremely diverse from place to place. This is best explained by Witchcraft and folk magic drawing its practice from its immediate land, culture, and what is available to people at that given time, from the vernacular of how villagers would speak to the familiar sights of a specific

---

17   Von Spee, Friedrich and Marcus Hellyer. *Cautio Criminalis, or a Book on Witch Trials*. University of Virginia Press, 2003.

community. Cultures are also constantly changing. Our magic and the magic in history always reflects the people of their time, just as art imitates life. (This also relates to the Craft's long history of using magic, curses, and hexes to fight back against oppression. People have always turned to the Witch when they sense threats or potential traumas and have the will for intercession and change. It's a commonly reoccurring phenomenon.) The Craft is definitely an art, first and foremost. We call it as such by its given name. However, it is also a lifestyle, a religion, a formula, and a method of understanding. All of these outlooks are part of its inherent multicultural make-up and not mutually exclusive to each other.

A Craft is in the doing, but we all bear Witchblood. The difference lies in what may awaken it. The awakening is in any engagement with the unseen and unexplainable forces that we intuitively sense and call out to. When they answer, we know. There is a quote handed down to me by a fellow Witch in my inner circle, attributed to the late Robert Cochrane: "A Witch is one who calls the spirits, and they come."

ORIGINS OF WITCHING NOTIONS TODAY

We, as a culture, have trended toward assuming validity of one's identity as a Witch based on bloodline. I believe that this is rooted in two very influential source texts on how Witchcraft was viewed and has contributed to the public's assumptions about Witches. The first is *The Malleus Maleficarum* (*"The Hammer of the Witches"*) written by Heinrich Kramer and Jacob Sprenger. The influence and popularity of this text cannot be over-emphasized when it comes to our history, modern popular culture, and individual notions of Witchcraft. Published in 1486, its misogynistic and twisted views still echo in collective memory centuries later. One idea it presents is the overarching sexist view that most, if not all, women are Witches and more vulnerable to the temptations of the Devil because of their sex.[18] They also had the secretive power to bear children. This, in and of itself, was viewed as a deeply mysterious and frightening thing to the men who knew nothing about the process of

---

18   Worthen, Hannah. "Early Modern Witch Trials." *The National Archives*, The National Archives, 4 Aug. 2022. www.nationalarchives.gov.uk/education/resources/early-modern-witch-trials/

reproduction. However, we know men were also accused of practicing Witchcraft, and many practiced but were protected by the male privilege granted to them by a patriarchal society. Women were demonized, while the male Witch was able to keep his Craft under the adaptations of an alchemist, magician, or folk healer. I think there is a direct relation between the specific depiction of femininity and womanhood presented in *The Malleus* and the modern archetype of the Witch.

Today, Witchcraft is mainly attributed to female Mysteries. There is a regeneration of the Goddess in art, media, and Modern Witchcraft. Many believe and pass on the belief that it is the Goddess who is the true initiator of the Witches. However, a Witch is a Witch regardless of their sex or gender when it comes to our practices today. We know that in some cultures' pasts, people who deviated from the gender constructs were often seen as being in touch with some other force and, therefore, could act as Witches, shamans, and healers, though these differences often led to either isolation or reverence.[19] Ignoring this history means missing the essence of the wholeness of the human experience as well as the true spiritual meanings of Baphomet, the Divine Androgyne, and the integration of our own masculine and feminine spirits. Simply put, the projective and the receptive forces within all things can be worked with in terms of polarity magic. Anything that acts as a set of different yet complimentary pairs can be used to express the idea of two things integrating or working together to make a magical change. This sense of polarity is a concept rooted in common beliefs of the Victorian Occult Revival and places where many first encounter traditional practices of magic.

Another reason why Witchcraft is attributed to the female Mysteries in *The Malleus* because of her genetics. Because of the vulnerability of her sex as a woman, the mother would pass along this Witchblood and, therefore, pass on her pact with Satan to all of her children.[20] If one woman was suspect, her whole family was suspect. Here, Witchcraft

---

19 One amazing resource that presents these histories and concepts beautifully is *Blossom in the Bone: Reclaiming the Connections Between Homoeroticism and the Sacred* by Randy P. Conner.

20 Roper, Lyndal. "Evil Imaginings and Fantasies: Child-Witches and the End of the Witch Craze." *Past & Present*, no. 167, 2000, pp. 107-139.

becomes not just a Craft or a tradition, but something frightening: a quality or moral evil in the blood that a person could not know about, passed on by a family member by simply being born.

The second important text is *The Witch-Cult in Western Europe* by Margaret Murray. Her works have almost all been dismissed as false by modern scholarship, but the views she proposed in 1921 were highly influential to how Witchcraft was (and is still) viewed. This work was a cornerstone of Gardner's development of the Wica, for example. One of the views she proposed was that Witchcraft is a long-held tradition held underground, a universal cult of Witches under the vestige of Diana the Moon Goddess and the Pagan Horned God of Nature. It was presented as an unbroken lineage of Witches being taught the Craft, kept within families for survival. It's not that far from what we know today to be true; Witchcraft is just not that specific or universal in its practice. In Murray's account, children would be initiated to the coven's Pagan "Devil," an embodiment or manifestation of the Horned God. This could happen as soon as they were born, and the child would later enter what Murray called the "Higher Mysteries" in their early twenties.[21] Although we know there was never a universal cult of Witches as Murray proposed, that does not mean there were not individual Witches who practiced in similar ways.

Often, gnostic, Pagan, or folk traditions discussed were indeed strictly kept in family lines. They were explained simply as "just the way we do things." This familial style of practice even goes back to traditional apprenticeships and guilds, where specific skills were taught and carefully passed from family member to family member or from teacher to apprentice. In trade groups such as the "horse whispers" or "toad men," these guilds developed another side of trade skills that were mystical, spiritual, and—as social trends add fuel to the fires—often diabolical.[22] One of the key characteristics of these groups was an initiation rite. There was revelry and power found in rebellion and blasphemy against

---

21 Murray, Margaret A. *Witch-Cult in Western Europe: A Study in Anthropology (Classic Reprint)*. Forgotten Books, 2022.

22 Howard, Michael. *Children of Cain: A Study of Modern Traditional Witches*. Three Hands Press, 2011.

mainstream belief. As the saying passed on to me goes, the Gods of the old world become the Devils of the new world.

Secretly preserving spiritual belief under guises and pageantry (rituals) helped teach the practical tricks of these trades. These initiation rites into the guild were core to the group's integrity and gave them specialized skills in the mastery of their trade, as there was also a living to be made in the work. Work is seen as a vocation, and for most, a calling, which implies spiritual fulfillment. The secrecy of keeping these ideas and practices in the family is not hard to understand, especially when looking at the history of the persecution of heretics and the overwhelming theme of demonizing anything "other." Yet, this is also part of how religious traditions adapt; there is a precedent for subscribing to dual-faith beliefs and still preserving the old (what we may look at today and consider Witchcraft or Paganism). However, it would never have been labeled as such in early conquest and Christian rule.

Languages and behaviors are dictated by their time. History is always rewritten by the winners and the dominant culture. Witchy practices often persevere in adverse situations, but often through the absorbance of the mainstream beliefs (such as Christianity for most of us in the US) and cultures of these families. For example, there was a vast amount of Pagan influence on Catholicism. Overlaps between Paganism and Catholicism are found in such practices as the veneration of the Mother of God,[23] the acknowledgment of the Divine female, holidays, and rituals from earlier Roman practices.[24] The practice of petitioning saints, many of whom were previous Pagan Gods, to intercede on behalf of the practitioner and the veneration of relics of the holy dead are truly not that far from petitioning nature and familiar spirits or a form of necromancy. Italian Witchcraft or *Stregheria* is a great example of not just dual faith practice but the incorporation of two systems, along with many other forms of magical traditions like New Orleans Voodoo.

---

23 Jordan, Michael. *The Historical Mary: Revealing the Pagan Identity of the Virgin Mother.* Ulysses Press, 2003.

24 O'Donnell, James J. *Pagans: The End of Traditional Religion and the Rise of Christianity.* HarperCollins, 2016.

WITCHCRAFT AND THE SEARCH FOR VALIDITY

Variations in people's practices make it that much harder to define the Craft as one specific thing in the search for understanding it and its validity. There is no unbroken line of genealogical Witchcraft but, rather, what we may be influenced by, orally taught, or practically exposed to. It is in these first brushes with inspiration from the Witch archetype that we are brought to the magical traditions. At the core of the Craft are the independent philosophies each individual holds. Any monopolization over "real Witchcraft" or the truest form of Witchcraft is a false and dangerous game to play. Everyone senses and works differently, and all practices are valid. I suggest we allow people's behaviors to tell you the value of their Witchcraft, as it will show you more than their claims.

All the traditions surrounding Witchcraft are simply *different takes on different histories,* from the wise woman's cottage at the edge of the forest in the fourteenth century to Gerald Gardner and the Witches of the New Forest, all the way down to Scott Cunningham's Wicca in the 1980s and the development of DIY "Witch-tok" through social media today. It's not for me (or anyone) to judge what practices are "valid," but it's worth knowing the cultural history of Witchcraft as an ever-evolving practice with new labels, subsects, and methods. Ultimately, people seek belonging, identity, acceptance, and community, and we use magic as a tool to achieve these things. Witchcraft has always provided many of those qualities of belonging for many of its members. The Craft has always been a tribe of the strange and different, and the Goddess needs those who answer that call to join in the dance.

CHAPTER THREE

SKULL AND BLOOD: ANCESTORS

Witchcraft practices have always acknowledged and venerated ancestral spirits. Everywhere we walk, we physically and spiritually stand on the bones of the dead. They are the scaffolding that built the world as we know it. Ancestor veneration and working with the dead is one of the Witches' main attributes in the power they hold with necromantic rites, mediumship, and our unique perspective on mortality. Some worldly examples of ancestor veneration are only a bone's throw away; we still have access to the traditional Witch's boneyard or churchyards to visit and engage with.

The graveyard is a place of legend where the Witch could sit and wait upon a stool or stump to engage in congress with wandering spirits. Here, they would be equipped with a lantern and a stiff drink to wait for the phantom roads to open. This simple ritual of silence and patience may very well wake the spirit of the churchyard to do the Witch's bidding. They could also go to the corners of plots to gather dust and dirt for dealings with the dead. The haunting image of the Witch who goes into the graveyard to hold conference with the dead still stays with me.

Growing up next to a cemetery, this was one of the first liminal spaces I loved to wander in. Praying for the dead was something always taught in my family so they could transition and continue to intercede for us. There is a great influence of ancestral veneration in America from such groups as the Spiritualist movement in the nineteenth century and Victorian mourning rituals rooted in folklore and elegant superstitions. We find it across the globe from Tibetan Buddhism to *Día de Los Muertos* in Mexico, and from Afro-diasporic cultures to the great tombs and burial mounds of the Megalithic period. Ancestral spirits work within the self and on our behalf. From their place in the afterlife, our ancestors can have a great influence on us.

Ancestors are not only immediate spiritual contacts of our blood descendants, but also of people who had a hand in shaping our experience, making us who we are today. The acknowledgment of those beloved dead as among a Witch's spiritual contact is crucial because they hold a deep personal connection. Our physical body and the land we tread upon are the same places and feelings that our ancestors once had and walked upon. The land and body of the Witch acts as a touchstone or portal where the dead can manifest because their connection and influence has always been present. This includes the dead known and unknown to us, as there is an invisible world all around. Remember that we too shall become ancestors one day.

You're always working with your ancestors, and you are the sum of all their parts. You are descended from millions of people, acting as the embodiment of their challenges and sacrifices, their givings and misgivings. Even if they're people you may not have had the best relationship with, there is still an opportunity to not only work with them but also to reconcile these relationships in their afterlife. They are in a plane of existence where this understanding and wisdom can change them as we knew them because they have entered a place of peace and liminality with the ability to cross between worlds. This is part of the beauty of what death has to offer. Witches have always seen death as not an ending or morbid concept, but another beginning or rebirth.

Ancestors are more than our blood relatives and friendships that we have known in this life. Looking at the Latin etymology of the word *ancestor,* the root words *ante* and *cedere* mean "before" and "go," respectively: simply "those who have gone before." Our bodies and blood, the land we live on, and the inspiration we carry are populated by a vast array of ancestral spirits. Ancestors are made up of several different classes. This classification is used as a tool to help us connect to all people who have gone before us but is never meant to put them into a box. While classification acts as a tool for our understanding of the vast expanse of the ancestral realm, this realm and these spirits (like all things) are still a Mystery.

THE ANCESTRAL REALM:
The Underworld, Summerlands, and Place of the Beloved Dead

Ancestors are the people who were once on the land of "the quick," or the living, and have died. They now exist in an unembodied spiritual state in the ancestral realm. The ancestral realm is the liminal place where the human spirits and the higher realms come together. They're able to intercede, work between worlds, and connect to all of the past, like a snapshot of time, linked with concern and guidance to our present time that coincides timelessly. (Time in itself is, of course, a human construct.) This realm assists in not just holding the consciousness of the universal human soul but is also a place where the personality of each individual spirit lives on so we can have access to one another.[25] The ancestral realm can be seen as a river or pool of flowing ancestral waters. Afterlife concepts are also sometimes presented as the banquet halls of Valhalla to the Nordic people, the Summerland to Theosophists, and Heaven to Christians.

The ancestral waters are meant to keep us connected and prepare us for our next transition between this life and the next. A great analogy for this would be the water cycle; we all manifest as individual water droplets, only to be reabsorbed into an ocean, a great body of water made up of many droplets. These waters cleanse away the persona of the individual so that it ceases to exist in the ancestral realm, allowing the eternal part of self—the soul—to be transferred and live on in the reincarnation cycle. The idea of having "three souls" or being made up of several energy points is nothing new to Witchcraft and metaphysical spaces. We, too, are a single individual made up of the many aspects of human experience. The waters flow all around and underneath us, connecting us to the worlds below and above as streams connect to lakes, oceans, and rivers flowing in and out

---

25 Personality comes from *persona*. A persona tells us that this is what is perceived, like a cosmic veil, hiding the true self of the eternal human soul that goes through the reincarnation cycle. The personality of people, what makes them individuals, their likes, dislikes, and human traits always stick around in time, memory, and on the ancestral plane of existence. This may relate to the idea of *the fetch, the lower self,* or *the ancestral soul* in the Witch's triple soul model seen in several traditions.

of each other. These streams work very similarly to the spirits, as water is one of the main conductors of ancestral power and communication.

These ancestral waters are often seen as living streams of memory, and what is remembered lives. Like water, ancestors ebb and flow with us, having more impact during specific seasons, especially Samhain or other harvest and reaping times for the death imagery of harvests and taking from the Earth. They also flow strongly during their points of entry and exit, like birthdays, anniversaries, and important dates of change or passing. They are the rivers of the ferryman Charon, the psychopomp guide to the underworld of the Greeks. These rivers are also rivers of our blood, sharing our material DNA as well as the spiritual reflection of the DNA shared with all those ancestral spirits who came before.

In many Witchcraft traditions, Water is associated with the direction of the West. It is no mistake that many tombs and burial places either face or are aligned to the West where the Sun sets or "dies," only to be reborn with a new day at the next dawn. It is to the West where we can still hear the echoes of the dead. In my practice, this is a direction where the ancestors reside.

ANCESTORS OF BLOOD AND BONE

The ancestors of blood are the people we are descended from genetically. They are made up of our mothers, fathers, grandparents, and all other relatives. This goes back to the customs and cultures they came from when looking at the history of our families' migrations and immigrations to new regions. Using our knowledge of their past places and customs, we can acknowledge them, as well as the heirlooms, the stories, and the otherworldly spirits they brought with them. In the United States of America, this transition to the New World is significant, as many non-Indigenous Americans came here either by the will for a better life or by force. Ancestral and generational trauma can all be visited in ancestor work as a means to not only heal these things passed on to us, but also as an act of redemption when we fall into the same traps. Once we acknowledge these ancestors, we gain an awareness of what it takes to improve and can learn from the successes and failures of those who brought us forth into the present.

Among our ancestors of blood, we find some of our most personal connections with those related to us. They include the departed family who have always been present, watching over us and our families since birth. Our ancestral line stretches back to the beginning of time, and they pay attention to each generation. They can share a lot of our traits, vulnerabilities, and genetic memories, and are the ones responsible for getting us to where we are today. It is in this respect that we can honor their lives, for their lives resulted in ours regardless of our ideological differences. We open the door to their advice and intercession once gratitude is made known.

All of our ancestors have experiences we can learn from and be inspired by; they all have something to offer, but our openness to them just depends on what we need and how their wisdom is interpreted and applied. A relationship with ancestors of blood always exists, especially if it was there before, and even if we may not have known them in their lives, they have known us in their death. This relationship, like all relationships, is reciprocal. The ancestral practice not only helps us build that relationship with them but also with ourselves. We are of their blood and bone, and it, like the Witchblood, holds a deeper power.

In and of itself, ancestors are a means of connecting us not only to the human soul but the fullness of the cosmic "world soul," or the universal consciousness of all living things on Earth. When we go back far enough, our blood relations were tapped into the cycles of nature and tribal ethics. They lived not just in alignment with the seasons, but at the mercy of the turning of nature and, of course, the land they walked upon. They relied on nature, and, from nature, they marked the great rites of passage and acknowledged a cycle of life, death, and rebirth.

ANCESTORS OF THE LAND

You may encounter the ancestors of the land daily, running into them frequently in the spaces you inhabit or visit. They may be called "ghosts," or simply seen as human spirits, but these are the ancestors of the land. They are the ancestors that dwell in our immediate surroundings because they have a connection with the land, having left their energetic signatures in these places. They too walked the same ground and lived in the same place. We may say they have attachments to the land, but they are always here because they left a footprint. They are made up of what I term "the builders, gatherers, local kinfolk, and craftsmen." They can guide us through the energies of our homes and the communities we live in. We are the continuation of the community they built, creating the legacy of our homeland. They can also be seen as *community spirits* because they are invested in guiding us through the spaces and communities we inhabit.

This is not to be confused with spirits who may be "stuck" or have "unfinished business," as they belong to another category. However, like a lot of ancestors, there can certainly be overlaps. Indigenous spirits have a strong presence in this category. Importantly, we may offer healing and reconciliation to them for the cruelties colonizers inflicted upon them, as in the US, non-Indigenous people live on stolen land. Indigenous spirits tend to offer a wealth of information and tap us into a deeper understanding of the folklore and customs that may still be in our regions today. It's important to remember that they were here first, and this always needs to be acknowledged. Many treaties had to be broken for non-Indigenous Americans to live where they do, and this knowledge and awareness of these surroundings is itself an offering to the ancestors of the land.

There is a slight difference between ancestral land spirits and the *genii loci,* or "spirits of place." The term originated with the Roman practice not just for the spirit of place, but for the guardian spirit or protector of place. This includes familiar spirits, daimons, animal spirits, and other shades or elemental beings. Although an ancestor spirit can certainly be part of the *genius loci* classification, they are a distinct class of protector land spirits, or, in an animistic worldview, the spirit of the land itself. For example, the animistic spirit of gates, walls, archways, and hearths are classic *genii loci*. The landmark would be associated with a spirit to be appeased in exchange for protection and holding the virtues of the land to those people inhabiting there, so that we can understand how the land presents itself in the form of an entity or spiritual attachment. Ancestors of the land are also not to be confused with elemental or animal spirits, as these nature spirits have their distinct vibrations.

ANCESTORS OF INSPIRATION

The ancestors of inspiration are some of the most accessible spirits to us, but also one of my personal favorites as an artist. These ancestors are anyone who ever inspired us, shaped our worldview, and who continues to speak to our spirit. They are made up of musicians, performers, writers, activists, historical figures, and those who fostered their creative spirits. Ancestors of inspiration share a common trait or vocation or hold a truth that we also find in ourselves and can be either known or unknown to us on a personal level. For example, my first teacher in theatre was the person who greatly inspired me in the path I chose as an artist, which contributed to bringing me to the Craft. However, some spirits I have a very close relationship with were before my time, and I could have never met them in person.

One of my closest relationships is with singer Cass Elliot. Her music shaped me into the person I am today, as she shared traits and artistic ideals that I still hold. She visits me in dreams for pep-talks and check-ins, and I know we have a connection. The nice thing about many of these types of ancestors is that their words, songs, and performances live on. We can visit and revisit the time capsule of film, books, and media that still exist. These carry on their vibrations captured at that moment because they are still present through that work. This is why art is so profound: all art captures and evokes the spirit of the artist, as well as the message of the art they convey to us. This includes historical figures, scientists, activists, and figures that deeply recognize us as we recognize them.

We find a connection in the mutual human experience. I say that these spirits are accessible because they became icons with legacies left behind in some way, immortalizing their feelings, performances, and words. They are wonderful resources for help with work problems, creativity, and, of course, wisdom we may seek out. Because we do not know them on a personal level, it is always important to ask for their permission before developing a spiritual relationship with them. This goes for almost all ancestors we may not have known, or for those ancestors we did know but who have very different spiritual truths from our own. Spiritual consent is so important to all relationships with the otherworld. If you respect them, they will probably respect you in turn.

ANCESTORS OF ADOPTION

Ancestors of adoption are those we adopt into our own chosen family and the ancestors and loved ones who have adopted us as part of their kindred. This, of course, includes all our friends and loved ones who are not directly related to us by blood. This occurs between families, partnerships, and relationships with our bonus families or stepfamilies in relationships, marriages, or even close friendships. This is when we become part of that family dynamic. It is not uncommon for one person's ancestral line to intercede in their significant other's life when they bond and a connection with the spirits of that family develops, even if they were before their time and unknown to that significant other.

Ancestors of adoption also include those of us who have been adopted into a family or have a stepfamily. Many people don't know their blood relations, but that doesn't mean you can't engage with ancestral work. Sometimes, the opportunity to know blood relatives is not accessible or even safe to explore for any number of reasons. The important thing to know that is we create our own chosen families, communities, and lifelong friends even after death. When someone is adopted, ancestral work can be a great healer in knowing where adopted or chosen families came from, not just genetic origins. What was shared continues and always exists in the ancestral realm. We just need to proclaim it, introduce ourselves, and reach out. Oftentimes, they will reach back.

THE WANDERING
AND RESTLESS ANCESTORS

The wandering and restless ancestors, sometimes referred to as the "Wandering Ones," are a class of people who may have unfinished business. They tend to be stuck in interdimensional planes and can occasionally be aggressive or difficult to manage. They tend to bother or create problems for the living when their space has been invaded or they feel they have been violated in some way. The Wandering Ones may also be attributed to shadow people because they exist in liminal places, but they might resist this sense of being in-between. This friction often brings the spirit to an uncomfortable plane of spiritual existence. They choose to distance themselves from spiritual passageways to the otherworld and are often closer to a sub-lunar, lower, or chthonic realm.

They are what many people might consider to be demonic or unsavory spirits. This type of spirit is not "evil," but instead is of a different vibration that, to us, can bring unsettled feelings such as intense sadness, anger, or, above all, fear. They tend to be a class of spirit with whom we often need to set clear and established boundaries. We need to honor and respect them at our discretion. We can make offerings or provide them with a "spirit house" in reverence, as this is our way of holding our boundaries with them. If these boundaries are broken, it is then, and only then, that a banishment or transitional rite to move that spirit to its plane of existence is employed, and this is very rare.

Many of these spirits may be in a state of trauma and pain, and when we attempt to heal this, they may work on our behalf. For example, picture the wandering spirit of a judge who was cruel, ruthless, and unforgiving in life. I employ his graveyard dirt when someone who is causing me ill must be brought to justice, or if I need his influence to rule with an iron fist in a troublesome circumstance. This is because I've taken the time not only to ask his permission, but also to acknowledge where his perceived negative traits may serve my life for the better. This is more of a necromantic or transactional relationship than a purely ancestral bond, but still one that can be done with proper protections, wards, and clear boundaries with the spirits of this type.

THE WITCH'S MIGHTY DEAD

The Mighty Dead is every Witch who was, is, and ever will be. All the people who shared our practice(s), spiritual lineage, and inheritance of the Witchblood awakened within fit in this category. This stretches back to antiquity, including Witches of ancient lore and history, such as Circe, Medea, Isobel Gowdie, Mother Shipton, and the Witch of Endor. It also includes famous Witchcraft tradition founders like Gerald Gardner, Doreen Valiente, Robert Cochrane, Alex Saunders, Gwen Thompson, and Eddie Buczynski. They are especially helpful not just as protectors but as spirits with the ability to add their own Witch power and amplification to any services we may need. They can even teach us their crafts, spells, and recipes from beyond by filling us with inspired speech, visions, and ideas. If we have psychic contact in life, we can also affect the living realm once we too become part of the Mighty Dead. Witches have a relationship with each other because of the calling to the Wyrd and the Witchblood that has been awakened. A recognition of that magic has been shared throughout time, bonding us together to a current of the Witchblood and, thus, Witch power!

WORKING WITH THE DEAD

ANCESTOR VENERATION

Ancestor veneration is the practice of building personal connection and contact with the dead. It includes offering an open dialogue, prayers, physical offerings, candlelight, incense, pictures, and heirlooms. Put simply, it is the act of reaching out to the ancestral realm. Veneration can take the form of making physical offerings or dedicating specific rites and spaces to those who have departed. Veneration can be described as anything that makes connecting with the dead easier for the practitioner. The dead are on another plane of existence, so the relationship is no longer physical but is instead disembodied. As physical beings, we can act as the conduit for them to continue their wisdom in our relationship. It's good to have a divination tool or skill handy to help build that contact and interpret the messages, dreams, and signs they may bring to us. One practice is to perform a "Dumb Supper," where we make a meal in honor of the ancestors and eat in silence, leaving them an offering plate of what we have made. We open the veil and, in the silence as we eat, we listen for their messages and feel their presence.

AN ANCESTRAL ALTAR

Everyone will have a different way of building an ancestral altar depending on their gnosis, spiritual contacts, and traditions. For me, my altar to the dead is simple and is set in the Western part of my house. I use pictures of all my dead, prayer cards, family heirlooms, and the daily or weekly offerings I include as part of my practice. I use a white cloth to cover the altar, representing the white light of spirit (or simply the color of bone), as well as purity, as I want to give my spirits a pure and sacred space to reside within my dwelling. I also have deeply personal items given to me by my deceased that act as a connection point to those who gave me that object. I maintain a practice of offering water in a clear glass every day, which can also be used as a scrying tool, for water is one of the main ways in which spirits travel and communicate. It also offers symbolic nourishment to make contact easier, and so we can continue to show our love and appreciation for them.

I also like to use sentimental perfumes and colognes, play music for them, and speak their names out loud when I open the altar for working and offering. You can offer coins for the ferryman as payment for guiding them through the realms; keys, which are related to Hekate in her role as psychopomp; and any symbolic offering that may help you turn your attention to the idea of "parting the veil" for an open dialogue with spirit.

I think it is important to include candles or lamps to bring illumination to the ancestral realm, to light their way not just through that realm, but to guide them to us, the spirit workers, for light is the purest energy source. I have offered prayers and poems that I have written, memorial artwork, herbs associated with the dead, incense smoke to carry my messages to them through the air, and foods and drinks they loved or that I know they would like. The center point of my ancestral space is a skull. The skull acts as the main focal point of connection as it is the ultimate symbol of the dead, for underneath it all, we and our dead will become one. It is the literal house for our spirit, or the brain, for always *memento mori*.

"In blood and bone
And in Spirit and place
By dust and skull
Is Death's holy face.
Land of the Quick
On hallowed ground, I tread
Between lands of the living
And lands of the dead."

THE FIRST VISITORS: GODS AND GIANTS

There seems to be a myth in most cultures about how interactions with power from the Gods, nature spirits, and divine avatar-like figures came about to explain the deepest unknowns of civilization. Witchcraft not only celebrates this lore, but also sees it widely acknowledged across several different cultures and folklores. As we touched on in Chapter One, the Witch-lore of our beginnings boils down to the myth of otherworldly or extraterrestrial visitors with greater consciousness and advancements coming to Earth to impart their knowledge, teachings, and love unto the human race. However, to avoid fundamentalist thinking, it is best to not take these literally, but to look deeper into these stories as a method of conceptualizing the unexplained and what is considered sacred.

The Gods, like us, have evolved through time, for they are of timeless places and continue to evoke the same human inspirations as they did in antiquity. There is a significant link to the universal story of engagement with the powers of deity forms in whatever context that may fall into, whether it be wandering through a forest and summoning a God to bring aid or empowerment in a specific working. Like most things in the world of Witches, we know there's so much under the surface when it comes to the origins of our conceptions of "God."

The philosophical question raised is whether we have created the Gods or the Gods have created us. However, us having created them in our image is the most likely explanation for what we have seen throughout history in all its specific cultures and reactions to the changing of human life. There is a natural need to give the Gods a face, a mythos, and a clear form as they have presented themselves in our impulses and inner sight, and it is clear that humans have done this since the beginning. Anthropomorphism is the result of our power of projection toward something alien or outside of our immediate conscious mind. It may be our natural inclination as living beings, our evolutionary trait from the need for survival, our need to understand the unexplained, and the human impulse to personify natural forces so we can identify with common phenomena and experiences. We create with symbols, and that which is behind the symbol is the true spirit we seek.

We give form, create structure, and then give meaning to the formless. As humans, we continue the work of one or more great creator(s) by giving order to chaos and body to the unembodied. With more exchanges and investment, these creations become very distinct and autonomous lifeforms that go back to the first storytellers, priests, and bearers of knowledge. The figure of the Witch is all of these things and more. *Deep magic* is the meaning-making and creation process of finding divinity in the day-to-day. This is why the Craft ultimately speaks to the power of love, compassion, and the acknowledgment of spirit being present in all things: it offers the opportunity to seek Divinity and what is of our sacred self. The journey of seeking is an exercise in love for us. It allows us the permission to dream and to visualize a better reality that, as magical people, we know is attainable.

"We are the music makers, and we are the dreamers of dreams."
—Arthur O'Shaughnessy

MASKS OF THE GODS

There are as many Gods as there are faces of humans. Each is distinct and connected, donning its garb of history, quality, and form. These concepts of the Gods can be taken literally or symbolically, as both forms exist and can be engaged with. They can be seen as archetypes or as living entities, having likes and dislikes and personalities that can be observed in folklore and myth. Many Witches identify as either soft or hard polytheists, monists, or another form of theist.[26] This identity depends on their experiences regarding working with a deity structure and how they decide to believe in the orthopraxic context of the Craft. Witches are truly meaning makers, and to seek meaning is not to merely accept what we may feel and see, but to find it reflected within us and shared amongst others, whether this be in history, folklore, or in the present day. How we believe in or engage with the Gods is ours to choose based on our experiences. These experiences could even be the very influence of the Gods manifesting through us, guiding us to the guise of their choice, so that we can understand and recognize the meaning, magic, and mystery in our own lives. This deeper experience of the discovery of meaning—the eureka of realization—is what they have to offer us as we take our first steps.

Polytheistic belief in all variations and diversities is something commonly seen in the ancient cultures of Hellenistic Greece,[27] Rome,[28] and among the Anglo-Saxons of Old Britain.[29] This was due to the multicultural nature

---

26 Monism derives from Neoplatonic thought as the idea that all things are derived from "the One Source," but that this source may present itself in several different forms and appearances. *Polytheism*, or simply, "the belief in many deities" can mean several things, depending on one's interpretation. The main two forms within Modern Witchcraft today are popularly known as "hard polytheism" and "soft polytheism." Hard polytheists recognize each God as a real, autonomous, and distinct being, while soft polytheists see the Divine as archetypal and personified faces or facets of the universe, better relating with the idea of *pantheism*, or that the manifestation of the universe is identified with the Divine and admits or tolerates all existences of deity.

27 Ankarloo, Bengt and Stuart Clark. *Witchcraft and Magic in Europe: Ancient Greece and Rome*. University of Pennsylvania Press, 1999.

28 Jones, Prudence and Nigel Pennick. *A History of Pagan Europe*. Routledge, 1997.

29 Hutton, Ronald. *Pagan Britain*. Yale University Press, 2022.

of these cosmopolitan places where the exchanges of ideas, new religions, and new Gods had taken place. Gods often take the shape and form that those around them can understand, especially in diverse places. The Gods of the Witchblood are *shapeshifters;* they can change their shapes, faces, and forms as easily as we can sense change in the atmosphere. The "other" has always used the symbols and sensations of the immediate culture, time, and spirit of place to communicate to the groups of people they are around, historically and today.

Each culture independently creates its own understandings of the Gods as communication with them develops, much as it does for each individual today. Each person or group has their rituals, structures, and taboos as a means of better honoring communication with a deity. Through time, that deity relates more prominently to that given form, language, and ritual with living entities of these cultures, working groups, and personal relationships. Naturally, these forces absorb varying and multifaceted tales of history, myth, and legends. This is why we have so many different expressions of religion.

Though this may be a gross oversimplification on my part, it is conceptually important to understand the idea of trade, absorbance, and the multiplicity of the many forms of deity throughout time. By understanding the origins and evolution of a God through the ages, we can better honor our mythos of meaning-making, which is also the making of magic itself. Our practice of engaging with these concepts is what makes mythos turn from a story to a realized practice that can change our lifestyle and deepen our gnosis.

In my opinion, each story or myth is a specific teaching mechanism that explains or leads the practitioner to an even greater truth. This deeper wisdom and the journey we take in a divine relationship causes us to experience what I call the *many masks of the Gods*, which is the face or mask we create to give form to the formless and knowing to the unknowable. We have to personify and relate with these powers by giving them a design that evokes their spiritual presence. Behind these masks are the powers of the Gods deeper still. The specific forms and faces of the spirits we see and connect with may change, because we have our Mysteries as Witches, as a collective, and as a world. As shapeshifters, the Gods will assume the shape that is the most fitting to our understanding, sometimes in the most ironic of ways.

The Gods are an Ultimate Mystery, and we naturally tune into the universal language of icon, storytelling, and symbolism to explore that Mystery. This may be human instinct, and most instincts are of the spirit because people experience emotion with that same tangible resonance. We may call it personification, but personification is one of the many ways that a form can be given to an abstract idea, feeling, or thought. Giving specific thought to a form creates a symbol, and a symbol has undeniable power that evokes a spirit, causing the symbol or icon to take on a life and independent form of its own. The symbol can be named, dressed, and given specific histories that share qualities and identifications with our ancient ancestors. All of these aspects contribute to the creation of *God*, just as the Gods may have created us from clay and fire.

The Gods I specifically explore and work with in my practice are the Gods associated with, adopted by, and who have a kinship with Witches; they are *the Witch Gods*, also known as "the Old Ones." Many of our idea of Gods has radically shifted because of the significance of the Abrahamic and monotheistic religions in the Western world. All deities truly belong to their classification of the vast array of spiritual intelligences that practitioners may encounter or be called to engage with. Notice how I said *called*, because as independent entities, they are not to be picked and chosen by us, nor are they to be inserted and invoked like a game of Mad Libs in our rituals or workings. The Gods call us in a very real way and aren't to be disrespected with blatant ignorance of their origins and histories.

Inspiration, fascination, repeated signs, symbols, and omens are part of the intrinsic way in which a deity may instill a call within us. When we feel this, we are instinctually guided to journey toward them, and often, they are right there behind us along the way. We meet the Old Ones at the crossroads, the liminal places where all things come together and depart once again. I emphasize critical thinking, personal research, and validity for the sake of showing honor and respect not just to the spirits, but to ourselves, as we too deserve truth to empower our experiences. Witchcraft is about reciprocal and authentic relationships, and a relationship with a higher power takes time, study, and understanding to truly honor how it works and what our role is in this spiritual relationship. Respect begets respect. Work and effort must be offered into any relationship for anything meaningful to come of it, especially among the spirits and Gods.

FIRE AND LIGHT

As we began looking up at the stars and wondering who we were, another aerial event likely took place: a bolt of lightning! The flash of stars gave fire from the cosmos to Earth, and humans were able to harness and recreate this primal element into a force that has aided us in every way. We wouldn't have survived without Fire as our first spiritual conduit. Fire is put at the center of ritual and ceremony; it is the place where all gather around to listen to the storytellers, priests, mystics, and wise people. For many, Fire represents a portal to the otherworld and is one of the working symbols of the *axis mundi*, the connecting pillar of the universe's realms. Fire is the light of Earth as the Sun is the light of the celestial sky. The concept of sky and light is of the utmost importance to the linguistic roots of the God and Goddess, deities, and a creator being. This is seen in the tales of Prometheus, the Irish *Tuatha Dé Danann* (also known as "The Shining Ones"), and the tales of Gods emitting a greater light, like a halo, as well as their intrinsic connection with the two planetary luminaries, the Sun and the Moon. Fire is the primordial power Witches know emits not just physical light, but also a psychic light. Light is the purest energy source, stimulating the consciousness and providing a wealth of information.

The etymology of the words *God, deity,* and *divinity* are very important and reveal a secret of the Witch's light. This takes us into the power of the Witch's voice, as the spoken word is a pure and powerful vibration of creation. The word *god* can be traced to its earliest roots of *ghut,* "that which is invoked," or the Irish *guth,* meaning "voice," both tracing to the earlier Sanskrit word *huta,* which means "invoked."[30] *Deity* and *divinity* are both traced back to the origins of the "dyeu."[31] This word has importance as an early form of the Indo-European concept of a sky divinity, or *deivos,* meaning "celestial ones."[32] The word *dyeu* presents a

---

30 Goswami, H.D. "The Etymology of the Word 'God.'" *H.D. Goswami,* 10 Oct. 2017, www.hdgoswami.com/the-etymology-of-the-word-god/.

31 *"dyeu-." Etymology.* www.etymonline.com/word/*dyeu-.

32 Watkins, Calvert (ed.). *The American Heritage Dictionary of Indo-European Roots.* 2nd ed., Houghton Mifflin, 2000.

connection to the shining planets. *Dyeu* means "to shine," similar to the Sanskrit word *deva*, meaning "shining one."[33]

In our origins of language, the recognition of the Gods was to the sky and thus, to the lights—*the* light—and the idea of a celestial order uniting to the Abyss, a pre-creative world of chaos. This idea of transforming chaos into order is one of the most universal motifs in the study of creation myths concerning a deity figure or figures.

Most Witches suspect that ancient peoples have always looked to and studied the stars and planets. Legend has it that when Gods came to Earth, they may have been responsible for building large and otherwise mysterious megalithic tombs, structures, pyramids, and stone circles. The most famous of these stone structures in the Western world are England's Stonehenge and Ireland's Newgrange, which become illuminated at midwinter, an important connection to the kingship of the Sun. Historically, the Gods were associated with elemental powers responsible for the natural landscape and the planets themselves. This is seen most prominently in the names we have given to the planets of our solar system, which are derived from the names of the Roman Gods.

These starry associations with the Gods can be traced back to the cosmopolitan beliefs and practices of the first Ancient Sumerians, the Persian Magi, and followers of the Zoroastrian faith.[34] The earliest recorded forms of the planets and their associations to the Gods can be seen in Egypt around 2000 BCE, with the acknowledgment of the Sun Gods primarily as chieftains, and the myriad of deities represented in the star groupings and constellations.[35]

For those observing these rotations of the cosmic bodies, movements in the stars were seen as the footprints of specific influences of power, like deities, that could contribute to the times of change, known as "magical tides," that were associated with specific alignments and cosmological

33 Prabhu, Mahesh. "Understanding Deva and Devi." *Vedic Management Center*, 1 July 2023, www.vedic-management.com/understanding-deva-and-devi/.

34 Baigent, Michael. *From the Omens of Babylon: Astrology and Ancient Mesopotamia*. Arkana, 1994.

35 Aldred, Cyril. *The Egyptians*. Thames and Hudson, 1988.

placement in the sky. It carried the foundations of metaphysical thought throughout the world. My favorite cosmic associations are seen in the forms of the Olympian spirits or Planetary Gods of the sixteenth-century grimoire the *Arbatel*.[36] Astrology has long been one of the many skill sets attributed to the Witch, as the vibrational pushes and pulls of the planetary powers have been known to affect life in an often very real and predictable way.

GIANTS AMONG MEN

Something unique about Witch-lore when considering the mythology of prehistory is several cross-cultural accounts of giants. The most common recurring motif in these tales is the defeat of the ruling giants or titan figures from their cleverer offspring, followed by a theme found in creation myths full of accounts of the relationships between mortal people and deities, their offspring destined to form a giant race. In many myths, these giants are presented as forceful natural elements who also act as the first creatures or spirits said to have ruled over the Earth, including the Greek and Mediterranean mythos of the Titans and how they were considered the first beings or *first Gods* arising out of Gaia (the Earth) and Ouranos or Uranus (the sky). The Titans were then overthrown by their wiser and more benevolent offspring, the Olympians, led by Zeus. The Titans are only the beginning of the long list of cultures that have a pre-history rooted in the concept of the giants and the Gods. Among the many are the Irish Formorians, overthrown by the Tuatha Dé Danann led by Lugh, and the Nordic *Jotnar* or frost giants overthrown by the Gods of Asgard led by Odin and his brothers. We see giant tales in the folklore of Brittany's landscape of the Gaelic *Gargon*, and even the Abrahamic faiths of the *Nephilim* or "fallen ones" mentioned as "men of renown" in Genesis 6:1–4.[37]

Does *giant* simply mean "large"? In this context, giants are a form of nature spirit, or a spirit embodying the chaos of beginnings and the timelessness of the past as it lives on in human memory. Among other nature spirits akin to giants, there are spirits of the *aos sídhe* or the faery folk, related to the Tuatha Dé Danann. As shapeshifters, these spirits are

---

36 Luppius, A. *Arbatel: De Magia Veterum*. 1575.

37 *Genesis 6:1–4.*

present in all shapes and sizes. Some beings, like the *sídhe* or the elf, have been held in public imagery as "the little people," but big or small, they are extremely different in size compared to our human stature—a way of giving an example of their primal or alien nature, perhaps. We also have classified spirits such as dwarves, knockers, trolls, and hobgoblins, all representing specific qualities of the wild and untamed nature of the land itself. They are the scavengers and watchers of the human world. Protectors of sacred sites and often the cause of some trickery and chaos to the humans they encounter, they exist within a dimension intersecting with our own.

Whether they are a giant or of the sídhe, they are of the otherworld and the macrocosmic universe, entities of the otherworldly places that we may encounter in the lands of elsewhere. You may see the giants as our most primal qualities personified, much like H.P. Lovecraft's Eldritch Gods. Being of the macrocosmic universe, giants are alien and frightening to us. Lore gives us accounts of serpents and dragons in the same way, but the giant has seemed to truly endure in a multi-cultural fashion. The best examples of this variety of creature can be seen in the Icelandic *Poetic Edda* and the Irish *Lebor Gabála Érenn*,[38] known in English as *The Book of Invasions*.[39] Just as skilled and gentle as a giant may be, there is tons of evidence in these texts that the giants are considered easily outwitted, physically different, and often frightening.

In short, collectively, giants are not benevolent to humans, as they may mean well but are so alien to us in our world that their mere presence can bring about chaos and disorder. There is also the idea that a giant refers to not just the idea of an older being, but of a larger and longer history and a higher or distinct intellect or experience. The giants represent an extreme part of nature, and it is they who possibly migrated or intersected with our world from lost lands or stars. Other cultures may have looked for connections between these beings and the Atlantic, from where we have the legends of the lost city of Atlantis.

It is the giant's age and wisdom that towers over others, not just their stature. The size of a giant is changeable when examining the accounts more closely, despite the language we may use. However, size matters...

---

38   Dronke, Ursula. *The Poetic Edda*. Oxford University Press, 2011.

39   Macalister, Stewart, Robert Alexander, and John Carey. *Lebor Gabála Érenn: The Book of the Taking of Ireland*. Irish Texts Society, 2009.

only sometimes, as later mythology credits giants as the makers of rivers, large mountains, islands, burial mounds, and even Neolithic sites, as well as stories of sleeping giants, or giants that have been turned to stone, which now make up the landscape of mountains and boulders.

The Assyrian cosmic bodies were portrayed as giants. This is also very telling about giants' role in mythology. The Assyrian story of giants is especially well portrayed with the larger-than-life Anu.[40] Anu was the chief God of the Mesopotamians, *the Anakim*, who populated Canaan.[41] Time and time again, giants are portrayed as primal nature spirits the first generation of Gods. They are described with monstrous or unflattering attributes, physically showing that they are frightening forces that not only shaped this world but also can and would threaten it—anti-Gods, if you will, for it is the giants that embody *primordial chaos*. Their shape and unique vestige may be that of an earlier and long-forgotten life form, or even previous faiths and cultures before the Indo-European settlers, purposefully depicted as not-quite-human in form. They were said to bear almost grotesque features of the natural world in comparison with the idealized images of their children, the second generation of Gods we even look to today.

Giants of lore were repeatedly overthrown by their descendants, with each incarnation growing more proficient in the guardianship and guidance of the Earth's living things. This taps into the idea of each generation improving, that the old is replaced by the new, and cyclical creation and destruction will never be complete, that each generation is "perfected," growing farther from a perceived malefic or "savage" form. With time, we grow more "civilized." Without conflict, there is no progress, and with no progress, there is no pursuit toward anything—meaning we learn nothing, and, therefore, nothing is our reward. This is why there will truly never be "world peace," for the cauldron is always stirring, never still, and there are many more battles to be won in the worlds beyond this world. Even the Gods such as the Tuatha, the Olympians,

40 Beaulieu, Paul-Alain. *The Pantheon of Uruk During the Neo-Babylonian Period*. Brill, 2003.

41 Sousa, Jonathan. *A Star from Heaven: An Introduction to Angelic Magic*. Self-published, 2018.

the Ennead, and the Aesir are portrayed as giants but evolved in ways that differentiate them from their parentage. Most are at least part giant and able to wield power in such a way as to bring order to chaos. The new Gods can bring order and defend against the frightening forces of the prior generation, which is perhaps an example of how continuation and change creates better functions in life.

The Gods provide not just personal relationships but a dwelling place where humans can abide. To a flourishing agricultural and Neolithic society, it is these deities that embody virtues of art, wisdom, and, importantly, *order* to defend the innate yet overwhelming unpredictability of nature. The natural and seemingly overpowering forces of drought, sickness, depression, and untimely death are linked with the tyrannical giants of the past in certain stories. The names of these beings often tell you what they represent to the culture or the harm they can potentially cause. In old Irish, *Fomorian* is translated as "those from under the sea" or "ghosts from beneath."[42] This demonstrates their deep unpredictable nature of cause and effect, that they are directly from under the earth, wild and dangerous.

This dangerous nature attributed to the giants could explain the reason so many different deities are mainly attributed to healing and protection. This would be the role of "good" Gods: to fight back against forces of harm and chaos, uphold a cosmic balance, and protect and guide their people on Earth. Each generation represents a continuation of improvement linked to the creation of humanity in the folkloric genealogy with classical texts of this mythical golden age where the Gods and humans could freely interact. It's quite possible to interpret the Gods as representations of our very earliest ancestors. The new Gods learned from their creators, the old giant Gods. Each generation was part of the repeated creation cycle, evolving for the better, rebelling against things that devour life like Kronos the Titan, and looking out for each other.

Myth is a way of explaining and understanding the unknown, especially in oral traditions. Each generation takes a story and repeats it, usually

---

42   Ó hÓgáin, Dáithí. *Myth, Legend & Romance: An encyclopedia of the Irish folk tradition.* Prentice Hall Press, 1991, pp. 232–233.

reworded as their own. We are separated from our ancestors as time passes, but their legacy is more embellished and larger in the stories we are told about them. This was possibly the most ancient way of carrying on stories, as stories independently act as a reflection of the people telling them. This reflection happens like the firelight casting strange shadows upon the cave walls around the storyteller's fire.

ANCESTRAL AND TUTELARY DEITIES:
Mythos of the Sacral Kingship

At the beginning of creation, there was power in a name, and a name was not just a title of a person's identity but a current of power's continuation that was placed upon them, empowered by the priesthoods influenced by a specific deity within the individual's cultural community. There is no absolute correct pantheon of spirits or one set of practices when we see the multicultural regions from which the Gods arose. This can best be expressed by exploring the concept of *tutelary deities* at a macro level in the grand scheme of diversity with deities, customs, and practices.

Tutelary implies the specific function of the deity: they act as a protector or patron of a location, tribe, skill, or lineage. Tutelary deities emerge frequently in folklore and are often rooted in lineage tales of a tribe's ancestor that closely embody the actual deity. This would make how divinity was seen in individuals and how many lay claim to divine parentage make sense, and would explain how and why the thousands of titles or epithets of deities across the world may have come about. (An *epithet* is a title that describes qualities and characteristics relating to a deity's attributes and manifestations, as there are several throughout time, especially regarding Greek and Roman worldviews.)

For example, the Goddess Hekate has several epithets or manifestations, including *Hekate Apotropaia* (she who turns away/protects),[43] *Hekate Soteira* (the world soul), and *Hekate Enodia* (lady of the roads).[44] Epithets are mostly literary, poetic, and ritualistic in their functions. It can best be

43   Long, Natalie (Glaux). "Hecate." *American Folkloric Witchcraft*, 29 Mar. 2013, afwcraft.blogspot.com/2013/03/hecate.html.
44   Brannen, Cyndi. "Hekate Enodia: Goddess of the Road (Recorded Class)." *Keeping Her Keys*, 6 Aug. 2022, keepingherkeys.com/home/f/hekate-enodia-goddess-of-the-road-recorded-class.

assumed that people were encountering specific versions of Hekate, each unique to that time and place. The tutelary deities are specific deities of that specific community or land from which they emerged. Through the beauty of art, nature, and symbolism, they became even more personal, and through their historical evolution, they became even more distinct, although they all share similar qualities and traits under the umbrella title of that one title or name.

Names individualize empowerment, and they act as divine representations also capturing the essence of the deity. Perhaps these names we find are of ancestral rulers with a claim to divinity. For example, this can be seen in ancient dynasties at Newgrange of related elite figures being buried at the sídhe mounds throughout Ireland, bearing important names of deity figures along with a continuation of a divinely descended family chosen from the elite class of warriors to be great rulers.[45]

First popularized by the folklorist James George Frazer in his publication *The Golden Bough* in 1890, we have the myth of the priest-king, the sacrificial king, and the monarch's role in antiquity as both ruler and magician.[46] This bond or sacred marriage to the land was the act of the king becoming the virtue-holder, the embodiment of the spiritual relationship between the community and the supernatural otherworld.[47] The sovereign, most likely stemming from the priesthoods of ancient societies, was committed to their role as they were those who could uphold their duty and act judicially and democratically, and spiritually function with the powers. Typically, the reign of the king was restricted to seven years before the crown would be given up or taken away and a sacrificial rite would take place to ensure the bond between the land's fertility and the health of the people.[48] There is an example of Swedish kings who would reign for nine to

---

45 Not just to be interpreted as a "*faery mound*" but more broadly as an "otherworld mound." The hills act not just as a burial place and an otherworld portal but also, in folklore, they are frequently described as "the seats of kings," none being more sacred than the seat of the High King at the hill of Tarra.

46 Frazer, J.G. *The Golden Bough*. Macmillan, 1966.

47 The land itself is an embodiment of the Goddess or supernal nature of a society's own cosmology.

48 Farrar, Janet and Stewart. *Eight Sabbats for Witches*. Revised edition, Phoenix Publishing. 1998

ten years before a sacrificial rite would take place during a festival at the temple of Uppsala.[49] However, if a king failed in his duty, the crops would die, and if he broke his spiritual oath, there would be famine, war, and disease—very real threats to early people. In the Irish *Dindshenchas,* there are stories concerning the *Machas,* part of the folklore concerning the Goddess of sovereignty, prophecy, and battle: *the Morrígan,* or simply, *the Great Queen.*[50] One of her several names is Macha, or, in some tellings, she is several different women all bearing the name *Macha,* all of whom are Great Queens bearing the title of the Goddess as well as possibly being the representative or incarnation of the patron Goddess to the community. The way she would assume this role as Goddess of the people was probably done in the rituals of seasonal festivals, marking times of planetary power, oracular rites, or ceremonies of trance possession where the Queen would channel the Goddess for her people. The Goddess would give prophecies and advice and be present through the priestess-queen. It was through trance possession that the Gods could be made manifest in a physical sense among the tribe.

Classically monarchal societies often existed as dynasties, possibly for the sake of preserving a special bloodline related to what was believed to be divine descent. It was through the descendants that these Gods were believed to still be on Earth. This is why we know there were several kings and queens bearing names of the Gods as part of their lineage.[51] By the time most of these ancient stories of the oral tradition were recorded, they were widely Christianized by the ecclesiastical monks of Ireland, and the reworking of once-Pagan heritages very soon turned to Christian ancestries.[52] The Gods very well may be our ancestors, depending on your interpretation.

49 Frazer, J.G. *The Golden Bough.* Macmillan, 1966, pp. 166-167.

50 *The Metrical Dindshenchas.* School of Celtic Studies, 1991.

51 N. B. Aitchison, N.B. *"Kingship, Society, and Sacrality: Rank, Power, and Ideology in Early Medieval Ireland."* 1994.

52 Clarke, David and Andy Roberts. *Twilight of the Celtic Gods: An Exploration of Britain's Hidden Pagan Traditions.* 1996.

THE OLD ONES: THE WITCH GODS

Certain deities have taken an interest in Witchcraft and guiding Witches, awakening an understanding in us of what it means to live a magical life every day. There is a certain responsibility unto the Old Ones in caring for something held as deeply sacred as the Craft because of the impact it has upon the world they assist and guide. The Gods presented here are my conceptions of them as a Witch rather than historic accounts of Witchcraft deities. I encourage you to let them seek you out through your engagement with the Craft and knowing your own Witchblood, which means exploring an array of spirits and what a God or Divine power may mean to you in your practice.

When a deity calls to you, you'll know. There may be something in your research that jumps out to you or inspires you, and if you're willing to work with these spirits, you may be able to make a connection. Inspiration is the gift of the spirits that fuels Witches' passions and pursuits of empowerment. If you feel called by a particular spirit, always ask for signs and omens, attempt to make offerings, and seek divination from someone who specializes in the Pagan paths. Notice where your inspirations lead you. Your interest was placed within you at one point in time, and this is worth exploring. There are no guarantees, but there is always room to attempt contact. Doing your research allows you to understand these spirits with much more practical knowledge. Even by itself, the journey of research is considered a solemn offering. It helps you to get to know the deity's cultures, origins, and how each generation has influenced the reshaping of the Gods. We can detect the forms we have given to these beings and how we have reshaped them with each new generation of understanding.

Witchcraft has never lacked divine inspiration directly from the spirits and their influences. Each Witch will have naturally created their own approach to the workings of their personal and group practices simply because our society is different today. A practice that worked in the past would not work as well for us now. Creativity is the wine of the Muses, the Goddesses themselves, and change is the Lady's power. There is a certain truth in the chant, "She changes everything touches. Everything she touches changes."[53] The evolution of the Craft is what makes it a stronger, enduring force today and for the future yet to come. Give yourself full autonomy when seeking deities within yourself so you may see them outside of yourself. This inner working is where we greet the Old Ones at the threshold of the core, heart, and head.

LADY OF THE MOON

The Moon Goddess is the primal Witch-Goddess specific to the commonalities in Witchcraft-oriented practices. The association with lunar Goddesses is seen in several pieces of folklore and history.

Diana, Hekate Triformis, Selene, Artemis, Aradia, Arianrhod, Artume, and Devena are some of the classically revered lunar Goddesses, but contemporary Paganism's "Triple Goddess" presented by Robert Graves is worth special attention. In the early 1970s, Paul Huson presents the Goddess Habondia in his book *Mastering Witchcraft,* forming a direct correlation with the Dame Abonde or Holda seen in Witch trials and Witch figure folklore.[54] His writing also discusses the evolving legacy of the Witches' association with the Goddess Diana as the leader of wild night hunts, as well as Diana's overall conflation with several other tutelary ancestor Goddesses (defined as an Ancestress of Pagans). Diana is described as a beautiful lady clad in regal garments and mounted upon a wild animal, leading hoards of the night's phantom armies. These nightly spirits under the Lady are rumored to be familiars of secret knowledge

53 Starhawk. "She Changes Everything She Touches." *Dreaming the Dark: Magic, Sex, and Politics.* Beacon Press, 1997, p. 226.

54 Huson, Paul. *Mastering Witchcraft: A Practical Guide for Witches, Warlocks, and Covens.* G. P. Putnams, 1970.

about the Arte. These dead offer unique skills and help practitioners in day-to-day life if they know how to conjure and seal a deal with them.

Pacts such as these exist for Witches like me today. There is always a contract in place between Witches and spirits, often marked by the cycles and tides of the Moon. Using any method—spell, chant, rite, or rhyme—the Witch sets out in the night to catch these tides of power. These tides are moments of huge magical power on the Earth as controlled by the Moon. (The Moon is the symbol of the Witch Goddess, hence her role as the leader of magical power by her right as the queen of enchantment.) These pacts and relationships are made in both religious and tangible ways. This passage is made, or rather "mantled," by the lunar Goddess, as the pale-faced Lady ensures entry into a familiar way and a fulfillment of the *sangreal*.[55]

> *"Beloved Bloodmother of my especial breed,*
> *Welcome me at this moment with your willing womb.*
> *Let me learn to live in love with all you are,*
> *So my seeking spirit serves the Sangreal."*
> —The Sangreal Prayer, William G. Gray[56]

VENUS

Venus has long been held as the brightest star of the night and referred to both as a Goddess figure and, in a Luciferian interpretation, as the brightest light in the heavens thus, the *Lightbringer, Lucifer,* or *the Morning Star.* As a Goddess figure, Venus is heavily associated with love, luxury, and prosperity. Later, she became conflated with the Greek Goddess Aphrodite and earlier sea Goddess figures. As a collection of guardian spirits of specific landforms and waters, she was also tied to the idea of virginal maidens and the figure of the *Koré*.[57]

---

55 The Holy Grail has deep Pagan undertones and connotations in addition to the grail's Christian Mythos, truly making it the womb and tomb of the Patron of the world. See the works of William G. Gray for more information.

56 Jones, Evan J. and Doreen Valiente. "The Faith: The Sangreal Prayer." *Witchcraft: A Tradition Renewed.* Robert Hale. 1999, pp. 26.

57 *The Koré (kor-a):* A figure or archetype of the "young maiden." Persephone is often referred to by this title.

THE EARTH MOTHER

The Goddess was most associated with the Earth Mother in ancient times and directly connected to cycles of birth and death. The idea of the Earth as a providing mother of all things comes from the land that brings forth life and is related to ideas of fertility and nurturing. The Earth Mother possesses the land itself as the body we reside upon, and her centrality comes from she who is also the space of the present. Like a mountain or tree, she climbs toward the spaces that are betwixt the kingdoms of the upper world, elongating her body to touch the oceans of the ever-expansive sea. Together, we view her as an all-encompassing figure of Earth, sea, and sky. She is the guiding habitat of all people and spirits of the Earth.

Sometimes, she is depicted as a vibrant red or green serpent, or sometimes as a stone woman. Most often, feminine imagery in the natural landscape, such as caves, mountains, and rivers, develops a Goddess association. Land masses are seen as ever-bestowing life and the powers of change. Red, of course, is a color connected with blood and women's Mysteries.

The Earth Mother can be seen in various forms as Frigga, Cybele, Demeter, Gaia, and Danu, but the most famous in modern times is her incarnation of Mother Earth in English Romanticism, a literary and artistic movement that strove to revitalize the essence of life and naturism between roughly 1800 and 1840.[58] This movement attempted to preserve the golden age of the forests and countryside before the advent of industrial city life. Technology was seen as moving humanity away from the majesty and preservation of Earth's beauty and sacredness. Romanticism fueled new cultural ideas through culture, art, folklore, and environmentalism, and its influence on how we view nature and the sacred is still seen today.

Hearth Mothers and Goddesses of inspiration and the home, such as Hestia and Athena in the cults of Greece and Hellenistic practices and Brigid of Ireland, existed alongside the Earth Mother. Brigid, of course, is revered as one of Ireland's three patron saints for her medieval Irish writings, her sacred fire still burning at the monastery of Kildare.

---

58 Hutton, Ronald. "Finding a Language." *The Triumph of the Moon.* Oxford University Press. 2019, pp. 1–34.

THE LADY OF THE CROSSROADS

Most famously associated with Witchcraft, necromancy, and her role as a queen of the dead, Hekate has made a huge impact upon the hearts of Witches. She is seen as the eternal Maiden, another "maker and taker" of Witch-kind in times of crisis and darkness, and is especially important for those who work in death-oriented practices like mediumship, divination, ancestor work, or death-midwifery. Yet her associations are vast; Hekate is much more than just a chthonic dark Goddess but is the mother of Witches. Historically portrayed as a torch-bearing Goddess of the night and the Magna Mater of Witches, she holds many faces and uses many tools. Among these tools are the sacred blade, the cords of initiation, and the keys to cross the thresholds. For more information on Hekate, see the works of Sorita D'este.

THE QUEEN OF ELPHAME

Faery queens of old are alive and well in traditional Witchcraft cosmology. The powers of faery run through the wild and lonely places where nature spirits and the "good folk" dwell. However, these spirits are often organized by an otherworldly hierarchical and monarchical system based on their qualities and virtues. All of them are ruled by a faery queen, in the same way that bees follow a queen. The most famous example of the faery queen and Witch-lore comes to us through the trial records of Isobel Gowdie in 1662 in the small Scottish village of Aulderan.[59] However, a common motif in Witch confessions was making a pact or having the blood awaken the power of the Witch via a faery queen, with another example of the queen of the fae from the 1576 confession of Bessie Dunlop.[60] It is hard to say if this was also a common practice originating in folk traditions or if it was molded by the influence of the persecutions. Both can and have existed, yet, like the Witches' Sabbath and the Devil himself, nothing is quite as it seems.

---

59 Wilby, Emma. *The Visions of Isobel Gowdie: Magic, Witchcraft and Dark Shamanism in Seventeenth-Century Scotland.* Sussex Academic Press, 2013.

60 Hodgart, John and Martin Clarke. *Bessie Dunlop: Witch of Dalry.* Hodder & Stoughton, 1995.

BAPHOMET

It is so important to include and acknowledge the Divine Androgyne among deities. The Divine Androgyne is present in all deity and spirit forms as spiritual essence is formless, attuning to form and incarnation as the practitioner casts it. Within a deity's liminal presence, and acting as a source of inspiration, is the figure Baphomet. Between the horns of the Sabbatic Goat of the world shines a mighty torch. He is androgynous, endowed and breasted, pointing to the Mystery of triplicity and the Hermetic principle "as above, so below." Baphomet, as a world soul and *axis mundi,* connects the worlds above, below, and center. This depiction is most famous from Éliphas Lévi, but also comes up in the legends of The Knights Templar, who worship this heretical androgynous being.[61] The *Bucca* of Cornish Witchcraft, as the white and black goat or *Bucca Gwidder* and *Bucca Dhu,* is seen as a Divine Androgyne.[62] Ultimately, the Divine Androgyne is a figure of the Horned God in dual nature and triplicity that is altogether beast, human, male, female, and sacred from the goat's otherworldly viewpoint.

THE HORNED ONE:
The Light, the Lover, the Stag

The Horned God is the quintessential counterpart to the Witches' Goddess. This God came out of tribal legends of the hunter-gatherer cultures and their dependency on and reverence for the horned animals that provided resources, food, tools, and wisdom. These horned animals symbolized the king of the otherworld, embodied in the form of an animal that provided all parts of itself for the tribe. One of the most enduring images of the Horned God can be found on the Gundestrup cauldron of Denmark, an ornate silver cauldron depicting scenes of the powers of nature, the kingdom of beasts, and the Horned God Cernunnos.[63] This artifact dates to the late Iron Age and offers a wealth of symbolism and insight into

---

61   Newman, Sharan. *The Real History Behind the Templars.* Berkley Books, 2007.

62   Gary, Gemma and Jane Cox. "The Bucca." *Traditional Witchcraft: A Cornish Book of Ways.* Troy Books, 2008, pp. 57–59.

63   Salo, Unto. *The Gundestrup Cauldron: Cultural-Historical and Social-Historical Perspectives: An Essay,* Institute for the Study of Man, 2018.

the mythos and beliefs of the different Celtic-speaking tribes as they migrated throughout Europe.

Images depicting this particular figure can be found not just in Ireland and much of the British Isles, but also areas as far off as northern Italy, parts of France, and Rome. Gaulish lore, coming out of ancient British, Irish, and Gallo-Roman practices, works to unite the Horned God with the Lord of Wild Places and the King of the Beasts. The Horned God was very much adopted and merged with the concept of the Witch's Devil, a God of duality, nature, and the Witch's magical life force. He is a keeper and a guide to the land's energetic powers that trail through the Earth, and a guardian of the Goddess herself. He brings new Witches to the Witch Goddess in whatever form she may take. He is a God of light and luminescence. The Sun rising and setting, living and dying each day, gives a glimpse into the cycles of life and rebirth that he holds the reins to.

Witch and Magister Evan John Jones referred to the Horned One as "the Horned Child," as he is born again at the winter solstice, retaining his creative vigor, and beauty, and is often described as having "a lusty passion."[64] He grows along with agriculture before he dies at one of the three harvest festivals of Lammas, Autumn, or Samhain. The life cycle and roles of the Horned One depend on the group and their mythos. What has worked best for me is simply feeling the seasonal pulls as they come. Since his primary role takes place at particular ritual sabbats, his place as Witch King is marked throughout the Wheel of the Year. His horns are also a vital symbol. Horns are a near-universally recognized symbol of divinity, sacrifice, and the roles of the hunter and the hunted. The hunted becomes the intermediary between the tribe and the underworld of death and is reborn to nature once again as he embodies nature's creative counterpart.

He is the Wandering One, leading Witching folk on the long and winding road of initiation, Witchcraft, fire, fertility, and death. He is also seen in Welsh folklore as *Gwyn Ap Nudd*, the King of the *Tylwyth Teg* or the fair folk, and leader of the Wild Hunt. These qualities are also strongly associated with Herne, the Hunter of Windsor Forrest

---

64 Jones, Evan J. and Doreen Valiente. "The Nature of the Rites," *Witchcraft A Tradition Renewed*. Robert Hale, 1990, pp. 47-60.

in English lore.[65] All this may appear in whatever guise the Horned God may present you, as your interests and understandings are a key component to your deeper understanding of his innate mercurialness. However, due to his dual nature—a God of life *and* death—he has a darker aspect as winter comes, occupying his throne as the Lord of Death and the underworld below.

PAN:
THE GOAT FOOT GOD

Pan originates in ancient Arcadia, a mountainous rural area contrasted against the booming industry and civilization of ancient Greece.[66] This rurality was treasured as an original homeland of the Greeks and was often romanticized even in the ancient world. Ancient Greeks valued Arcadia for its distance from busy city life, its glorious mountains, and the herds of goats that roamed there. Because shepherding and husbandry were among the main skills and practices of the region, the Arcadian God was visualized in the form of a goat, representing the spirit that goats provided to people as trade, livestock, and companions in the wild landscape. This goat-God figure, Pan, shares many traits with his father Hermes. The two figures may have been the same at one point, as they were both patrons and protectors of roads, travelers, and pastures.[67]

Pan's patronage specifically fell over the pathways taken by goat herders and the animal handlers themselves. Arcadia's geographical isolation also designated Pan as a solitary figure, a God who wandered alone with his troupe of nature spirits, most of whom were nymphs. Despite this solitary nature, he is often depicted alongside deities such as Dionysus, for his love of wine and pleasure, and Artemis, as they both occupied wild places.[68]

---

65 IndyBabalon. "Faces of the Holly King." *Crossroads Coven*, 25 May 2018, crossroadscoven.wordpress.com/2011/12/04/faces-of-the-holly-king/.

66 Pausanias, *Description of Greece*.

67 Mankey, Jason. "Pan and the Other Horned Gods of Ancient Greece." *The Horned God of the Witches*. Llewellyn Publications, 2021, pp. 47–66.

68 Ibid.

As a solo God, Pan is also the God of masturbation, contributing to his lusty nature depicted as more concerned with the sexual pleasure of the moment. He is indiscriminately spontaneous in his expressions of sex, fertility, dance, and music. These activities are all sacred to him, as they may not be the necessities of life, but they sure make life worth living—we all need fun, mirth, joy, and ecstatic pleasures every once in a while. Many classic paintings depict him chasing nymphs and often failing in his attempts toward sexuality, but he chases regardless. Overall, Pan is attributed as the God of joy, said to delight the other deities of Olympus despite his strange bestial nature.

The romanticism of Pan as a figure emerged in artistic splendor throughout Europe, specifically famed during the Italian Renaissance's chronicling of Roman beliefs and deities. He evolved into the role of the God of all things, for *pan* in Greek means "all" or "everything." This all-encompassing outlook, as well as his attachment to rural, rugged, and wild places where magic is sought after, is widely attributed to the spread of his image.

Later, during the Victorian English Romantic movement, Pan became known as *Orphic Pan*.[69] Pan was now symbolizing the God not as physically seen, but rather felt in the presence of the natural landscape, the soft breeze of wind across your face and the playing of soft panpipes in the distance to announce the God's presence. Pan was seen as the All-God, inspired by the following in different circles of the Homeric and Orphic Hymns and captured in poetry by Aleister Crowley, Oscar Wilde, and Robert Frost. Pan is known to appear in several novels, artistic motifs, and even home decorations of the late nineteenth and early twentieth centuries.

The most famous Witch attributed to venerating the God was Rosaleen Norton, an artist by trade and devotee of Pan, who arose in the media during the Witchcraft revival of the 1940s through the 1960s. She considered Pan to be the patron of all Witchcraft, the vitality of all sexual passions, and the essence of life itself. To Norton, he was the natural chieftain deity of the world and a spiritual conduit of all magical operations.

---

69 Robichaud, Paul. *Pan: The Great God's Modern Return*. Reaktion Books Ltd, 2023.

DIONYSUS:
The Earth-Shaker and Liberator

The cults of Dionysus are rooted in the ecstatic practices of exploring liberation and returning to the healed self. The Dionysian praxis often uses all forms of the arts, sex, and a variety of substances in conjunction with a variety of trance and possession techniques, which allows the devotee to transcend freely between states of consciousness and explore their deepest inhibitions. These rites were based on a seasonal death-and-rebirth theme, common among agricultural cults surrounding the main cultivation of the grapevine for sacred wine. As the life of the vines is sacrificed by pressing the ripe grapes into wine, the fermentation of the juice, as if by magic, resurrects the bloodied grapes into a reborn nectar of wine. Thus, the wine became an identifiable symbol of the God and his mythological life cycle, similar to the relationship between Demeter and grain like that of the *Eleusinian Mysteries*. Early origins of the Cult of Dionysius can be seen in Crete and Asia Minor. These practices are like the Osirian Mysteries in Egypt, likely taking shape in Minoan Crete from about 3000 to 1000 CE.[70] The name *Dionysus* exists nowhere other than in Crete and Greece as an earlier form of Zagreus, known as the first Dionysus.[71]

Theatre originated with the *tragōidia*, consisting of the Greek words *tragos* and *ōidiē*, meaning "goat song."[72] To begin the drama, a sacrifice of a goat was made to the wild, ecstatic God of nature. This is the origin of the ritualistic nature Greek drama still holds, connecting us directly to the Gods of comedy and tragedy.

As the double-natured God, Dionysus wears the masks of joy and rage, creation and destruction, and, importantly in theater as we recognize it today, of comedy and tragedy. Attending a play is part of continuing the broader tradition of storytelling. It remains an active ritual where the audience is also an active participant in the rite or the play by receiving

70 Burkert, Walter. *Greek Religion*. Cambridge, Mass: Harvard University Press, 1985.

71 Meisner, Dwayne A. "Dionysus in the Rhapsodies," *Orphic Traditions and The Birth of the Gods*. Oxford University Press, 2018, pp. 237-278.

72 King, Kimball and Brett Rogers. "Greek Tragedy and Satyr-Drama." *Western Drama Through the Ages*, Greenwood Press, 2007, p. 12.

the performance. The tradition lives on in the storytelling itself as a play or ritual is witnessed. With no audience, there is no conduit for the story to continue. The plays of ancient Greece were often sacred in the context of deities, heroes, and enlightened or fallen ancestors.

The ritual of watching tragedy forces the audience to experience *catharsis,* a word that here means "to cleanse" or "to purify." The purging of emotions that may have been pent up and needed a release is a big part of what we gain from the rite. We, the audience or ritual attendants, are then, in unison, triggered by the performance. We reflect on the shared human experience and connect with the purging of knowledge for the sake of enlightenment. In this way, Dionysus becomes the world's mirror, forcing the audience to stare directly at the shared extremes of human sorrow. He is theatrical in his behavior, which is also how he is commonly perceived. For many, Dionysus is the balance between the extremes, and he is also of pure celebration and the joy found in his festivities and the satyr play.[73]

Dionysus and his Mysteries, depending on how they are perceived, are very much made up of queer Mysteries, consisting of opposing concepts. As a goat-horned God, he is found as an androgynous deity in mythos, shapeshifting and one with the essences of both gender expressions. This concept was made famous by the Christ mythos and the works of Frazer's *The Golden Bough.*[74] Often depicted in the *Orphic Hymns,* "double-natured, thrice-born" is one of Dionysus's many epithets.[75] He is the balance between the extremes: as a borderline or liminal God, his teachings and his nature present us with the truth that "what goes up must also come down."

He is that which holds the center between two existing opposites where both are equally valid, another form of the Hermetic principle of polarity that is found in common Occult or Witchcraft circles.[76] He

---

73　The Satyr play is a comedy rooted in tragedy told from the point of view of the satyrs, often with crude humor, exaggerated costuming, and comedic effect by the chorus playing the rowdy band of satyrs.

74　Frazer, James G. *The Golden Bough.* Macmillan, 1955.

75　Athanasakēs, Apostolos N. and Benjamin M. Wolkow. "The Orphic Hymn #30 to Dionysus," *The Orphic Hymns.* Johns Hopkins University Press, 2013.

76　Polarity is not exclusively about gender or sexual orientation in Hermetics, but rather two opposing things that come together and balance each other out.

holds the center with his *thyrsus,* a pinecone-tipped wand representing his powers of magic, fertility, and wisdom. He is the maintainer and catalyst of the flow, and as an ecstatic God, you may never know when he will stir up that balance or foundation he holds in his form as either a goat or a bull. Dionysus is joy and rage, ecstasy and madness (wisdom and knowledge), wine and joy (life and fun), and creation and destruction (magic itself). His epithets include titles of "earthshaker" and "liberator" for a reason: realizations and aftershocks of any experience can be life-altering.

He is also the keeper of wine, the blood of the Gods. The wine of Dionysus is the potent symbol of he who holds the cup that overflows, empties, and refills itself. It is the blood of the deity or Dionysus himself, as the grapevines (life) are harvested (death) and fermented (rebirth) into the sacred wine. The wine itself induces an altered state of consciousness, and the spirit of the wine can act as any sacred offering and symbol of change, which is why it is an important libation to the working of Witches. To many, wine has long been part of the sacred and religious contexts of offerings, ritual, and community sharing.

SHAPESHIFTERS

The Morrighan is a prime example of the liminal nature of a deity with the ability to shapeshift into any form desired. Shapeshifting, by means of presenting themselves to us in an unexpected way when working with their power, is a clear example of liminality. This is not only associated with anthropomorphism or animal spirits but also with gender expression, symbolism, and even behaviors and mannerisms. Spirits work within the self, but the external expression is made by the Witch, the sacred artist, and the bard, who tells the story that brings them into existence. As Witches, we are open to receiving the pieces of deity that relate to us the most. In this way, we build an individualized dialogue with our spirits and often receive validation of our experiences with these beings by looking into their histories.

CHAPTER SIX

ARADIA: GODDESS OF THE WITCHES

The Creation Myth of Aradia is a story like many of the ones we may already know in the Western world. It's always best to start at the beginning, so please enjoy this original piece of storytelling and poetry, *Incarñata Dīvāna.*

> *In the beginning, there was but the spirit of Diana in the vast abyss in a time out of mind. She was the one being before creation, for it has been said that within her were all things. From herself, she divided into the light and the darkness, giving birth to Lucifer as her consort, other self, and the light, becoming the Moon and He the Sun. Diana, still of the night in the dark abyss, fell in love with this splendorous being that came from her. She sought to consult the spirits before the first spirit, the mothers and fathers of the beginning. Those were the giant, celestial Elder Gods. They told her that to capture the heart of Lucifer, she must go to Earth incarnated as a human woman. In a totemic shapeshifting chase began Diana's hunt of the night for her union with the light. She was the cat and he the mouse:*

> *The hunt of the cat and mouse occurred*
> *As the wheel of seasons turned and turned*
> *In a Solar eclipse of the cosmic light*
> *Diana's pursuit took winged flight*
> *Those two became one and then became three.*
> *To make children of the Earth beloved and free*

To then after soothe the angered, fallen son
The Mother's cord in motion, had already begun
Splendor had coupled with the shadow of his twin
To vanquish the curse of the false God's sin.
Diana, unto ever-loving Lucifer's plight
Sang unto him the song of Night
And on her wheel spun moonlight
For Aradia, savior, birthed in sight!
So Diana's wheel of fate still turns
As Lucifer's fire of gnosis burns
Making her spindle go round and round
Affecting the fates of mortal ground
For Aradia taught them the Mysteries of all that be
To Dance! Sing! Under the Moon, naked and free!
She awakened the blood, the power within
'Round temple and groves of the people therein,
For incarnated the voice of Diana spoke!
The power of faery, together with Folk.

After the fall of Lucifer (or possibly during that same fall), Diana came to Earth in her human form as her daughter, Aradia, and created and taught the Witchblood to the children of Earth, teaching them the arts of magic, poisoning, and sorcery. It was she who led the creation of magic as an art of protest and rebellion against the tyranny of the Church and the enslavers of the poor, the paupers, and the marginalized. This form of sorcery was protest, revolution, and liberation, all from she who became known as the first Witch and priestess of the many. In this way, and by her charge of the Mother Diana, she was passing unto them the Mysteries of the Witches.[77] Not just for Witches, but for all. The Gospel is for all those willing to learn it. Aradia is a Witch for all Witches, the Mother Incarnate, and the voice of the Great Goddess herself, she is the body of the people, their refuge, and their altar.

As it was, as it is, and as it ever shall be.

---

77 Seen in this aspect as the Queen Goddess of Earth, sea, and sky, associated with the mountains and leader of the wild hunt of night, with troops of the dead. The Witch's night-flight or phantom procession.

Aradia, The Gospel of The Witches (The Vangel) by Charles Godfrey Leland was first published in 1899. Leland originally published three volumes of folklore from 1892 to 1895, and *Aradia* (also referred to as *The Gospel*) was the final publication of the series. The first two texts published, *Etruscan Roman Remains* and *Legends of Florence,* are standard collections of European and Italian folklore available at the time.[78] However, *Aradia* that has an extraordinary impact on the views of Witchcraft, lending itself to the creation and understanding of some of Pagans and Witches' contemporary practices. The origins of this mystical text are as mysterious today as they were in antiquity. The text either revived or created a pantheon and praxis specific to the Witchblood, as well as a living Goddess to whom Witches can connect the awakening. She is birthed by Diana, the Moon Goddess who is now associated as the queen of Witchcraft or the queen of fae.[79] Aradia is the divine avatar of herself and her gift to humankind as the "first" Witch.

"For Diana so loved the World, She gave her only begotten Daughter."[80]

Aradia is presented as a liberator, initiator, the Witch's teacher, and a Goddess incarnate on Earth. Specifically, she relates to peasantry, the marginalized, and oppressed groups who are still at the mercy of the land and closer to nature. She related to the class of people associated with folk practices, healing, and divining, who experienced scrutiny from the church. Witches were historically associated with members of these social classes, which contributed to their liminality as workers between the worlds.

According to the text, Aradia is the true Witch-Maker through the symbol of her mother, Diana the Moon Mother. In addition, Lucifer, the Sun, brought her into being for the specific purpose of rebellion and action against enslavement, oppression, and tyranny, taking magical and vengeful action upon the oppressors of the common people with

---

78 Leland, Charles G. *Legends of Florence.* MacMillan and Co, 1895. See also: Leland, Charles. *Etruscan Roman Remains.* Routledge, 2002.

79 Referring to what would be considered faery folk, goblins, and spirits of nature that share the same theology as Witches mentioned in the text.

80 A variation of my own inspired by *The Gospel of The Witches.* I took creative liberty in blending the verse John 3:16, inspired by my upbringing as a Witch with some Christian influence.

the gifting of Witchcraft, bestowed by the Great Goddess's daughter upon the world. The powers of the Witch embodied a living vessel exemplified and defined Aradia in her role as the first Witch on Earth.

The tyranny of the Catholic institution is commented on directly in the text and is very much a part of Leland's belief structures.[81] As stated in *Triumph of the Moon* by Ronald Hutton, Leland was candid "to protest against what he saw as the unhealthy benevolence towards the Middle Ages expressed by 'all historians' of that time. To him, this remained a time of monstrous abuses and tyranny of church and state."[82] Hutton also explains that every time the Gospel presented a malefic spirit, Leland went to extra lengths to identify it with a pre-existing Pagan deity. However, Hutton did point out that, among Leland's informants, folk magic itself was seen not as a religion but more of a sorcery, stating that "it did not add up to a religious system" and that it was "something more than a sorcery, and something less than faith."[83] When Diana, in her human form as Aradia, made the Witches, she gave them intercession by also teaching the faery realm, the realm of the goblins, and the familiars or *foletto*.[84]

The text of *Aradia* itself can be seen as thematically gnostic and Luciferian-inspired. It presents the reader with a very militant text that uses Catholic influence against itself and blends it with Roman-Pagan cultures, a feature of many Italian Witchcraft practices. Such is the dual practice of the old religion (*La vecchia religione*) and the new (Christianity). The pantheon of Aradia was inspired by and based on Christianized motifs and characters such as Cain, the "man in the Moon," and Lucifer himself as the saving Sun God and liberator of inner knowledge.[85] Aradia becomes a Christ-like figure, meant to both teach and save the people enslaved by the confines of their oppressive society and to liberate them by the power of magic and the Gods of Old. Later, this lore is conflated with the figure

---

81   Pennell, Elizabeth Robins. *Charles Godfrey Leland: A Biography*. Houghton Mifflin, 1906.

82   Hutton, Ronald. "Finding A Witchcraft." *The Triumph of the Moon*. Oxford University Press, 2019, pp. 147–156.

83   Ibid.

84   Spencer, Craig. *Aradia: A Modern Guide to Charles Godfrey Leland's Gospel of the Witches*. Llewellyn Worldwide, 2020.

85   Howard, Michael and D. A. Schulke. "Casting New Light on Wicca?" *The Luminous Stone: Lucifer in Western Esotericism*. Three Hands Press, 2016, pp. 90–98.

of Herodias and her daughter Salome (the Dancer of Seven Veils) from the New Testament.

The conflation of Aradia is likely an example of Pagan and Christian characters synchronizing, in the same way as Roman deities were derived from the Greek pantheon. This occurred as ecclesiastical writings greatly influenced the way legends and lore were passed on, changing everyday schools of thought and blending lore as "fact." By the twelfth century, Christianity forcefully blended all pre-existing legend and lore concerning the Witches' Sabbath and the subversion of Witchcraft as a diabolical conspiracy against the Church. This conflation was performed directly in the *Canon Episcopi* of the Council of Ancyra in 314 CE, stating that Diana/Herodias held one-third of the Earth "away from God."[86] This claim of Herodias being the same as the Goddess Diana then became cemented among the people in Europe. Although very different, the two figures were already widely viewed as the same; there was a previously established widespread belief in Herodias's wandering nightly spirit which The Council of Treviri had identified specifically as the wicked spirit of Herodiana. This council outright blends the names Diana and Herodias as Herodiana together.

Misunderstandings also arose as these spiritual travels through the night were thought to be actual flights, not the spiritual practices of astral travel, the psychic journey to consult with spirits, and the workings of mental magic. The *Canon* stated that these ecstatic journeys of "hunts and flight" were led by Herodiana and even Dame Abonde as the legend started to blend through the regions.[87]

An attitude threatening the veneration of Pagan spirits and deities emerged as cultural transitions took place from Pagan to Christianized societies. This aversion stemmed from the cultural transition toward demonizing things that were not sanctioned by the Church, though the Catholic saints could still be petitioned.[88] This change in cultural approach impacted religious attitudes regarding Witchcraft. Italy had a unique way of intertwining Roman and Catholic religious influence in its blending of

---

86 Valiente, Doreen. "The Forerunners." *The Rebirth of Witchcraft*. Robert Hale, 1989, p. 24.

87 Magliocco, Sabina. *Who Was Aradia? The History and Development of a Legend*. Pomegranate, 2001, pp. 5–22.

88 Walter, Philippe and Jon E. Graham. *Christian Mythology: Revelations of Pagan Origins*. Inner Traditions, 2014.

folklore and Christianity, acknowledging the possibility that Witchcraft and Catholicism could exist together.[89] In this context, it is important to understand how specific times and places affect legends, and how they change quickly as worldviews and cultures transform synchronically.

Aradia was published well before the philosophies of Margaret Murray and her Witch-Cult theory. However, Leland may have been the origin of such a claim. As an amateur American folklorist, Leland claimed that he had discovered an underground cult of surviving Witches from the Tuscan region of southern Italy.[90] According to his report, this tradition was unbroken and unchanged by the influence of the Catholic Church, surviving through families.

Leland claimed that he came into contact with one woman, Maddalena, who is truly a huge figure in the creation of *The Vangel* (*The Gospel of The Witches*).[91] With the success of the text's publication, it is possible that it served as fragmented evidence and inspiration for Murray's proposal of the Western Witch Cult in 1921. However, despite both Murray and Leland's works having been widely discredited by scholars, there is evidence of the survival of Witchcraft and Witch-lore in Italy, just not in the ways they claimed it existed.

One of Leland's main influences for *The Gospel* was the novel *La Sorcière* (1862) by French historian Jules Michelet. However, Leland claimed his Gospel was not a work of fiction but a sacred text of true Pagan Witchcraft and was not at all influenced by the religiousness of the Catholic Church. One look at the text and its contents tells us a very different story, as there are clearly Catholic overtones in *Aradia*'s language, motifs, and biblical comparisons. These overtones may be attributed to different regional translations that had spread throughout

---

89 Grimassi, Raven. *Hereditary Witchcraft: Secrets of the Old Religion*. Llewellyn Worldwide, 1999.

90 Spencer, Craig. *Aradia: A Modern Guide to Charles Godfrey Leland's Gospel of the Witches*. Llewellyn Worldwide, 2020.

91 Blended European folk beliefs of Witches and cunning folk state that powers were drawn from a sacred or black book. In this popular belief, Leland presents this alleged text as "the Book" discovered by his informant, Maddalena. This, of course, may not be historically accurate, but rather reworkings of previous folk-beliefs and practices along the Witchcraft narrative of his time (see *Mystical Origins*).

Europe, as the Church influenced not just people's spirituality, but their entire lifestyle, classes, and political structures. In short, the Church had a way of rewriting folklore, history, and people's own magical beliefs, including the Church of the early modern era as the legends shifted. With writers like Gardner and Valiente responsible for the revival of Modern Wica, *Aradia* was one of the most important texts that inspired the rhetoric of contemporary Paganism and spiritual movements alike.

The lunar associations of Diana and Aradia offer insight into Witch-craft-oriented folk traditions that existed in Italy and evolved with the already-coinciding Christian symbolism that became part of the magic of Italian Cunning and Folk Traditions. Certain figures evolve with time, and although Leland's work may not be proven to be fact, there are underpinnings of a deeper Mystery at play, though they may be fragmented and presented in a reinterpreted text.

Leland was a folklorist of his time and his fascination with what he considered to be "True Witchcraft" is what went on to become what we now hear in Pagan circles, especially through the writing of Doreen Valiente and her Charge of the Goddess. Regardless, magic has given birth to the figure of a Lunar Goddess who "saves the people" and empowers them to fight back! It's an inspiring work of Witch-lore, telling of the creation of Witches and all their magic being worked today. This tale of a Witch Goddess also evolved due to socio-cultural norms of storytelling, and, in this way, stories of magic always live on as they generate a spirit of their own.

MYSTICAL ORIGINS:
Maddelena

The Mystical origins of the creation of *The Gospel* lay upon the work not just of Leland but of his informant, Maddelena. After meeting Maddelena in 1886, Leland presents her as a skilled Witch from a Hereditary family who had been able to procure the stories and folklore from her fellow Witches. Leland said he "employed her specially to collect among her sisters of the hidden spells in many places all the traditions of the olden time known to them."[92] Maddelena herself has mysterious origins, as according to Roma Lister, a peer of Leland's, her real name was Margherita. Yet, she signed her letters as "Maddelena Taluti" and

---

92 Leland, Charles. *Aradia or the Gospel of the Witches.* Samuel Weiser, 1974, p. VII.

was Leland's main hired informant for Italian and Roma folklore for his first two published works.

She may have been Leland's main connection to entering the world of the Occult. Being well-traveled, upper class, and studying much of minoritized and Indigenous myths, Leland was well-versed in approaching superstitions and spiritual traditions of "the folk" with Victorian scientific rationalism. However, he believed in preserving the sacred and omnipresent beauty of nature.

As recorded by Ronald Hutton, Leland was also known to have a history of revolutionary political ideologies as he participated in the French Revolution of 1848, and earlier in life, was present at the battle of Gettysburg in the American Civil War.[93] His travels were a driving force of his love of Europe, and he settled in Florence by 1888. Hutton recorded Leland's hatred of absolute monarchy, the glorification of the medieval and Renaissance periods, and the Roman Catholic church.[94] He most likely brought his style and influence to the translation he received from Maddelena, as it is also clear to several historians that he was not fluent in Italian, nor the dictations of Maddelena herself. With this tampering of the translation, the original Italian loses its nuance, and perhaps with that, part of the complexity of the text. Elizabeth Robins Pennell, Leland's niece and biographer, recorded in 1888 while Leland was located in Florence that "he was [introduced] into the Witch-Lore of the Romagna, an [introduction] that was to bear fruit in a whole seris [sic] of books."[95] In his manuscript notes, Leland describes Maddelena as the reason he was informed about the existence of such a Gospel of the Italian cunning folk that may have been in existence circa 1886. With much enthusiasm, Leland urged her to discover such a text. She mailed a hand-written manuscript on January 1, 1897, producing what would become Leland's *Vangel* or *The Gospel of Aradia*.[96] However, without warning or any known reason, Maddelena mysteriously disappeared without a trace, never to be heard from again.

93   Valiente, Doreen. *The Rebirth of Witchcraft*. Robert Hale, 1987.

94   Hutton, Ronald. "Finding a Witchcraft." *The Triumph of the Moon*. Oxford University Press, 2019, p. 153.

95   Pennell, Elizabeth Robins. *Charles Godfrey Leland: A Biography*. Houghton Mifflin, 1906.

96   Leland, Charles. *Aradia or the Gospel of the Witches*. Samuel Weiser, 1974.

THE WITCH MAKER AND MESSIAH:
ARADIA HERSELF

Aradia's name gives us clues to her role and origins as the Witch before all Witches, as well as her conflation with Herodias, the "wickedest" woman of the New Testament. The name Aradia does not appear in any pre-existing religious text or manuscript of Italian folklore. According to author Jeffrey Burton Russell in his book *Witchcraft in the Middle Ages*, there is no evidence that *Aradia* provided an accurate depiction of Italian Folk Witchcraft.[97] This does not mean she didn't exist, but her real existence was not the same as the incarnation that Leland gave us, as his descriptions were heavily poetic and inspired by the English Romantic moment of his day. He likely drew some of his conclusions about the nature of Witchcraft's survival in the current art and literature of his day.

When it came to the identity of Diana and her tie to Herodias, *the Gospel* very well may have been shaped by the sensationalism of Oscar Wilde's one-act play, *Salome* (1891).[98]

The meaning of the name *Aradia*, when looked at in Latin and Italian, relates strongly to her role as Divinity. This has been gloriously presented in the work of Craig Spencer's *Aradia: A Modern Guide to Charles Godfrey Leland's Gospel of The Witches* (2020).[99] The Latin translation breaks down as "altar, refuge protection, or voice" for *Ara* and "by day, or relating to Diana" for *Dia*, whereas the Italian translations are roughly "altar" for *Ara*, "give, grant, or bestow" for *Dia*, and "Goddess" for *Dea*.[100]

Leland claimed that Aradia may have had a connection to Jewish Folklore, specifically the eighth to tenth century work *The Alphabet of Ben Sira*'s portrayal of Lilith (*lilitu*), but this may be a matter of poetic inspiration rather than historical fact. However, there is a connection between the figure of Lilith to Aradia's role as a Goddess and her connection to the figure of Cain. Lilith's rebellious and spirited nature

97   Adler, Margot. *Drawing Down the Moon: Witches, Druids, Goddess-Worshippers, and Other Pagans in America Today.* Beacon Press, 1986.

98   Wilde, Oscar. *Salome.* H.M. Caldwell Co, 1907.

99   Spencer, Craig. *Aradia: A Modern Guide to Charles Godfry Lelands's Gospel of the Witches.* Llewellyn Worldwide, 2020.

100 Ibid, pp. 14–15.

may remind some of the similar relationship to the Witch Goddess Naamah, the wife and seducer of the fallen Lucifer or Azael from the Legends of Tubal Cain and Qabalistic teachings.[101] Some relate Aradia's naming to the story of Herodias and the beheading of John the Baptist in the Book of Mark, likely because of the connection with Salome and Herodias as biblical figures and their associations to Pagans and heresy. Herodias is held responsible for pushing Salome to perform *the Dance of Seven Veils*.[102] The legend says that St. John's decapitated head doomed Salome, blowing her to the night sky with his holy breath, thus connecting Witches with flight and the Moon.

Herodias became popularized in the visual arts as the instigator during the medieval and early Renaissance periods, and in fiction and theatre of the Victorian Age. She very quickly became a popular character and was also referred to in medieval Italian as "Erodiade," which is very similar to the name "Aradia" used today. Her Goddess and Witch associations first made an appearance in the ecclesiastical records of Regino Abbot of Prüm's *Canon Episcopi*. Even the main character's name in *La Sorciére* by Jules Michelet is Herodiade.[103] Since this novel is one of Leland's main inspirations in the construction of Aradia, I think it is one of the most direct traces to the inspiration for Aradia/Herodias for Leland as a writer.

In Italian regional lore, we see such titles and characters as *Mama Erodas* (Mama Herodias) and *the Sas Mamas* (The Mothers). At one point in time, these figures were connected to children's boogey stories. In even earlier lore, the Madonna (Mary) of Catholicism became associated with Diana. *Madonna Oriente* (Milady of the East) was found in ninth-century trial records and ecclesiastical documents from northern Italy, western

---

101 Huson, Paul. "Introduction." *Mastering Witchcraft: A Practical Guide for Witches, Warlocks and Covens.* G. P. Putnams, 1970, pp. 9–10.

102 This would have originally been a Sumerian temple dance based on a Babylonian story of Inanna or Ishtar about birth and rebirth, but was made famous with the revival of Salome and Herodias in pop culture, literature, and the works of Oscar Wilde and Richard Strauss.

103 Michelet, Jules. *Légendes démocratiques du Nord; La sorcière.* Ernest Flammarion, 1895.

Germany, and southern France. Also present are the figures of other night-riding Witch Goddesses *Dame Holda, Frau Holda, Abundia, Perchta,* and *Bonsoria* (The Good Sister).[104] In Sardina, these tales became the *Sa Rejusta,* a folk tale of a Witch under a boulder, as late as the 1980s from the folklore of a demonized Night Witch.

In the recorded Witch trial of Sibella of Milan in 1384, compiled and discussed by Carlo Ginzburg, Sibella was convicted and killed for the crime of confessing to participating in these so-called "games of Herodias/ Diana" in 1390.[105] Sibella explained that the Witches' Sabbath was led by a dark man named *Lucifelus,* and the Witch Queen who oversaw the region, *Queen Befania,* which is a reference to the Italian Christmas Witch, *Befana,* as well as to *Madonna Oriente* and *Signoria Oriente,* the Lady of the Game. "Game" in this title possibly refers to Diana's Hunt, as well as to people escaping into the woods at night to feast, drink, sing, and make love as a joyful and diabolical celebration of the Goddess and of life itself. All these associations may be derivatives of the Cretan Goddess figure of *Ariadne* and the Etruscan evolvement to *Areatha* or *Arathia,*[106] meaning "the luminous ones."[107]

As Witches today, we can tell that "Aradia" may have been a title of a High Priestess of Diana, derived from several names in Witch-lore. What is clear is that *Aradia* means "living altar," a shining Goddess, and bestower of magic, creating a shelter and a refuge for all people to learn in times of great need. Effectively, *Aradia* means "to bring justice to the world," "to come before an altar when needing guidance," and "to give thanks."

In Italian folk-spiritual traditions, within the Journeying or dream-tranced state, the Witches Sabbath, a coven setting is presented as the

---

104 Magliocco, Sabina and Ronald Hutton. *Aradia in Sardinia: The Archaeology of a Folk Character.* In Dave Evans and Dave Green (eds.), *Ten Years of Triumph of the Moon.* Hidden Publishing, 2009, pp. 40–60.

105 Ginzburg, Carlo. *The Night Battles: Witchcraft & Agrarian Cults in The Sixteenth & Seventeenth Centuries.* Routledge, 2015.

106 Mengoni, L. (ed.). *Aradia, il Vangelo delle streghe di Charles Leland.* Firenze: Olschki, 1999.

107 Mayani, Z. *The Etruscans Begin to Speak.* Simon & Schuster, 1963.

Tregenda.[108] This is the Witch's meeting, a place to work their magic and offer their services to the public in need. The idea of a priestess embodying a living altar also has traces of the sacred king motif, where the king would marry the land, as discussed in the tradition of Crowley's *Gnostic Mass.*[109] This theme of being or becoming a "living altar" harkens to the idea of the body itself being sacred, for even the Bible states that the Holy Spirit dwells embodied and within the self in its descriptions of the body as a temple.

Tools we use as Witches are true reminders that each part of ourselves is an instrument of magic and that being "of the blood" is an innate, indwelling spirit within all whom *The Gospel* may find. Awakening that blood is the journey of finding our own chosen people and discovering our path, power, and magic. We all have our own yellow brick roads to follow "home." For me, "home" is the process of becoming, as we all are finding the fullness of what it means to be a human, to enjoy "all acts of love and pleasure," and to embody a refuge of kinship with those who may find their way to the Witches.[110]

Aradia, from the Latin translation, also means "voice." This presents the same Goddess motif seen in Irish lore of allowing the Goddess to awaken within oneself and speak through a person able to channel her. Every Witch can harness this power of oracular and embodied trance, surrendering the ego and letting the spirit within do the rest. Ancient societies have engaged in this practice, and participation calls back to the ancestral heritage of not just dressing in the skins and furs of animals, but in becoming the totemic beasts we are inside. This is part of the Witches' *fetch:* the primal soul able to shift and shape on the dream or trance level of work. In Aradia's case, she embodied the spirit of Diana, shining with the moonlight behind her and illuminating her as the Shining One, as she spoke with Diana's voice and uttered the Witching secrets to her chosen people.

---

108 Spencer, Craig. "The Sabbat." *Aradia: A Modern Guide to Charles Godfrey Leland's Gospel of the Witches.* Llewellyn Worldwide, 2020, pp. 22–23.

109 Crowley, Aleister. *Liber XV. Liber 15—The Gnostic Mass.* https://www.sacred-texts.com/oto/lib15.htm.

110 Leland, Charles. *Aradia or the Gospel of the Witches.* Samuel Weiser, 1974.

DIANA:
QUEEN OF ALL WITCHERIES

Legends of night flight or dream and trance work, ecstatic celebration under the Moon, and connections to folk healers and diviners became common motifs of Diana as she evolved. These motifs refer to even older folklore, specifically to night-flying specters, weavers and spinners, and the phantom armies led by a Goddess of Night.[111] Diana also became more conflated with Hekate as *Diana Triformus:* a Triple Goddess figure consisting of Diana, Hekate, and Selene, Goddesses all associated with the dead and the Moon. Diana's survival into modernity was not just the work of the Romantic movement, but of her all-encompassing nature from civilization, the Moon, and the natural realm along with the wild beasts. She is the only Pagan Goddess acknowledged in the Bible, as found in *Acts 19:1–41* when Paul goes to Ephesus. With this biblical preservation, she becomes attributed even further with Witchcraft, faery, and night flight via ecclesiastical writings. Over time, she was seen and worked with by practitioners as an all-life-giving Great Goddess figure. Now, she is called the Moon Mother of Witcheries.

We have already covered her name becoming equated with the biblical character of Herodias, but Diana/Artemis has long stood for all people, as she is said to see your heart and nothing else. People from all social classes were welcomed in Diana's temple. She could be found everywhere, as the Moon was still watching whomever "[Her] desire was the dawn."[112] The name *Diana* is traced back to a Latin title, like many deity names discussed, meaning "shining, divine, or heavenly," emphasizing her celestial connection with the Moon.

In Diana's Italian origins, she identified within the Etruscan Goddess *Uni,* from where she was associated with youth, wholeness, and women.[113]

111 Lecouteux, C. *Phantom Armies of the Night: The Wild Hunt and Ghostly Processions of the Undead.* Inner Traditions, 2011.

112 Leland, Charles. "Chapter III: How Diana Made the Stars and the Rain." *Aradia, Gospel of the Witches.* Samuel Wieser, 1974.

113 Thomson De Grummond, Nancy. *Etruscan Myth, Sacred History and Legend.* University of Pennsylvania Museum of Archaeology and Anthropology, 2006, pp. 78–84.

She is known by many names, including *Uni Anti* or "First Mother." In southern Italy, she is known as *Tanith* because of her symbols of the Moon, the scared tree, wild places, and the animals therein. Tanith is also linked to the ruler of the Carthage Pantheon. It is not until the expansion of Greek civilization that Diana fuses several times with other Goddesses, the longest lasting being her conflation with Artemis. Diana also fused with Athena, Persephone, Aphrodite, Hekate, and, importantly, Hera.

As a Native Goddess or *die Indigetes* Goddess, she was always revered first. Diana was more accessible to the common or plebian folk of Roman society, while Hera was more elite as the Queen and Consort of Jupiter, so she had more popularity among the higher class of patricians. It is interesting to note that in Italy, Diana was considered the consort or counterpart of both Jupiter and double-faced Janus. With the classism of the two cults of the Goddess changing in the world, Diana became associated with the commoners and Hera or Juno with the elite devotees of the Goddess of wealth, fertility, and marriage. This is best explained by Rev. Navi Sousa (formerly Johnathan Sousa) of Wolfheart lineage in *The Coven Cani di Artimi*. They present in their book, *Reflections in Diana's Mirror*:

> *"Many assume that Her identification with Artemis was the one and only fusion for either of these Deities. This identification first officially occurred during the later Roman Republic though there were possible earlier precedents. However, Diana was most usually identified (in Magna Graecia) with the Goddess Hera. This was especially prominent throughout Calabria, the island of Sicily (amongst the Siculi), and in the city of Benevento in central Italy. [Why Hera? We must look to the archaic concepts of Diana as Queen of the Starry Heavens. Two of Her epithets, Lucina and Lucifera, were also shared by Iuno. Both titles referenced the role of a bringer of light (both physical and metaphorical)."[114]*

Diana's role as the Queen of the Forests and of the land itself is important to consider, for this is a way to trace her associations with nature spirits in the lore, or queen of faery, goblin, and familiar spirits,

---

114 Sousa, Jonathan. "Diana: Her Mystery and History." *Reflections In Diana's Mirror.* 2015, pp.14–17.

and the spiritual processions and trails of the roaming dead. We know that in *The Gospel*, it is Diana who teaches magic and sorcery to the races of Witches and Janas, faery folk, goblins, and the spirits of the wood. This is important to note because, in certain folk magic practices, practitioners would not consider themselves entirely of the bloodline of Adam as the biblical creation story became a normalized belief in society. Rather, in some cases, people adopted or claimed a lineage to Cain, who became the first wandering magician after he killed Abel.

This is a nod to the fact that people used lineage even then to trace themselves to an even grander origin (influenced by what was available at that time). Since magic was also taught to nature spirits, Janas, and the faery folk, it can be assumed that these spirits could have been seen as independent lineages of non-human descent, possibly tracing to other origins. Witches are included in this category as they would have considered themselves descendants of "a fallen race of angels," or related to or sharing the same Indo-European blood and origins of the "elder Gods," the Jana, or the fae.

The Jana is specific to women, as in the ancient world, women had the very important skill set of weaving and spinning, an art closely related to magical practice. The process required energy, practice, and concentration, all foundational skills for the Arte, and, of course, produced something transformed: wool to threads and threads to clothing. There is said to be a spell of this energy flowing through making and twisting of thread, one of the prime symbols of the Goddess, such as Fate (the Moirai), Ariadne, the Norns, Frigga, Arianrhod, and Athena.

Diana's associations with the forest are probably the oldest, as Diana was seen as not just a *die Indigetes* but as part of the spirit of the land itself, specifically sacred stumps or cedar trees. Her oldest representation is said to be a simple mask of her face set upon the limbs of trees to signify her all-encompassing nature as the spirit of the wood and all the animals and inhabitants who lived within the wood, "for in her were all things."[115] Of course, with her lunar association, she is already a Goddess presiding over the nocturnal activity of the woods and overgrown places. This makes a strong case for her evolution and the workings of Witches and all that may go bump in the night.

---

115 Leland, Charles. *Aradia or Gospel of the Witches.* Samuel Weiser, 1974.

ARADIA'S TEACHINGS:
Reading the Gospel

When you read *The Gospel of the Witches*, you may notice some specific themes and storylines that classically lock in with the Witch-lore you have discovered. I encourage everyone who may be seeking a path to read this as a source text and explore what it means for you to embody the spirit of the Witch today. Are there valuable insights from Leland that you may want to incorporate or add to your practice? There may even be some things you already do that can be found in *Aradia*.

THE ESBAT

"Once in a month and better it is when the moon is full."[116]

As an extension of the cult of the Goddess Diana, we can trace the Witch's association with working the Craft as aligned to the lunar tides of power and the full moon. We acknowledge the changing and moving tides, seasons, and power that the Moon brings and takes. In *The Gospel of the Witches*, Aradia gives the Charge to her followers. This connection with the Moon takes precedence over the cyclical framings in Witch-meetings of energy waxing and waning, dark and light, showing the many aspects of the Goddess in Witchcraft. This push-and-pull is part of the Witches' working foundation to develop sensitivity to energy, spirits, and hidden wisdom and inspiration.

FOOD AND DRINK

The Gospel, and its subsequent historical lore, shows the importance of "the Witch's Libation" and "the Witch's Feast." Food and drink play an important role in the celebratory nature of Witchcraft. Each ritual is as much an offering to the Gods as it is to the self, nourishment of the body and soul. This notion takes its form in food. In much of the folklore, there are stories of peasants attending the Witches' Sabbath with hordes of rich food, only for it regenerate itself once eaten. The crescent moon-shaped cakes act as offerings and nourishment for the Witches, complete with

---

116 Leland, Charles. *Aradia or Gospel of the Witches*. Samuel Weiser, 1974.

the conjuration of flour; the grain that the Mother gives from her fertile Earth in coordination with the shining of the Sun represents a unity in two things working together.

There is also the pollination of Diana's bees and fireflies touching and blessing this grain, the salt of the Earth, and the honey and its sweetening quality. (There is a particularly large amount of folklore when it comes to the uses of honey.) Food is not just an offering. There is an inner alchemy achieved in the body through eating. By eating food, we too become divine and can have communication and intercession with the Gods we feast with. We invite them to our banquet table where, through us, they laugh, sing, make love, and feast! The food itself is made as a blessing for the Witch to absorb and take the qualities of the divine we seek into ourselves. This is the pre-Christian form of a *eucharist*. It is the consecration of raw elements into something special that transforms itself and the consumer when we acknowledge what it is like to not just eat but to devour, taste, and fully enjoy the human experience under the watching eyes of the spirits.

THE CHARGE OF THE GODDESS

The Charge of the Goddess is perhaps the most influential and well-known piece of Wiccan and Pagan liturgy we have today. It was made famous by Doreen Valiente's adaptation of the Leland text as she was working with Wica founder Gerald Gardner. *The Charge* can be seen as a message from the Goddess directly as a call to action for how we, as practitioners, can celebrate the sacred. Its major themes are liberation, personal freedom, and, above all, loving and being loved while allowing the Goddess's spirit to permeate the entirety of our activities. It also speaks on perseverance, and on finding the willpower to never give up one's freedom or identity of self until "the last of your oppressors shall be dead."[117]

The Charge has taken on several variations over the years, with Doreen's adaptation taking place sometime around 1957. The evolution of the Charge's usage, as described by Valiente in her book *The Rebirth of Witchcraft*, is very interesting as it would have been used to fill that awkward silence in ritual when the Goddess did not come through. To truly embody a spirit—or any deity, for that matter—it was and is

---

117 Leland, Charles. *Aradia or Gospel of the Witches.* Samuel Weiser, 1974.

incredibly important to develop some mediumship skills or a trance level of psychic working. One of Gardner's first initiates, Barbara Vickers, was famous for these qualities.

If the person working as the Divine representative during invocation did not have anything come through or any inspired speech activated, Valiente's *Charge* would have been there to use in its place. It is not meant to be recited but serves as a backup in case nothing comes through the oracular working of the Goddess. The original writing of *The Charge* by Garnder is also closely related to Aleister Crowley's *Priestess Speech* from his *Gnostic Mass*.[118] Doreen discusses this candidly in her book, and, due to Crowley's dreadful reputation and her great dislike of him, is part of the reason why she set out to rewrite *The Charge* completely.

CHARLES LELAND'S CHARGE

"When I shall have departed from this world, whenever ye have need of anything, once in the month, and when the moon is full, ye shall assemble in some desert place, or in a forest all together join to adore the potent spirit of your queen, my mother, great Diana. She who fain would learn all sorcery yet has not won its deepest secrets, then my mother will teach her, in truth all things as yet unknown. And ye shall all be freed from slavery, and so ye shall be free in everything; and as the sign that ye are truly free, ye shall be naked in your rites, both men and women also: this shall last until the last of your oppressors shall be dead. (And ye shall make the game of Benevento, extinguishing the lights, and after that shall hold your supper thus)."[119]

DOREEN VALIENTE'S CHARGE (ABRIDGED)

"Mother, darksome and divine,
Mine the scourge and mine the kiss
Five-point star of love and bliss
Here I charge ye in this sign.

---

118 Crowley, Aleister. *Liber XV. Liber 15—The Gnostic Mass.* https://www.sacred-texts.com/oto/lib15.htm.

119 Leland, Charles Godfrey. *Aradia or the Gospel of the Witches.* Samuel Weiser, 1974, pp. 132–133.

Dance about mine altar stone.
Work my holy Magistry,
Ye who are fain of sorcery,
I bring ye secrets yet unknown.

No other law but love I know,
...And all that liveth is mine own,
From me they come, to me they go."[120]

LUNAR POSSESSION
AND GRECO-ROMAN RITUAL

The ritual of Drawing Down the Moon, often simplified to "Drawing Down," is among the main rituals attributed to Witchcraft and lunar rites. Gardner popularized this rite, which has several variations for use as a tool of communication and interaction with deities associated with trancework. This ritual not only invites the Gods to participate, but also invites them to be invoked so that they may physically manifest within a person with a "shining voice." The idea of being a shining voice is a direct reference to *Aradia*, as every time Aradia speaks, she can channel her mother Diana, allowing her to become a Goddess in the flesh. We know the term "Drawing Down the Moon" originated in the Greco-Roman world and may have involved the reflected Moon on a mirror, bowl of water, or other reflective surface to focus and work with the lunar energies.[121] The idea of drawing power from the Moon can also be seen in such legends and tales of *The Witches of Thessaly*, *Medea*, and *Circe*, to name a few.[122]

120 Valiente, Doreen. "Working with Gerald." *The Rebirth of Witchcraft*. Robert Hale, 1989, pp. 59–62.

121 Edmonds, R. G. "Defining Magic in the Ancient Greco-Roman World." *Drawing Down the Moon: Magic in the Ancient Greco-Roman World*. Princeton University Press, 2019, pp. 19–34.

122 Ibid.

CHAPTER SEVEN

THE GRIGORI

"And it came to pass when the children of men had multiplied that in those days were born onto them, beautiful and comely daughters. And the angels, the children of Heaven, saw and lusted after them, and said to one another, 'Come, let us choose wives from among the children of men and beget us children.' And these are the names of their leaders: Semiazaz (Azazel), their leader. Arakiba, Rameel, Kokabiel, Tamil, Ramiel, Danel, Ezequeel, Baraqijel. Asael, Armaros, Batarel, Ananel, Zaqiel, Samsapeel, Satarel, Turel, Jomjael, Sarel."[123]

—The Book of Enoch

A lot of Witches will immediately dismiss the idea of angels to avoid any entanglements with Christianity, but I encourage you to remember that much of ancient practices have also been adopted by and preserved in the Church. Today, certain spirits may appear under the guise of a saint or as part of a new prayer practice. It cannot be denied that Paganism was naturally absorbed into the new religion of Christianity. While angels are ubiquitous and found in countless cultures, Christianity is the most mainstream contemporary religion that heavily involves angels. Like angels, many Gods and spirits have been described as extraterrestrial

---

123 Lumpkin, Joseph B. *The Books of Enoch: The Angels, the Watchers, and the Nephilim, with Extensive Commentary on the Three Books of Enoch, The Fallen Angels, the Calendar of Enoch, and Daniel's Prophecy.* Fifth Estate Publishers, 2015.

beings of light that came to Earth and taught humans the secrets of magic, mysticism, mathematics, science, art, and technology.

The Watchers are often seen as the source of Divine parentage with humankind. They have a particular interest in the protection and teaching of Witches and those ignited with the gnostic, masonic, and initiatory themes of an initiatory experience and pursuit of the Witchblood. They are specific angels who, after falling, began populating the Earth with a magical bloodline and who have a Divine duty to watch over those Divine descendants of Witches and the Earth's trajectory for human evolution.

Angelic "beings of light" and messengers are associated with the creation of a shared bloodline between humans and the heavens by way of a race of beings that fell in with the world as the sons and daughters of Earth. They are the mighty men of old and renown, very much like the giant beings discussed earlier. In the cosmology of the ancient ones, these beings came to Earth to teach civilization and magic. They were also responsible for the giant race of the Nephilim, but being of the Nephilim may be separately meaningful, as Nephilim is an even older bloodline directly related to the angelic realm of these specific angelic race's free will to separate from the will of Yahweh and to take mortal wives, with whom they fell in love. The Nephilim are seen as the giant and half-mortal offspring of the Watchers and could be seen as a literary parallel to the Greek Titans.

In the mythos, the Nephilim can be understood as the founding council of Gods and the forebears of the arts, Witchcraft, and spiritual intervention to humankind. Even within Christian theology, it was the Watchers who were punished and imprisoned on the Earth. Holy mounds became replaced with tales of fallen Devils residing in the mounds, yet the Pagan pulse still engulfed folk belief. As long as magic was successfully performed within the confines of the Church, it was called a miracle; by approaching magical workings under a Christian lens, working with the spirits of angels and saints became acceptable. However, even if the results were the same, working with the old spirits became an act of heresy and a challenge to the power of the "One God."

We must often stop and check our perceptions and preconceived notions about the origins of these angelic beings classically associated with the cosmos and the planetary and elemental guardianship over the universe by the Divine Creator or Architect.[124] There are traces of the Western

---

124 "Architect" is a term often used in Masonic spaces.

esoteric traditions of freemasonry, gnostic Judeo-Christian sects, Witchcraft, mysticism, and, most famously, the system(s) of Solomonic magic in this lore. Many practitioners relate their mythos and teachings of blood kinship to the legions of the fallen angelic realm through the Watchers or *the Grigori*. This kinship began long before Christianity or any ancient religion, but rather when a visiting spirit of the otherworld began altering the tapestry of human life through an epic fall from paradise. These spirits are interpreted by most Witches as angelic beings who, in their autonomy, choose to help evolve humanity. They were said to have taken mortal wives and created offspring capable of learning the secrets and Mysteries of the universe, the language of the cosmos, and the ancient speech of the angels.

Through this lens, we can start to understand why angelic beings have been historically associated with Witches. Witches are commonly seen as embodying the rebellious catalysts of change, acting as seekers of personal freedom and agents of wisdom through connection with planetary influences from those who rule the stars and hold the four corners of the universe. A large area of the Witches' power can be found in the ability to work Angelic magic.[125] The fallen angels, the Watchers, and Elemental beings described in mystical thought were written on animal skins found among the Dead Sea Scrolls.[126] Most, if not all, of Angelic lore and its interconnection with the realm of the Gods was taken not from the Bible as we know it today, but before its formal "finalization" at the First Council of Nicaea in 325 AD when Christendom was at its height.[127]

For some, the Watchers act as the guardians of the spirit roads to different realms, and often intercede to carry out the cosmic order of the universe, associating themselves with constellations, planets, and the natural forces that carry out those planets' power. Notice how, in the biblical myth, every time an angelic being is presented, the first thing they say is to "be not afraid," as if to warn of their nature, which is said to give off a fiery presence that is deeply overwhelming for humans in their company.

---

125 Angelic magic is ancient and diverse, referring to not just High Magick but also to petitioning angels in a spell. Often, angels are called "Lords of Flame" in Western esoteric organizations.

126 Burrows, Millar. *The Dead Sea Scrolls*. Gramercy Pub. Co., 1986.

127 Stewart-Sykes, Alistair. *The Gnomai of the Council of Nicaea (CC 0021): Critical Text with Translation, Introduction and Commentary*. Gorgias Press, 2015.

ANGELIC ROOTS:
Sumerian, Canaanite, Hebraic, Zoroastrian, Solomonic, and Greco-Roman Traces

What are angels and from where do they originate? The simple answer is Sumer, home to the city of Babylon.

The Great Gods of the Sumerians were known as "The Starry Ones" or the *Igigi of the Anunnaki*. The Yazidis and Zoroastrian faiths intermingled in the cosmopolitan region under the Zoroastrian Magi, introducing a formal hierarchical system of their deities.[128] The Anunnaki were the Gods of Earth created by the Igigi as the guardians of the human world. This class of guardians was known as the *Karibu*, from which we get the Hebraic form of *Kerubim*, or "choir of angels." Honoring the *Apkallu* or the *Abgal*, the Seven Sages who tended, guarded, and protected the Tree of Life, were also present in this system. There was also the Sumerian spirit *Mukhalu*, who is very easy to trace to the later figure of the Archangel Michael.

After the Sumerians, there was a division created along the line of how the starry ones were viewed between the Earth and the stars, or, if you like, the heavens above and the underworld or hell below. The starry ones can be seen as angelic spirits and the power of the cosmos above, and the fallen angels or demons in the darker worlds below and between. Under the direct influence and teachings of the prophet Zoroaster and the Iranian-Persian *magi,* from which we derive our modern word for "magician," a new grouping of angelic beings appeared.[129] Zoroaster's legends recounted the creator of all that was good, *Ahura Mazda,* and the creator of all evil, *Ahriman.* It was to the God Ahura Mazda that the *Amesha Spentas,* or the "seven holy immortals," assisted the good creator as the helpful and noble spirits of health and regeneration along with the legions of the *yazatas* or "angels."

The mythos of beings of light who descended to the Earth is preserved in Sumerian, Persian, Hebraic, and Greco-Roman lore, though how these beings are classified in pantheons and other hierarchical structures

---

128 A living Indigenous ethno-religious group in Kurdistan, a region of the Middle East that include parts of Iraq, Iran, Syria, and Turkey.

129 Sousa, Jonathan. "Roots of the Art." *A Star from Heaven: An Introduction to Angelic Magic.* Self-published, 2018, p. 10.

may be different. Classically, most hierarchies tie these beings with the number seven, the planets, and the role of priests or kings and guardians revered and honored by ancient peoples. For instance, the Hebrew word for angel is *malakim,* meaning "kings" or "royalty." This relates to the idea of divine kings, such as David's role in the Bible.

The connection between the divine and the community leader is an important ritual undertaking, whether this is several deities, the Hebrew God of the Abrahamic *Adoni,* or God of the Israelites as the sworn creator of all.[130] This was made, or rather expressed in the covenant made with Abraham throughout the bible, the mosaic covenant being a prominent feature of the Old Testament.[131] In the Psalms of David, the Hebrew God convened said "Council of Gods," which is the parent of Canaanite-Semitic culture,[132] possibly borrowing its influences from the people of Chaldea.[133] A native Chaldean was renowned for being familiar with astrology or a student of the initiatory mystery cults. Chaldeans were hailed throughout the ancient world as mystics and sorcerers and held kinship with the seven planetary Gods or Seven Gatekeepers.

With time, the Archangels or the *Nagiddim* were recognized as choirs or legions of angels. The key difference between the Hebrew and Hellenistic ideas of the power of Archangels was how they viewed the angel's free will. While the Olympian pantheon was polytheistic and each spirit was considered to have a degree of freedom and individualism, within Judaic and, by extension, Christian thinking, angelic beings had no free will, only exalting and carrying out the will of Adoni. Every time there was a great event (namely the flood or the destruction of Sodom and Gomorrah), it was the angels, sent by God, who carried out the specifics. Their powers were able to create, herald, and destroy.

A different structure of viewing angelic entities was introduced to the Catholic Church in the early sixth century by Neoplatonic Christian

---

130 As attributed to the monotheistic theology of the Abrahamic faiths.

131 *Exodus 19:5-10*

132 *Psalms 8*

133 Sousa, Jonathan. "Roots of the Art." *A Star from Heaven: An Introduction to Angelic Magic.* Self-published, 2018, pp. 10-15.

theologian Pseudo-Dionysius the Areopagite. (He was the Athenian man converted to Christianity by Paul the Apostle mentioned in the Book of Acts.)[134] This structure consisted of nine choirs of angels divided into three spheres. The first sphere of angels is said to directly surround heaven's throne, made up of the *Seraphim, Cherubim,* and *Thrones.* The second sphere is the *dominations, powers,* and *virtues,* consisting of angels who govern the physical world and all the spirits that live within. The third sphere belongs to the angels of *messengers, guides,* and *guardians* over humankind. These are the Principalities and the Archangels. (Please know that there are specific angels that hold place in multiple choirs simultaneously; this is not a strict categorical system.)

This scheme gave rise to new offshoots and sects of mystical angelic lore emerging prominently in the beliefs of the Ottoman-ruled Middle East, *Magna Graecia,* and the Italian Renaissance.[135] They were common within gnostic thought and ancient Abrahamic mysticism (Jewish, Christian, and Islamic lore).

Many images of angels in popular culture come from more modern Christianized conditioning, and the actuality of these figures is rarely part of their common conceptions. Visions of the Seraphim Angels were seen as a fiery serpent or *Saraph,* especially in references taken from the book of Isaiah.[136] There is also a reference to the vision of great eyes on circular gyroscopic wheels described in the book of Enoch.[137] The depictions of angelic beings throughout most of ancient history are often not of lovely men or women with wings, but something much stranger.

---

134 *Acts 17:34*

135 *Magna Graecia* is an era termed by the Romans as a time when the areas of southern Italy were densely populated with Greek settlers, bringing with them Hellenistic life and religious practices. This era took place during roughly the first half of the eighth century.

136 *Isaiah 6*

137 Lumpkin, Joseph B. *The Books of Enoch: The Angels, the Watchers, and the Nephilim, with Extensive Commentary on the Three Books of Enoch, The Fallen Angels, the Calendar of Enoch, and Daniel's Prophecy.* Fifth Estate Publishers, 2015.

The English word "angel" comes from the Greek word *anglos* or plural *angelio* and was a title addressing angels of the third sphere from the prominent spiritual hierarchy. *Daemons* are another class from this spiritual hierarchy, from which the English word *demon* is derived. It's worth it to note that, as a Minos of the Minoan Tradition, Crete holds what may be the earliest evidence we have for an angel-like being. The equivalent of an angel or a daemon traces back to Minoan Linear B script as *"A-Ke-Ro,"*[138] although there is no concrete proof there was ever a connection between Sumerian and Minoan people.[139] The meaning of *A-Ke-Ro* is translated as a spirit that acts as a messenger (like an angel from the third sphere) parallel to how *daemon* and "demon" are translated.

Angelic and demonic workings were prominent among those who worked with the earliest forms of ceremonial conjuration, utilizing the Abrahamic and Greek philosophies that started merging into the concepts of Hellenistic Neoplatonism from the third century on.[140] From this blending of philosophies, one distinct schema under Neoplatonist influences occurred, birthing this classification of spirits:

- Hypercosmic Gods
- Empyrean Deities
- Archangels
- Terrestrial Deities
- Angels
- Heroic Souls
- Daemons
- The Souls of the Dead

---

138 "The Linear B Word A-Ke-Ro." *Palaeolexicon*, www.palaeolexicon.com/Word/Show/16647.

139 Macquire, Kelly. *"The Minoans & Mycenaeans: Comparison of Two Bronze Age Civilisations." World History Encyclopedia*, 4 Sept. 2020. www.worldhistory.org/article/1610/the-minoans--mycenaeans-comparison-of-two-bronze-a.

140 Sousa, Jonathan. "Roots of the Art." *A Star from Heaven: An Introduction to Angelic Magic*. Self-published, 2018, pp. 9-20.

These terms and classifications increased with new interpretations and a broadening understanding in the Church's adoption of varying Neoplatonic thought, but also functioned as broad titles for spirits. This meant they could be used to describe numerous kinds of ancestral spirits, deities, or nature forces encountered by the Church or conjurers and magicians.

ANGELS VERSUS ARCHANGELS

Angels are the source of pure natural force that exists everywhere, and Archangels are a subsect of angels that are the forces or teams of forces that govern and guide the powers of planets, stars, or constellations. They live on a level of existence that is right above us, allowing easy access to them when we wish to call upon and work with these forces. Long held in the magical and Occult orders, they are petitioned in specific environments like a magic circle to create a clear boundary and provide protection from the Elemental powers summoned during our rites. This is because they govern and guide those forces of pure power that could become overwhelming or feel unstable for the practitioner. However, angels (by description) can be quite scary or overwhelming when interacting with humans, in part due to being on a different plane of existence than humans. In this respect, it is better to cast specific protections and wear protective talismans, charms, and insignia so we may interact with the spiritual world more easily.[141]

FALLING FROM GRACE

The gnostic and ceremonial teachings of the angels are not the same belief as the Watchers falling from grace, as this was a fall that was much more profound. The Watcher's fall was the act of falling in love with the people of the Earth. It was with care and investment that these stellar beings assisted in the conscious awakening of humanity. They fell in love with humans (literally and figuratively), taking spouses and teaching them about charms, spells, crafting, metalwork, and agriculture. However, angels and humans created offspring like no other before. It's said that

---

141 In Ceremonial and Solomonic magical systems, this is commonly referred to as a "lamen." This is an enchanted breastplate meant to cover the heart for protection and the focus of magical energy.

this offspring was the renowned great men of old, yet they also produced a monstrous giant race. The giants caused so much toil in the eyes of the Hebrew God in biblical myth, and it was for that reason that the great flood was sent to Earth to wipe out all of civilization except Noah and his ark. Some claim that Noah himself was of Watcher descent, per oral tradition in some mystic and Masonic spaces.

THE RENAISSANCE:
SOLOMON, ENOCH, AND JOHN DEE

The Renaissance brought a resurgence in the workings of grimoire traditions. These grimoires act as textbooks, working journals, and outlines of rituals, conjurations, and invocations to different spirits. The most well-known are *The Greater and Lesser Key of Solomon,*[142] or simply *The Key of Solomon* and *The Goetia.*[143] This magical working system was highly popular during the Victorian era, as it was made famous by Samuel Liddell MacGregor Mathers, Occultist and co-founder of *the Order of the Golden Dawn,* one of the oldest orders. This grimoire deals with angelic and demonic spirits, as well as the same spirits commanded by Solomon in the building of his temple. Solomon himself is a figure steeped in magic and is commonly acknowledged by Freemasons, Rosicrucians, and Witches alike.

The other main text concerning this type of ancient magic is called *Enoch,* and it can be traced back to early myths, legends, and translations throughout time. There are three distinct versions or found scripts of *Enoch* with the text's origins in ancient Ethiopia.

Whenever *Enoch* is mentioned, we must acknowledge the legacy and influence of the practices of Enochian Magic created and channeled by Elizabethan Magus, Dr. John Dee, and his "scryer" or clairvoyant, Edward Kelly. Together, they channeled the language of the angels, both spoken and written, and the term "Watchtower" is often attributed to them from this practice.[144] Their rituals were long and evocative to

---

142 MacGregor Mathers, S.L. et. al. *The Greater Key of Solomon: The Grimoire of Solomon.* 1888.

143 De Laurence, L. W. *The Lesser Key of Solomon: Goetia, The Book of Evil.* Scott & Co., 1916.

144 Turner, Robert. *Elizabethan Magic.* Element Books, Ltd., 1989, p. 24.

properly create the atmosphere for an angel to appear. (Atmospheric creation and mood setting is one of the best-kept secrets in any ritual or magical undertaking.) The Golden Dawn then greatly expanded upon the Watchtower system, in which tablets bearing sacred names and talismans were used to summon each of the Cardinal Angelic points with the tools and symbols of their nature.

MADELINE MONTALBAN

Madeline Montalban was a contemporary of the Golden Dawn, Crowley, and British Traditional Wica, greatly contributing to the contemporary understanding and practices of Angelic magic. She often goes under the radar as a true child of the night, overshadowed by some of her more well-known (and published) contemporaries. Her approach was practical and of its time, and it was not as theatrical as some of her contemporaries' esoteric circles. Drawing from the grimoires of Solomon and others of the Italian Renaissance period most notably Francis Barret's *The Magus,* Montalban developed the *Order of the Morning Star,* and it's as deliciously Luciferian as it sounds.[145] She focused on magic and real-world results that were both poetic and simple, as far as practicality was concerned. Her greatest theurgic work was that of her own developed theology and working relationship with the angelic being whom she called *Lumiel,* or Lucifer, the leader of all the Watchers who fell from heaven, the light-bearer of the arts and metal craft. Her Angelic system was utilized in the Alexandrian Tradition to further magical development for initiates of the tradition. This is best credited to the works of High Priestess Maxine Saunders in The Temple of the Mother.

In his beginnings after the flood, Lucifer had fallen out of love with humanity and sacrificed his eternal flame of spirit into all physical matter upon Earth. Other mighty fallen ones came with him as teacher angels. Part of Lucifer's sacrifice was his reincarnation as a sacred prophet or king to renew the inner flame of knowing in any given age, at any time before or after our own. The mystery burns where one's gnosis fuels its flames as the Watchers themselves may not give a damn about small and petty affairs, only concerning themselves with specific powers and civilizations. We'll talk more about Lucifer in Chapter Eight.

---

145 Barret, Francis. *The Magus.* 1801.

HERALDING THE LEGIONS

The Watchers are summoned by Witchblood: the rush of intent, the will to summon, and the daringness to speak your universe in existence. Like a flash, this leap of emotion stirs the blood, leading you into a place of sovereignty and standing in your capabilities. This respect for the cosmos is expressed in the call to invoke, called by spiritual guardians that hold a kinship with the inner workings of Witches.

A call such as this is an *invocation,* or the bringing in the presence of specific spirits, arising as one of the fundamental rites of the Witch. In this context, invocation is the ability to summon or conjure some of the most powerful forces of spiritual intelligence—the angelic and celestial beings—to open a way for them to intercede in our space or dimension while the work is performed.

This calling out starts with chills or the feeling of being watched, and the feeling as though your voice could call out across the surface of the entire universe. This powerful technique can occur after the Witchblood is awakened and you enter a state of altered consciousness with help from concentration and visualization techniques. These techniques help the self to ground into the goal of the working and allow you to draw in spirits with the most important tool: the portal of your mind and your mind's inner eye as a call or conjuration is made.

APPROACHING THE DIRECTIONS
OF THE WATCHERS

For many, the directions of the Watchers are part of the initial setting of space and cleansing before a ritual or making a sacred space. This setting can be done by the well-known ritual of the Lesser Banishing Ritual of The Pentagram.[146] In this ritual, the Archangels are summoned in alignment with the body while stepping into the Kabbalah's Tree of Life, empowering oneself and the space with the powers they hold in each direction. Older systems summon the four winds of the Greeks,

---

146 The best resources for this are Modern Magick by Donald Michael Craig and Circles of Power by John Michael Greer.

and the Chaldean system of the Watchers of Heaven fixed to the Four Royal Stars can also be used. This looks like:

- Aldebaran is Michael: The Eye of Taurus, linked with the Bull of Mithras
- Regulus is Raphael: The Heart of Leo
- Antares is Uriel: The Head of Scorpio
- Fomalhaut is Gabriel: The Mouth of Pisces

You may petition these Archangels directly in any manner of work, prayer, or spell. They are also said to act as intermediaries to the Elementals and powers of natural magic. In my own experience, it is the Archangels who are linked with spiritual, theurgic, and community-oriented concerns, while the planetary angels are linked with material and physical concerns. Finally, Archangel Gabriel serves his role as the messenger and, hence, the gatekeeper. In my style of Angelic working practice, I advise starting a working relationship with him first to open your gates and connect with the current of angelic practice.

The following are my correspondences.

THE ARCHANGELS OR THE GOOD WATCHERS

- East: Raphael
- South: Michael
- West: Gabriel
- North: Uriel

THE PLANETARY RULERS

- Sun: King Michael, Prince Raphael
- Moon: King Gabriel, Prince Gabriel
- Mercury: King Raphael, Prince Michael
- Venus: King Haniel, Prince Anael
- Mars: King Kamael, Prince Samael
- Jupiter: King Tzadkiel, Prince Sachiel
- Saturn: King Tzaadkiel, Prince Cassiel

The Olympian Spirits

- Sun: Och (transformation, healing, wisdom)
- Moon: Phul (longevity, divination, Water magic)
- Mercury: Ophiel (the arts, knowledge, cunning)
- Venus: Hagith (love, luxury, beauty)
- Mars: Phaleg (self-defense, military affairs, fitness)
- Jupiter: Bethor (wealth, truth, healing)
- Saturn: Aratron (reconciliation, magic, medicine, restriction)

The Olympic Angelic Rulers

- Sun: Michael
- Moon: Gabriel
- Mercury: Raphael
- Venus: Haniel or Anael
- Mars: Samael
- Jupiter: Zadkiel
- Saturn: Cassiel

The Arch-Fallen Watchers

- North: Earth, Turiel (teacher of the art of stones, crystals, and sculpture)
- East: Air, Remiel (teacher of the art of logic, rhetoric, and weather-working)
- South: Fire, Azazel/Lucifer/Lumiel (teacher of cosmetics, alchemy, magic, sorcery, and smithcraft)
- West: Water, Shemyaza (teacher of illusion, persuasions, and root and herbal healing)

EYES OF THE SKY:
AN AWAKENING CHARM OF THE GRIGORI

There are the sleeping embers of the Grigori within me. By passion, epiphany, trauma, or accident, I know, I dare, I will, I silently possess the winds of fate to blow upon my burning embers. Ignite the fire of the forge! My relation is to those beings of light and shadow of the otherworld. I stand physically entwined within the blood of the clay that is my body, the temple, and my works. For I am not just a mere mortal, but of the cunning, healer, night wanderer, and the Goddess of Earth, Sea, Sky! Kin of Cain, of the cave below where the sleeping soul of the wandering soul dreams of the new dawn under all creation!

Blood within me, bubble, summon, work for me now, and stir forth!

Feel its circulation and tune into the feeling of your heartbeat.

And so I hold my power!

CHAPTER EIGHT

LUCIFER: THE BRINGER OF LIGHT

There is but one figure we still need to fully address, but those who have been paying close attention may have already caught on to the importance of Lucifer as a figure in awakening the magic of the Witch within. He is known by many names, including *Old Nick, Christ Sunday, Old Scratch, Auld Hornie, The Devil,* and *Azazel.* He remains a hidden remnant that connects mystical and theologian understandings of human nature. I've come to know the presence of the light-bearer through the results of fruitful magic. The bringer of these gifts is credited to the Witch-God of crafts and metal, cosmetics and beauty, enlightenment, and rebellion. The Witch's Devil is not pure evil, but simply he who is the light dwelling in darkness, the other half to the balance, both destroyer and a creator.

Growing up, I was told tales of the angelic nature of Lucifer before his fall: that he was the most beautiful Angel in heaven and music would play from his steps as he walked. Even as a child, it was hard for me to believe that anything that went from extreme good to evil would be completely void of the good forever, doomed. In the tangible world, nature simply exists in its cycles of change with no motivations for good or evil. The Devil, like nature, invites the Witch to explore the unknown and wild places. Horned and cloaked, he beckons those who dare to test their limits into the woodlands, and like those woods, we find him much more complex than ever anticipated.

The subject of anything to do with the Devil, Lucifer, or Satan in any form of Witchcraft may be met with immediate shock and pushback. For the past few decades now, many Witches have been the victims of

Satanic panic and bullying for associations made between the Devil and Witchcraft.[147] This is something still alive and well today and as a result, several public figures who practice the Craft announced a clear divorce from the Witch's Devil altogether. There is good reason for this, and not every Witch uses Luciferian concepts or symbolism in their practice. However, that doesn't mean the Witch's Devil has never existed, and it needs to be stated that Witches have always kept a secret: the true identity and function of the Light-Bringer, the God of the Mysteries taught to humankind, as told in Enochian and Angelic lore.

This theme of meeting a Devil-like or trickster figures in folklore has been around a lot longer than some of the modern conceptions and traditions of the Craft. What motivated my spiritual work with the Devil taboo was the complete absence and mention of him in Witching spaces. I yearned to find a community that was willing to revisit the medieval and renaissance Angelic workings consisting of the fallen ones. Deep down, I knew that these types of spirits had an interest and connection to the practice of Witchcraft. The Witch's Devil and his role in the Pagan worldview is also influenced by Christian mythology. There is, then, the complexity of some Witches being of dual faith and how our stories too often cross and collide together as time and culture reshape tales. Through remnants of the old religion and rebellion against the Church, a new kind of diabolical folk deity arose.

There are several kinds of Devils we need to consider in order to understand the Witch's version today. There was bound to be misunderstanding in the cross-cultural exchanges of Luciferian and Gnostic points of view as students of the Occult became influenced by Christian teaching. There was the influence of the Roman Lucifer as mentioned in *Aradia* and actual reports of meeting the Devil (or several Devils) in the Witch trials of the early modern period. The Devil had a snowball effect as new tales of Devils, imps, and ghouls made their way across Europe thanks to Witch-hunter manuals, and demonology started to blend with the many trickster characters of folklore and fairy tales. These figures become the villains of the story often without full consideration of why these adversarial characters are conceptualized differently by each

---

147 Hughes, Sarah. "American Monsters: Tabloid Media and the Satanic Panic, 1970–2000." *Journal of American Studies*, vol. 51, no. 3, 2016, pp. 691–719, doi:10.1017/s0021875816001298.

generation. In the original holy form of the Light-Bringer, Lucifer is not the same as Satan, the Church's Christian figure the world has come to as the evil big baddie.

The Devil figure in Western esoteric circles by his many names takes classical associations as both a trickster and a Promethean figure, gifting the light of the heavens and imbuing the Earth with that holiest fire of self-knowledge. This literal dawn of consciousness brought on the knowledge of seasons, cycles of time, and mortality. His Mystery for me awoke me to my mortality after almost dying. Yet, we all carry a personalized Devil that constantly tests our beliefs. For me, this seems to strengthen my sense of self, but this back-and-forth between our sense of self and belief is a dance with the inner demons.

Heed the personal Devil's legions of ill feelings and shame. If we repress them, it only gives these emotions the strength to taunt us further. This process of confrontation can be frightening, and often feels as if we are being pursued by something sinister. By doing this work, however, we learn from this particular Devil. In becoming of a Witch, we seek the gift of self and perception. Perception acts as our inner light, illuminating the hidden and forgotten pieces of self; that is very much the realm Lumiel has manifested within for me. As much as I've felt him stalking the circle's edge at the observance of rites and engagements, he brings on the noticing of perceiving what has changed, been broken, and healed.

Some say he has fallen, but the light still shines in the palms of the artist's hand! The spirit of the Witch's God spirals and slithers into the Earth as the firstborn serpent from Eden. By the virtues of the Queen of Enchantment, the Moon: the light of the cosmos colors the dawn as winds quicken from the north, the stellar aurora borealis. The perception changes. Blood quickens with a flash of conscious thoughts, feelings, tastes, smells, and sensations known to the Witchblood as the original Fire that awaits the lost. In the retelling of the myth from a storyteller's tongue is the magick of Eden still growing. Earth is reclaimed by those who are of the Gods, those who became Gods, and those Gods becoming even in the moment of today.

Light heightens our perceptions. It illustrates what is before us. Having a keen sense of magical perception was taught to me as the mystical state of having full awareness, allowing the discerning Witch to build meaningful, innate relationships with spirits, self, and sorcery. Magic as a lifestyle slowly becomes something planned and spontaneous, ritualized and at a whim. This sense of innateness and of being one with the outcast speaks to the entire concept behind the titles of a Light-Bringer and the leader of the Watchers.

One of the key Mysteries I received in my practice was validated when fellow Witches shared my ideas about the aspect of the Witch ultimately being the guardian and torchbearer of the Promethean flames of Witch-fire. This guardianship occurs because Witches are often lost and disconnected from each other. These are the same fires of Divinity and consciousness that fell with Lucifer from the heavens. When these fires came to Earth, they became scattered like that of a broken mirror; each tiny flame would link itself to the heart of humankind. Through the holy fire of the cosmos, the world has been challenged to reclaim all pieces of its innate Divine light that are separate and disconnected within itself. The descendants of the men of renown became the initiators of these great Mysteries, as they were taught by the Angelics themselves. The mission of Lucifer is to liberate all of creation by awakening them to their hidden knowledge. In the cultivation of community, there is a stirring of the fires in the belly. Through gathering, there is the building of knowledge. This is the power to know and to be God-like.

There are alternative messiah concepts, as Luciferian and gnostic practitioners often see the link to liberation and savior as being our own duty to the divine self. This power is that we too are of the Gods, and this knowledge is a seed to some of Witchcraft's deepest principles. Whether born out of love, pride, rebellion, or hubris, this secret knowledge is attributed to the angel who was cast out and is the herald of that particular message. The Devil is probably not the Devil you think you know, but if you seek him out, you may be able to enjoy the Witch's gifts and live a truly delicious life.

"HOW YOU ARE FALLEN FROM HEAVEN, O LUCIFER, SON OF THE MORNING"

This section's title is a quote directly from *Isaiah 14:12*, the biblical passage to which we owe the synchronization of Lucifer with the theologian's idea of the Infernal Satan.[148] *Satan*, originally a Hebrew word simply meaning "any adversary or accuser," "to oppose" or even "to plot against."[149] There are several enemies in the biblical canon, depending on the viewpoint you bring. However, Lucifer meant something splendiferous, and in my experience, this God—if not all Gods discussed previously—holds a power that is of the unseen realm. Lucifer translates out of the Greek word *heosphoros* or "dawn bringer."[150] In Latin, this is *Lucem ferre* (light bringer) and *Luciferum* (morning), implying the connection between Venus and the morning star itself.[151] Yes, Venus and Lucifer are closely related. Not only is Lucifer connected to Venus, but Lucifer's domain or influence holds over the kingdom of Earth and, importantly, the Sun.

Understanding the astrological importance of Lucifer is helpful to this. Astrology, of course, is a divinatory system rooted in the stars and planets, writing out destiny in the stars. Rather than physical planets being summoned, these planets act as divine-like forces that govern and hold power over the specific attributes. These planets are led by the Sun, which contributes to these motions from the center of the cosmos. The Sun and even Venus, known to a few as the "black Sun," are both planetary virtues that are important symbols of the Lord Lumiel.

The Hebrew phrase *Helel ben sahar* is the title hurled towards a Babylonian king who has fallen into the horrors of war.[152] This could be a reference to other Canaanite myths that became deduced in the

---

148 *Isaiah 14:12*

149 Kelly, Henry. "Hebrew Backgrounds." *Satan: A Biography.* Cambridge University Press, 2007, pp. 28–31.

150 Grey, Peter. "The Dawn Breakers." *Lucifer: Princeps,* Scarlet Imprint/ Bibliotheque Rouge, 2015, pp. 13–16.

151 Ibid.

152 Day, John. Y*ahweh and the Gods and Goddesses of Canaan.* Sheffield Academic Press, 2002, p. 166.

Isiah narratives to simple traces and poetic themes as investigated in the book *Yahweh and the Gods of Canaan*.[153] The title is sharply directed in comparison to the king's downfall and to the literal cosmic motions of the planet Venus.[154] These translators were likely using their word for "morning star," which was a direct link to the celestial body rather than the fallen angel figure. The conflation of the two forever captures the imagination of those who see Lucifer personified in the various manifestations of something cosmic *and* infernal.

Venus has an interesting story, not just for this angelic connection but for how its celestial movements make it appear as if it is falling onto Earth's horizon as the year goes on. Besides the Moon, Venus is the brightest star in the sky, often first seen before the Moon in the evening and last seen at sunrise, creating an illusion of a false or black Sun every morning.[155] As the year goes on, the planet's movements draw closer to the horizon every morning, as if Venus is being swallowed up by the underworld below. The underworld or under-earth association has even deeper relevance to Venus and her being representative of the Goddess Inanna in the tale of *The Descent of Inanna*.[156] Venus was viewed in her aspect as the queen of heaven and ruler of stars. This is not just found in Sumerian myth but also in the Hebrew faith, as they had absorbed the Canaanite Ashera in similar roles.[157] In Greco-Roman myth, the morning star was personified and esteemed as a God in his own right, son of Aurora, the Goddess of the dawn. All figures mentioned so far are torch-bearing and light-associated Goddess figures, as the term "light bringer" or "torch bearer," *Phosphorous,* was applied to several deities

153 Albright, William F. *Yahweh and the Gods of Canaan: A Historical Analysis of Two Contrasting Faiths.* Athlone Press, 1968.

154 Grey, Peter. "The Dawn Breakers." *Lucifer: Princeps.* Scarlet Imprint, 2015, pp. 13–16

155 Howard, Michael and Daniel Schulke. "The Latent Radiance." *The Luminous Stone: Lucifer in Western Esotericism.* Three Hands Press, 2016, pp. 14–16.

156 "Inana's Descent to the Nether World: Translation." Electronic Text Corpus of Sumerian Literature, 2000. etcsl.orinst.ox.ac.uk/section1/tr141.htm.

157 Howard, Michael and Daniel Schulke. "The Latent Radiance." *The Luminous Stone: Lucifer in Western Esotericism,* Three Hands Press, p. 13.

in the Greek pantheon, from which we derive the epithets of other torch-bearing deities outside of the Greek and Roman pantheons.[158]

So why does conflation between stars, planets, and the Devil happen? I propose that the apocryphal books of the Bible still influenced the translators and priests at the pulpit. Even though such texts were not considered canon, books like *Enoch*[159] and *The Book of Noah* were so incredibly influential that they were bound to affect how other texts were viewed.[160] This even shows up in the later biblical writings, such as when Enoch is mentioned in *The Book of Jude*.[161] In second-temple Judaism, Enoch was indeed wildly popular.[162] When Enoch started to make its way to early Christians and Jews alike, people saw the story of the fallen ones referenced in *Isiah* not just as a planet but as a name. The story is of the Watchers, led by the Light-bearing figure, Lucifer or *Azazel*.

FIRES OF AZAZEL

"Azazel" is one of the names used to refer to the fallen leader of the cosmic light amongst many modern traditional and folkloric practitioners. This name is steeped in interesting connections that bridge the symbols of the Devil, the Hebrew concept of *Satan* or "adversary," and the Occult symbols still used today of the goat. This cross-firing of understanding is woven together to bring about a figure who acts as a gifter of Witch-fire. It has long been held in popular Witch tradition that the fallen angel described in *The Book of the Watchers* and in the Enochian texts is one of

---

158 Grey, Peter. "The Dawn Breakers." *Lucifer: Princeps*, Scarlet Imprint/ Bibliotheque Rouge. 2015, p. 14.

159 Lumpkin, Joseph B. *The Books of Enoch: The Angels, the Watchers and the Nephilim, with Extensive Commentary on the Three Books of Enoch, The Fallen Angels, the Calendar of Enoch, and Daniel's Prophecy*. Fifth Estate Publishers. 2015.

160 Hirschman, Jack. *The Book of Noah: Also Called the Book of the Mystery from the Book of Raziel*. Tree. 1975.

161 Jude 1:14-15

162 Boccaccini, Gabriele and John Joseph Collins. *The Early Enoch Literature*. Brill. 2007.

the many initiators into the Witchblood.[163] In summary, the story tells of how Azazel led the Sons of God and men of renown in the pursuit of falling in love with the mortal women, creating the offspring of the Nephilim. Azazel is the angel who not only leads this quest but divulges the secrets of the universe to the mortals. Azazel also was the bringer of fire, as he taught the mortals the art of the forge. He is attributed with introducing mankind to war and battle by introducing fire, blacksmithing, and making swords and fine metals, as well as the art of decoration and self-expression. He taught them charms and enchantments and the secrets of plants and medicine. Azazel also was the one who taught them the art of cosmetics and pleasure, implying the classically held attributes of the Witch in matters of seduction, lust, and love magic. Specifically, he is attributed to the awakening of sexual pleasure, promiscuity, and other activities deemed blasphemous by the Hebrews passing along the lore of the Watchers.[164]

From the blood atonement rituals described in the biblical texts, it is clear Azazel holds a thread of lineage that will directly take one into the Mysteries of magical teaching, hidden wisdom, and inner liberation. He is the symbol of the Sabbatic goat wandering through the desert. Whether it be sin-offerings he receives, or if he is indeed the teacher of all magic to the world, I find myself steeped in a magical atmosphere while chanting his name, knowing he gives refuge for the fires of the Witchblood. Notice how we return to the symbol of goats and their association with Witches, the Horned God, and the Devil. The goat has always been one of the most well-known symbols of the outcasted and otherworldly. This animal makes the distinction between the rough, rugged, and wild places that mankind fears and the soft domesticated farms of lush fields. The goat rides the boundaries as the Witch does between the borders of threshold and crossways, and yet maintains his vigor. Goats have a lusty and sexual connotation and

---

163 Lumpkin, Joseph B. *The Books of Enoch: The Angels, the Watchers and the Nephilim, with Extensive Commentary on the Three Books of Enoch, The Fallen Angels, the Calendar of Enoch, and Daniel's Prophecy.* Fifth Estate Publishers, 2015.

164 Collins, Andrew. "Demonic Doctrine." *From the Ashes of Angels: The Forbidden Legacy of a Fallen Race.* Inner Traditions, 2007, p. 25.

very much remain a phallic symbol among Witches. Their square eyes signal to the Witch that they are animals that can exist between the worlds, and goats have held a place of power in the Witch's symbolic worldview since antiquity.

The name Azazel usually translates to a title instead of a name for the leader of the Watchers. The root word of *azza* is translated to English as "the strong," or *uzza*, meaning "strength."[165] I believe this shows that Azazel could be a spiritual or directly Angelic force, which refers to a spirit upon the Earth itself. Azazel is another entity altogether, existing as a separate and solitary spirit in the wilderness, from my interpretations of his mythos. With the popularity of other apocryphal texts, Azazel and Lucifer became seen as the same entity over time. Every time Azazel is used, it has a direct association with the Levitan-Hebrew tradition of the scapegoat.

The origin of the scapegoat can be traced back to other parts of the ancient world, including Syria and the third millennia of ancient Ebla.[166] The offering of a scapegoat was of special concern to the spiritual leaders when a ritual of purification, atonement, or banishment was needed on behalf of the community, as the ritual had to work on a communal level. Atonement can be found in the pages of *Leviticus 16*, describing the annual holy day Yom Kippur.[167] We derive the term "scapegoat" from this ritual, which was central to cleansing away sin from the entire tribe. It takes the form of specific animal sacrifices performed by the High Priest or leader of the tribe, including divination, as lots would have been thrown to decide which offerings would be given to God and what was to become the scapegoat to go into the wilderness known as the abode of the God Azazel. The Priest would enter the temple several times, offering incense and the blood of all the sacrificed animals as they would be slaughtered and then burnt on a pyre. Next, the High Priest would place his hands on the head of the scapegoat, confess, and transfer all the people's sins on it by the act of energetic or magical transference. This is then symbolized by wrapping a scarlet red thread around the head of the goat like a blindfold.

165 Collins, Andrew. "In the Footsteps of the Watchers." *From the Ashes of Angels: The Forbidden Legacy of a Fallen Race.* Inner Traditions, 2007, pp. 252–253.
166 Johnston, Sarah Iles. "Scapegoat Rituals from Ebla to Rome." *Ancient Religions.* Belknap Press of Harvard University Press, 2004, pp. 33–37.
167 *Leviticus 16*

This is found in *Isaiah 1:18*, where we also get an amazing biblical charm that turns the people's sins into the thread and lays out a series of ritual praxis.[168] They would then have to lead the live goat to the desert to wander and be lost in the wilderness and land of "the other"—to Azazel—taking with it all the sins and transgressions of the people. Finally, a symbolic stone would be tied to the scarlet thread and the goat would be pushed off the rugged cliff, ending the rite.

> *"But the goat was chosen by lot as the scapegoat shall be presented alive before the Lord to be used for making atonement by sending it into the wilderness to Azazel."*
>
> —*Leviticus 16:10*

This imagery creates an emphasis on the magical taboo of blood rites. In the kingship model of the early Israelites, it is clear there was a sacred duty that mirrors the divine king mythos that is performed and found in several cultures with a divine hierarchy. Offering blood is sacred, powerful, dangerous, and possesses yet another hidden power of forbidden knowledge, even as it relates to Azazel. These taboos are where the Witches dwell.

> *"And Azazel taught men to make swords and knives, and shields, and breastplates and made known to them the metals of the Earth and the art of working them. And bracelets and ornaments and the use of antimony, and the beautifying of the eyelids, and all costly stones, and all coloring tinctures—Semyaza taught enchantments, and root-cuttings, Armaros the resolving enchantments, Baraqijal astrology, Kokabiel the constellations, Ezequiel, the knowledge of the clouds (weather), Araquiel the signs of the Earth, Shamsiel the signs of the sun, and Saraiel the course of the moon."*
>
> —The Book of Enoch, Chapter VIII

Even in this excerpt, there is a classical planetary structure that puts Azazel first, representing the Solar magician transforming and inspiring by imbuing the freedom of consciousness and self into mankind. In Rabbinical tradition, he is associated with caring for the virtues of the planet Mars

---

168 *Isaiah 1:18*

for the obvious war and metal association. For some, he is the Sun as *Negral,* the Babylonian God of the infernal Sun in the underworld.[169] As the Solar Sorcerer, he later takes on the same guise as the first blacksmith in the Bible, Tubal-Cain, mirroring the goat rite of atonement. Abel is slain and Cain becomes the scapegoat, leading the people of other blood lineages of Angelic Witchblood, which is why one of the many titles of Traditional Witches following these interpretations of lore is known as The Children of Cain, being the patron representative of the angelic fire and initiator into the Craft. He connects those to a mythopoetic bloodline that represents the qualities of the otherworld and the outcasted rather than being children of Eve.

THE FOLKLORIC DEVIL

As mentioned earlier, it is not safe to say that one works with the Devil. The Inquisition, the threat of torture, public bias, and the fate of losing everything because of such a claim are still present in how Witches have adapted to the public climate. Therefore, we have said (or, as a group, have allowed it to be said) that there is no Devil in the Craft whatsoever. What is meant by this is that the idea of the Christian Satan is not in the Craft, but there *is* a Devil who is an independent force separate from Christianity. However, even he has been transformed by the oppression of the Church. In a way, history has handed back a figure who is much more evocative of nature's darker aspects. The Witch's Devil is far closer to the figure traditions found in folklore and family folk customs. He is either dismissed out of fear, ignored, and replaced with a more acceptable or joyous, horned figure in Neo-Pagan groups. However, the term Witch has historically been aligned to these darker aspects. A Luciferian Priestess and solitary practitioner who retains a private practice, who wishes to remain anonymous, says:

> *"He is central in old folkloric craft lore to the mythos of seasonal tides and the opening of the cunning roads and secret passageways. He acts as an Initiator and awakener of the forbidden artes for those who seek him and wish him to come. In my last working, there was a more*

---

169 Jackson, Nigel and Michael Howard. "The Children of Heaven." *The Pillars of Tubal-Cain,* Capall Bann Publishing, 2000, p. 32.

Mercurial and trickster-esque [energy] in his role as the gatekeeper. I guess after the experience, there is some truth to his unpredictable and wild nature; he's not of our world. He is everywhere and everything, very much how I would think of Pan. For me, it seems he can intercede with us a little more closely, being of the fallen and closer to the Earth."

I knew exactly what she was referring to when she brought up Pan. The all-God of the Greeks was naturally absorbed into the image of the contemporary Witch's Devil. Places like Mount Herman are also home to the Cults of Pan in history.[170] The lore of the Watchers landing here led by Azazel is a fascinating cross-over in biblical myth. The places that these stories cross are too obvious to not take some delight in realizing a figure's origins.

The Witch's Devil is the artistic and spiritual symbol of enlightenment. He is the patron of the outcasts, personifying the pursuit of the authentic self, and the creator of counterculture. He reflects the Dionysian Mysteries of the underworld journey to find hidden Divinity in the darker places of the self. One of my first encounters with these ideas of seeing the Devil in a new light was in the stories discussing the origins of Lucifer's mark as it related to Witches. In some versions, this is the famous sorcerer's stone of lapis lazuli or emerald that fell during Lucifer's fall from heaven, the stone from his crown becoming the land itself. In the praxis of the Cultus-Sabbati, wherever the feet of Witches walk, that land itself is the Luciferian stone.[171] For some Folk Witches, there are those who know how to search for the mark of Cain on their fellow crafters. In these tradition's oral lore, if a certain mark, symbol, or blemish appears in the aura or upon the forehead or the third eye area, it is a telltale sign that the individual is one of the descendants of the biblical men of renown led by Lucifer himself.

The Witch's Devil can be seen in any form but appears most famously as the Man in Black approaching with his book. He holds the role of gatekeeper and guardian of the liminal spaces. One local tradition I've

170 Berlin, Andrea. "The Archaeology of Ritual: The Sanctuary of Pan at Banias/Caesarea Philippi." *Bulletin of the American Schools of Oriental Research*, no. 315, 1999, pp. 27–45. doi:10.2307/1357531.

171 Howard, Michael and Daniel Schulke. "The Hidden Stone." *The Luminous Stone: Lucifer in Western Esotericism.* Three Hands Press, 2016, p. 112.

had correspondence with uses the Old One to open the Gates of Hell and Saint Peter to open the gates of Heaven, but this is just one example of how the Devil is worked with even in gnostic and mystic groups that have independently formed in the past century. The Witch's God follows his own rules, and regardless of what we like to think, the Devil and the Witch do have a relationship. The Horned God of the Witches arises from as many of the same sources and concepts as the Devil.[172] This may not be true for all of Witchcraft and every tradition, but that doesn't mean it doesn't exist at all. It certainly stands to be an old, well-documented Witching tactic that, in a classic rebellious Luciferian fashion, has been reclaimed, as magic will continually be reshaped by the vision of a better world. In my personal view, I think the term Devil and Lucifer is still used among Witches who follow these kinds of practices because Witchcraft is rebellious by nature. This, of course, is exemplified in the story of the fall and rebellion against God as tyrant.

It is important to note that the oppressed, impoverished, and marginalized—those inherently a part of the land—are the ones recorded to have made pacts or attempted to have made contracts with the Folkloric Devil. Lucifer himself is the one who was cast out of heaven, the original outcast fallen from grace. For people with the folk memory of the old ways, it seems natural that they would turn to any spiritual presence, no matter how taboo it meant, if they were able to seize their fate. Like most people who are marginalized or outcasted, the need is to simply get results. If the Christian God cannot provide for them, I think it would be human to turn to another force that would. His image has been adapted and recreated in the forms of several older European horned deities. Naturally, he evolved to become a distinct champion of a completely different spiritual conduit for those who have always sought him out of sheer need for fulfillment.

For us today, we still find the thrill in speaking the taboo out loud, and we take even greater joy in rebelling against tyranny when it's for a good cause. This is the essence of Luciferian thought, which is both loving and arrogant, selfish and generous, and paradoxical and dual-natured like the Devil himself. We don't blame a wild animal for being wild, and the Devil is, like us, also an animal. He is a cunning businessman,

---

172 Mankey, Jason. "The Devilish Horned God." *The Horned God of the Witches.* Llewellyn Publications, 2021, p. 157.

and whiskey is poured out to him at occasional sites and places where we may suspect a gate to the wild and lonely places. If there is anything to learn, it's that whether he be a man in black, a black dog, a seducing woman, a serpent, or even a many-winged dragon, he is a changeable person who is all and one at the same time.

In reclaiming the Devil, we are claiming Witchcraft for ourselves, sometimes without realizing it. Witchcraft has always been inherently transgressive and, therefore, heretical. We can take joy and pleasure in the activities and expressions that were deemed evil by the church. Dancing, making love, and free will were all once ruled by the Devil himself. For most, Witchcraft as a practice is a choice. We choose to practice what we do because of the empowerment it brings in choice by itself. Like Eve and the fruit, empowerment is in the choice made and yet to be made when we are consciously living. The challenge is in seeking what we *truly* desire. For Witches, magic is a practice that directly asks us that question and helps us achieve it at the same time. We liberate the internal fires of Azazel to be awakened again with each working when an ember from the sleeping Grigori is fanned to the shining blue flame of the Secret God or a Divine higher self. For some of us, the Witch's Devil remains a point of opening secret passages for the terrain's wisdom. By this, he prepares us for the Great Initiation of life, death, and rebirth.

RECOMMENDED READING

- *Lucifer Princeps* by Peter Grey
- *The Luminous Stone: Lucifer in Western Esotericism* by Michael Howard and Daniel Shulke
- *The Devil's Dozen* by Gemma Gary
- *The Horned God of The Witches* by Jason Mankey
- *The Pillars of Tubal Cain* by Nigel Jackson and Michael Howard
- *Masks of Misrule* by Nigel Jackson
- *From The Ashes of Angels* by Andrew Collins

PART TWO

CHAPTER NINE

RITUALS AND SPELLS OF THE WITCHBLOOD

"By the pricking of my thumbs, Something wicked this way comes.
Shall come against him. What's done cannot be undone."
—The Witches of Macbeth[173]

Witches are known to prick their fingers from time to time. This could be for spiritual empowerment, symbolic sacrifice, or as a solemn expression of their practice of Witchcraft. However, use caution, discretion, and sterile practices when working with blood. Blood is sacred, and hopefully one would know that Witches are not performing gory rites. That being said, there are times that practitioners may prick their fingers using a sterile tool to produce a drop of blood to empower whatever they're doing. Blood is a personal and vital symbol of life, and the Witchblood is the vault of personal experience the Witch has had that has awoken the abilities of the Witch within. By no means is this decision required or something that every Witch must do to be considered Witch enough. Using any bodily link is completely up to the discretion of the practitioner and is not a requirement for magic. To me, using blood in your practice is an extremely personal choice, just like getting a devotional tattoo or piercing. If you are going to incorporate blood, then you should always consider safety first, using sterile tools in a safe environment, and doing sufficient research beforehand.

---

173 Shakespeare, William. *Macbeth*. Act 4. Scene 1. Lines 57–58.

Blood magic is both potent and personal. In all rituals, it's a good rule to thoughtfully consider the implications of what you are doing and, more importantly, why you are doing it. Blood is the life force of the physical body and the Witchblood is the life force of Mystery. It's unique to the Witches as the prime movers of magic because they are the traditional workers overwhelmingly attributed to the production of magic. Even the name "Witchblood" implies its specificity to Witches. Magic only happens when it's actively being performed. The Craft offers all the theatrics, tools, and techniques to engage in an active performance rather than a passive one. This, of course, makes the ritual even more effective by getting the practitioner even more involved and in control of their spiritual lifestyle.

> *"If one who claims to be a Witch can perform the tasks of Witchcraft, that is, they can summon the spirits and they come, can divine with rod, fingers, and birds. If they can also claim the right to the omens and have them; have the power to call, heal, and curse; and above all, can tell the maze and cross the Lethe, then you have a Witch."*[174]
>
> —Robert Cochrane

As a practice and Craft, Witchcraft celebrates personal growth over time. You may feel your magic growing each day, creating more subtle manifestations of change. As our magic grows stronger, we become more aligned with true desire, allowing the correct forces, feelings, and attractions to enter our lives. We may notice the change in ourselves, but these small observations will most often be noticed by other people first. I've noticed that when a person first starts a magical practice, they tend to start developing this aura of magic that attracts them to the correct situations and opportunities. Whatever you cast tends to leave an energetic signature that vibrates off you for a time, acting as a signal to the otherworld. Most of the time, this is first sensed by other Witches. Remember Witches *are* magic, and we tend to find each other despite the odds.

---

174 Richardson, Alan and Marcus Claridge. "Drawing Down the Moon." *The Old Sod: The Odd Life and Inner Work of William G. Gray*, Skylight Press, 2011, pp. 127–128.

These rites and spells are yours to explore, alter, and change as you see fit. Your Craft is your own, but everyone wanting to engage in the Arte has to find their way into the methods or techniques that speak to the soul. Sometimes we find ourselves at a brick wall in our practice, and the answer is returning to our basic foundations as magical practitioners. By being an eternal student of the Craft, we will never lack new ways of working with our spirits. You must see yourself as worthy of accessing these powers. Therefore, practicing regularly with confidence is important to create your magical sense of self. Once you find the techniques that work for you, you should practice them until they can be done on command. The practice of starting a Witchcraft-focused path starts with baseline awareness and cognizance of what motions and techniques get the attention of the spirits. Your perspective is your greatest tool.

Magic has, is, and always will be an accessible option for Witches. Everything a Witch embodies and wields is magic. It is the birthright and root of the Witch's Craft, and it will show you the interconnectedness of the world and possibly even unlock new insights and interests. Like a scientist, tracking what works and what doesn't in your operations is a matter of trial and error. The process of rituals, spells, and other forms of magic all train us to have the capacity to easily turn our mindsets, giving us the full benefit of self-control. Witchcraft's core functioning principle is the building up of a magical atmosphere, because a magical atmosphere permits everyone's natural powers to become unleashed.

"The generation of atmosphere, the aura of the uncanny, is one of the most important secrets of magic. It contributes to the willing suspension of disbelief, the feeling that, within the circle, or in the presence of the magical shrine, anything may happen."[175]

—Doreen Valiente

The generation of atmosphere is, in other words, performance. It starts in the building of the internal and external space with the imagery we build within our mind's eye that then trains all our senses. Performance, at its most basic level, is the transmutation of storytelling.

---

175 Valiente, Doreen. *An ABC of Witchcraft: Past and Present,* Phoenix Publishing, 1986, p. 372.

A good ritual tells a story of who we are collectively, what we need, and where we are headed in life. It should leave us feeling personally empowered but, storytelling aside, the principal component of Witchcraft is in *the doing*. Witchcraft is an important art form and a craft first and foremost. Like many crafts and performance styles, it's all about the subtle changes in the environment and the attention to detail in the act of performing itself.

Be careful what you wish for. The Witching seed plants a strong root when the willing seeker rises to this commitment. As a weaver of fate and worker of magic, you have a responsibility to uphold. There are certain unspoken rules and taboos you may encounter. Each tradition and practice is unique unto itself, but your discernment is what unlocks the door.

CHAPTER TEN

PREPARATIONS OF THE ARTE

RITUAL MINDSET AND ALTERED STATES OF CONSCIOUSNESS

The ritual really begins with preparation. Ritual happens through a series of repetitions and the altered state of consciousness that occurs through that given structure. Yet, through the Witch's willpower is what some call *crossing the hedge,* going back to the Witches' skill of "hedge riding" or crossing the symbolic boundary between this world and the other. This crossing is performed in a state of trance, deep meditation, or astral projection, and doesn't need to happen through hours of trance or complex rituals. Simply, the practice starts and ends with letting our everyday mindset become occupied by attention to the breath, guiding us through imagery, feelings, and other psychic stimuli.

Truly any piece of a magical operation starts with a single thought. In one of my favorite Occult documentaries, Gardnerian High-Priestess and Witch Eleanor Bone quoted philosopher Paraclete, saying, "The beginning of all acts of magical operation begins with determined imagination."[176] Most Witches can create a vivid mental picture of things, then project their conscious willpower upon that image, creating a desired effect. Creativity and clear thought are the seeds that germinate on the astral planes, manifesting as a spell. This exchange

---

176 Eleanor Bone in *The Occult Experience.* Directed by Frank Heiman and Nevill Drury, CineTel Productions Ltd and J.C. Williamson Ltd, 1985.

happens once we do an action (the rite or gesture itself) and decide to speak something into existence (the word or the spell). We are giving creative license to the universe as a co-creator of our lives to manifest that focused imagery we have willed into existence with our words, actions, and visualizations.

This goes to show the responsibility Witches take with our stream of consciousness and the true meaning behind our words, striving to live life mindfully. We can believe our conviction as Witches; our words have an unforgiving power when used with willpower. Through these chosen words, we create the world around us, and when spoken with clarity and gusto, our words get the attention of Gods and spirits alike.

The Witch's trance state encompasses techniques and methods that are embodied and accessible, directing the magical goal. Many consider it the mental practice of meditation used beyond the bounds of inspiration and clarity. The body itself becomes the most important tool, as the practitioner becomes the middleman between the elusive worlds of thought and spirit. When delving into the psyche, it is generally best to do a physical and mental check-in before undertaking any sort of work. When we can find the innermost self, we can feel magic is afoot and better use our senses openly to work said magic. This starts with relaxation and an awareness of the breath. We are still in control of our faculties and can retain memory through most of the rites unless a deeper working state is called for. (Meditation is one of the means this state can be achieved but is certainly not the *only* way.)

Know that to do this individually developed kind of magical work, we must be fully aware and in control of these altered states. In magical communication with the other, we have to be able to communicate our will and desires clearly. We are living on autopilot in most of our day-to-day lives. We let our minds wander and drift into daydreams without realizing that this, too, is another altered state. Being a Witch teaches you not only to shift these states, but to notice them when they catch us off-guard. Essentially, the practice of magic sets us up with the skills to live life mindfully, consciously, and creatively. Obstacles in life become invitations to sit at the altar to gather new energies, reflect, and ultimately change or use them to our benefit. In this way, we use obstacles to our magical advantage.

When looking at the practices of trance work and meditation, the body is responding to how these practices affect the brain waves. There are four types of brain wave specifically concerning the Arte in modern Occult practices:

- Beta: Alert, everyday, or "normal" consciousness. 13–20 hertz.
- Alpha: Meditation, intuitive "magical working state." 8–12 hertz.
- Theta: Light sleep, trance, deeper journey work. 5–8 hertz.
- Delta: Deep sleep. 1–4 hertz.[177]

When practicing, we are going to want to be able to go from beta and comfortably maintain an alpha or theta brain wave frequency. That sweet spot is somewhere between seven and ten hertz. When we can enter these mental states effectively, we can achieve states that allow us to gain direct knowledge from spirits yet also generate power from the inner teachings of the Witchblood itself. This in turn creates an energetic exchange of power, between our world and the other world, further bridging the Witch as a conduit. When large amounts of mental energy are generated and built up, it can be used to catapult the practitioner (or the coven, if done collectively) into another level of trance altogether. This alters the moment's existence and fuels the magic of the ritual.

Shifting from beta to alpha wave states with ease is what fully brings the spirits into our wake. It may bring visions. You may start hearing words or the music of the otherworld, bringing about states of intense emotion, giddiness, and claircognizance, especially if these altered states are done in conjunction with other techniques like music, dance, sensory stimulation, and what are known as *pathways of power*.[178] At the heart of the practice of altered states is the Witch simply allowing the information to come. The sense of fluidity is part of how we sense the ebb and flow of the spiritual traffic around us. When we can ritualize our process of changing our everyday perceptions, we have an easier time making the shift to magical states of consciousness.

Any time meditation is brought up, there is often the misconception that it has to be a very specific crossed-legged, thoughtless experience of a blissful state. Although this is one method, it is one of many we can turn to. Please note that some methods of meditation or trance may work for you

---

177 Penczak, Christopher. "Brainwaves." *The Gates of Witchcraft*. Copper Cauldron Publishing, 2012, p. 20.

178 Claircognizance: The ability for a person to acquire psychic knowledge without knowing how or why they knew it or how it came to them.

but not for others. We use these techniques not to escape our material world but to enhance it, setting out with purpose to create a conscious partnership with the world around us. Meditation is simply another method of *mindful concentration*. I also would like to break the misconception about the length of time one needs to meditate. What's important is not the length of time you meditate, but the feeling and results you get out of the experience. There are days where all I need is a five-minute tune-up, and other days where I need a forty-minute-long journey. How you listen to your surroundings and intuition is yours to experiment with. It is a matter of trial and error, but, more importantly, it is a *practice*. The more you try, the easier it becomes.

To start with the basics, you can focus on a single thought, item, or sound. You could speak a short mantra or focus on an icon of a deity to channel inspiration from the imagery. We can use visualization, silent prayer, or holding focus exercises. The gift of these practices is the hidden wisdom we may not have realized we could receive. The secret to all these methods is the Witch's breath.

THE WITCH'S BREATH

The breath is the fuel and the secret of all magical alignments. The awakening of the blood starts with the breath. At the beginning of every spell, there is an inhale and an exhale. In taking time to connect with each coven, we begin with the breath. As life starts with the first inhale, life ends with the final exhale. In the same rhythms of life, we become hyper-aware of breath in order to create magic. The breath, and our control of it, is what allows everything from relaxation to empowering an item. In folklore, the breath of the Witch is said to revive someone from illness, blow storm clouds away, and whistle up the winds. Yet, there is a shred of truth that breathwork is a solid foundation of meditation, trance work, and psychic regulation. It starts with the famous cleansing breath: in through the nose for a five count and out through the mouth for a ten count.

The breath is the body's sky. It's expansive and has the job of carrying the vital oxygen we need. When the mind starts to wander, get distracted, or even bored during meditation, we always remember the breath. This is partially why guided meditations are so helpful to start with at first, because they give you the suggested imagery and focal points needed to help you make the journey, and they have built-in countdowns to regulate a steady breathing pattern. However, meditation can be done anywhere at any time. For me, focusing on why I'm meditating or what I'm going to use my meditation to do and then using my breath and some repeated words transports me instantly. My mind will still wander—that is what minds do—but all I need to do to refocus is bring it back to the breath. When in doubt, just bring it back to your breath.

My practice of Witchcraft allows me to be fully engaged and aware of myself and my surroundings while, at the same time, drifting mentally between states of mind. This has helped me achieve my sense of personal empowerment as a practicing psychic worker. As a professional reader, it's so important to have the ability to switch this ability on and off in a work environment and operate in this state for long periods. I found this to be most helpful in my breath control. Developing this internal haven of controlled breath, or what some call the inner temple is vital to the safety and psychic hygiene of the practitioner.[179]

Start with finding a rhythm that works for you and use a full breath that expands the entire diaphragm. Relaxed shoulders and in a comfortable position. Many are fans of *four-fold* or *four-square* breathing, which has benefits in reducing anxiety and regulating the heart rate. Sometimes just starting is the hardest part. Here is a basic cleansing breath formula to help enhance the powers of air that move and blow within you:

> *In through the nose for a four-count*
> *Holding that in for a four-count*
> *Out through the mouth for a four-count*
> *Holding the empty for a four-count.*

BREATH OF AWEN

After every line, use this pattern of breathing at a slow and steady pace:

> *(Breathing in for one…two…three…four…five…six…seven…,*
> *out for one…two…three…four…five…six…seven.)*
> *Breath of the unseen! Blow through me.*
> *Breath of Athem! Move me.*
> *Breath of Awen! Inspire me.*
> *Breath within me! Cleanse me.*

---

179 Penczak, Christopher. *The Inner Temple of Witchcraft*. Llewellyn Worldwide, 2021.

GROUNDING

Grounding is staying present. When we are truly grounded, we are fully present and fully embodied in that time and place. Grounding is how we maintain the connection to the Earth, which, after all, is our main power source. Earth is the mother of life, where we live, and where we tune in. Grounding exercises keep us anchored to our bodies, which are grounded to the power source of Earth.

Grounding the self helps us do two things. First, grounding stabilizes us. It keeps us energetically in check, so we don't get carried away and suffer some annoying effects of being overstimulated. When we are grounded, we are safe within ourselves and reduce the risk of drifting off or becoming overwhelmed with psychic information. Grounding also helps us keep the intention of our work at the forefront of our minds. This razor-sharp focus ensures that our will becomes our desired result. This keeps group members in a coven setting in tune with each other and with their group mind or the coven *egregore.* As for the individual, it prepares and helps them tune into their will and surroundings, which is often where the most visceral encounters with spirits are held.

Grounding is sometimes described as cleansing and placing our energy where it needs to go at our core and our roots. This is sometimes called *centering.* For me, centering refers to the sealing of this grounded energy and to the process of then aligning myself to the goal of the work I'm going to be doing magically.

ALIGNING AND ALTERED STATE TRIGGERS

Having a good imagination is a crucial part of the Witch's foundational skill set. This is the innate tool we have to formulate information in visual or artistic form, allowing us to hold concentration for spellwork. Even if it's not exact or done with the mind's eye in a visual sense, that's okay! We all have inner senses that are waiting to be noticed. For instance, if I describe a beach with sand and bright blue skies, can you see it? Do you smell the ocean? Do you feel the breeze off the water? Notice what senses are the most aware. Generating imagery also brings the importance of building concentration and maintaining it for long periods.

For many, imagining for long stretches is still a practice, and take it from me—patience is required for this. Some of the best rites and rituals I've had the privilege of attending tuned into the feeling of the collective group working the rite. As a result, the ritual leaders took the time necessary for everyone to ease into a steady trance with impeccable concentration on the magical goal. There was a clear given focal point and a collective spiritual dialogue internally happening during the ritual. This achieving of group-mind is best referred to as a type of alignment, but also as a validation of centering the group as a whole.

When I get up in the morning, I try to take a second to breathe and stretch. In the first few breaths of waking, there is a slight adjustment to the new day. We align with our daily goals and planetary energies. We give thanks to the spirits at work and take that moment to allow our bodies to subtly readjust to the new energies of that day. If one has had a particularly busy night of dreaming or astral travel, doing a quick cleansing and rite of cleaning is best. This is part of staying psychically adroit but also checking in with our physical, mental, and spiritual health. In some traditions, like Anderson-Ferri and The Temple of Witchcraft, there is the practice of honoring the Witch's three souls in what is called a *soul alignment*.[180] You may be familiar with other Eastern systems like the chakras. However, as a Witch, I find more resonance in this particular system of alignment, working power centers we hold in the physical body.

The more trance and meditative work you perform, the more familiarized with that internal space within yourself you will become and the easier it will be. It will take time to learn how to relax the body and allow each tiny noise and twitch to be an outside reminder of the stillness you hold. While you develop this, you can create and assign yourself a simple hand gesture or facial movement that, for a while, you will only do while in your trance. This is you classically conditioning your body to respond to this gesture so you can drop into this same meditative state quickly if you need to. Rather than

---

180 Faerywolf, Storm. "The Personal Trinity." *Betwixt & Between: Exploring the Faery Tradition of Witchcraft.* Llewellyn Worldwide, 2017, pp. 51–70.

physically moving, you can make this gesture by signaling to the body to drop the brainwaves in the making of that movement or gesture. Practice and renew it frequently. For me, this started with the simple crossing of my index and middle finger, however, this could be a head movement, a specific breath on the palm, or making the signs of the horn in your left hand. Having an instant psychic trigger is helpful for small acts of magic, regulating self-check-ins, calming down heart rate, and finding deeper wisdom amid chaos.

As you begin to *consistently* work with your practice and rituals, you will notice many other psychic triggers that will automatically take you into that deeper zone. These may all be sensory or visual, from the sight of the candles illuminating your space or the smell of a specific incense, the music you may choose to play each time, or the weight of your ritual jewelry that you only wear for your practices. This is so all these items retain their sense of magic and protection, but so it honors the fact that every time you use it for your craft, it activates that familiar part of you. The moment our other awareness is keyed in is the moment we activate the Witchblood.

By definition, a ritual is a set of practices in a specific sequence. When we do something over and over, it becomes programmed into the mind and body. This is why it's important that ritual structure is consistent. Repetition creates these healthy triggers. The more you practice, you will notice yourself becoming increasingly tuned in with little to no effort. This is why Witches keep some items *only* for magic, separate from mundane tasks and everyday use. When we put on a piece of ritual jewelry or a robe, the physical senses recognize that as a signal to begin the process of *the becoming* or *the awakening*. When something is used again and again, it builds power, also known as *morphic resonance*. Morphic resonance is best compared to the snowball effect of something building stronger and stronger the more power it collects by our investment into it. This also means all objects, the space you practice in, and your body will build up this supercharge of Witch-power over time, but only if you use it wisely and correctly will it work for you consistently, as it's not a parlor trick or a game. To work, it must be respected.

LOCATION

The space you choose to perform your magical workings is critically important to building the right atmosphere for you to slip into a state of psychic activity and receptivity to what you are doing in ritual. The space must be three things: safe, private, and free from distraction. Granted, there may be places of power you don't have access to in private, but this is the ideal for rituals that require more time and coordination. Keeping these three things in mind gives the necessary precautions for a comfortable working environment. Sacred spaces should also always be safe spaces. For most of us, this is the bedroom. Some of us have the privilege of having a separate room purely for practice, and some are even luckier to have access to private natural landscapes without fear of interruption. I prefer to work outside whenever I can, as the connection and results are always more immediate.

You should be able to acknowledge the power of the place you are using, though it is a force you can't see with the naked eye. This acknowledgment of power, then, is what creates an energetic shift by identifying and respecting the land's natural current or vibration around you and is why grounding is so important in the Craft. As grounding helps you tune in to the land itself and still be anchored in your physical body, the body becomes filled with the power of the Earth's tutelic force that you can manipulate, project, and use at will. Everywhere has places of power where it seems that the spiritual world overlaps with our own. Old milestones, crossroads, woodland areas, and locations steeped in legends are some of my favorite places to find. Nature is your temple, and it is in the wild places that Witches are said to walk. With a darkened room and candlelight, even a dorm can be temporarily transported to the classic Witch's den.

When exploring new spaces or visiting locations you have never been to before, it is always best to take time to tune into your feelings and notice how moving through the space affects you. Psychic information often comes in quick flashes and translates itself to us as feelings and sensations. Some places are uncomfortable and spooky, but they still make very good places for Witches to work. Part of my learning was confronting that anxiety about what could be out in the dark woods as I worked magic because the spirits are not of my vibration, they are or can be *uncomfortable*. Therefore, it is always a good idea to address the land spirits and the land itself as a visitor, introduce yourself, and ask its permission to be there. In some places, we are welcomed, and in others, we are told to stay out. The power is in that acknowledgment. As animists, we try to allow spirits to have choices concerning the relationship we mutually hold with the otherworld.

THE MAGIC CIRCLE

The circle itself is an archaic shape known to Witches and always has been revered in symbols such as the ouroboros, the pentagram, and the Celtic cross. A circle is also the same shape as the Sun and Moon from how we observe them from Earth, and so the ancient people probably knew that to mimic their shape was to align or summon influence from the sky. The circle is the symbol of everything: the Wheel of the Year, the constant unbroken infinite of life, death, and rebirth. The ritual of casting a circle is the practice of sacred space building and creating a temple as the chosen place of magic. The circle's roots, as mentioned before, are echoes of the ceremonial magicians' working setup for the conjuration and commanding of spirits. For this reason, the circle is there for the magician's protection from rebellious spirits or harmful energies that may infringe upon the space. So, the first reason to use a circle is for protection. This could additionally protect you from any outside influences or distractions, as they are neutralized and blocked out from the circle during the initial casting rite. However, in my personal experience, there are often very few malevolent energies or spirits you may encounter.

With this in mind, it is a well-known taboo to break the circle so as not to provoke these nasty spirits in the ceremonial magician's mindset. It's said that breaking the circle can cause the power raised within the space to leak out. It is suggested that you set your circle in a place without distractions or reminders of the mundane world, so pushing back furniture and taking down the clocks from your home or finding a safe location outdoors is best.

Witches believe in the attunement of frequency, being able to work psychically by tapping into these frequencies of light, sound, and feeling. When the circle is cast, it carves out and separates this world from the spirit world. The willpower of the Witch anchors us in between the worlds of human and spirits. The circle is the portal into a place of timelessness where we can be in a raised frequency to commune with the other. Therefore, the Witch walking between the worlds has one foot on Earth and the other in spirit. Just like if you have a pot to hold boiling water to cook food or to change one substance into another, the circle is the container of power the Witch uses to commune with the presence of the Gods. For some, stepping into the Witch's circle is stepping into a cave or womb of the Great Mother herself. Here, the Goddess keeps her bubbling magma of change, and everything she touches, changes, lives, dies, and changes once again.

When we mark where we cast a circle, we may only see it as that single ring of energy, when in actuality it is a sphere, a mill tower, and sometimes can be cast as a fluid sphere that moves and expands with the movement of a group. It is a mingling of energies from the power raised as we pull power up from the land itself. The magic will hold firm to the visualization created by the practitioner and used time and time again as an established piece of astral signaling.

In modern Wica, the traditional measurement for the circle is nine feet in diameter. This holds a good-sized group fairly comfortably, although it can be quite snug in large or particularly active groups. You just have to learn to adapt so as not to break the circle. But why nine feet? Going back to Gardner and the development of his Witchcraft tradition, we can look at one of his source texts, *The Key of Solomon*.[181] The nine-foot measurement is most likely an alteration of Gardner's convenience in comparison to the key's eighteen-foot circle measurement. Imagine him trying to fit that in a small English cottage! I think it a clever alteration on Gardner's part, keeping in mind the mystical accounts of the number nine in numerology and its association with Witchcraft and Malefica. The number of three times three is a popular formula among Witches.

Circles and proper casting are fantastic for the formality of setting up our rituals and stepping into ritual mindset in terms of consciousness triggers discussed earlier. Again, circle casting serves as the foundation for magical creation to set aside a timeless space. I was influenced by the teaching that circle casting is making a microcosmic world within the macrocosmic world we live in, a ritual imitating life within the great circle which is our everyday

---

181 MacGregor Mathers, S. L. et. al. *The Greater Key of Solomon: The Grimoire of Solomon*. 1888.

existence. There are times when a full circle casting may be inconvenient and downright *extra*, and several interesting conversations have sprung up in recent years among Witches asking about the need to cast a circle in modern times as a result. We might prefer to perform throughout the day or when we get the time to do so, especially in cases such as spell working, the crafting of magical objects, and practical workings.

A circle functions best when it is used for rituals of immersive working, energy building, and proper formality as dictated by one's intuition or tradition. However, spells are intensely driven prayers and no circle is necessary for casting them, although a circle also helps to raise energy. It's entirely up to what feels correct to you. You may also choose to not cast if you're already in a natural place of power or a location already energetically awake. This could be your regular location for magic where you have done work repeatedly over time. Andrew D. Chumbley has summed it all up best for the future generations of Witches. He said that when you stand within the working circle, you "cast true about you like the horizon itself, your presence preserves the lineage and tradition of the Witchblood, i.e. those who have gone before in the craft and those who have incarnated today who are their magickal and spiritual successors. In this way, those who belong to the craft in modern times are tracing or retracing in the circle the footsteps of their ancestors and ancestral spirits."[182]

THE RITUAL BATH

After I've chosen my space, set up my altar, and am ready to begin with my circle, I take a ritual bath. Being in a candlelit bathroom, taking a ceremonial shower or salt bath, is an immediate trance trigger for me. When we are bathing, not only are we cleansing and purifying ourselves so we feel cleansed and ready to work, but we can declare ourselves as pure when presenting ourselves before our spirits. I find it a matter of spiritual politeness to be free of any debris or interference from what I carry with me. Dirt, oils, emotions, and unhelpful thoughts from my day-to-day life are bound to retain psychic interference or things I may not want to bring into my sacred space. Part of the preparation is the complete neutralization and cleansing of the space *and the self* beforehand. The act of taking a

---

182 Howard, Michael. "Casting The Circle." *Liber Nox: A Traditional Witch's Gramarye.* Skylight Press, 2014, pp. 50–52.

purifying bath is not only a healthy trigger for the Witching state of mind but also makes the practitioner fully receptive to the powers being worked because they are cleansed on both spiritual and physical levels. In this way, the old saying that "cleanliness is next to godliness" is true.

Most ritual baths are set with holy or Epsom salts that have been consecrated and exorcized by the Witch's word, bringing out its natural cleansing properties. This is giving the salt a charge or a direction to manifest its purifying virtue. The salts are then used in the bath or used to scrub the body in the shower. Salt is the purest form of the Earthen element, and it harkens back to the creation of life from the sea and the solubility of the womb. As we strive to awaken and become ourselves, we return to our most natural or purest state. The salt and water mixture creates holy water, the original potion of all giving life. We may decide to add certain herbs, flower petals, or even seashells to imbue the bath as the pool to the otherworld for us to renew ourselves in. It is also helpful on a magical level to burn specific incense to enhance the properties of the bath. This also adds to the bathing ritual by creating a hazy, dream-like atmosphere. To me, it feels like being in a chamber of rebirth, and in many ways, when we take the cleansing bath, we are washing away our mundane worries and cares. We step out of the bath cleansed and rebirthed, and ready to enter the sacred space different than before.

BUILDING ABILITIES

Take fifteen minutes to do a muscle-by-muscle relaxation exercise, starting from the top of your forehead and going down to the soles of the feet. Do this intentionally by tensing up each muscle, holding it, and then allowing yourself to release it and feel the relief. I suggest you develop your personal series of seven to thirteen symbols, or even just a series of colors to visualize and hold in your mind's eye for a minute or two each. Make this vivid and lifelike to the point where you can touch each symbol or color and know what it feels like.

As you do this, keep in mind the symbols should be clear and not complicated so you can do this quickly and effectively when the situation requires. By closing your eyes for two to six minutes and using deep breathing, you're able to drop your brainwaves and enter this proper meditative state. With the symbol set or using a countdown system, you can personalize a fast and recognizable system that takes you into this

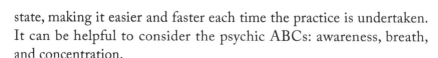

state, making it easier and faster each time the practice is undertaken. It can be helpful to consider the psychic ABCs: awareness, breath, and concentration.

Count down from seven to one, starting with the crown of your head (just an inch or two above the top of your head) to the bottoms of your feet. Take time to focus on each planet, working your way down the list. Visualize their colors, their qualities, and how they present themselves to you. This looks like:

- White: Moon. Intuition, psychic ability, guidance.
- Yellow: Sun. Virtue, health, honesty.
- Orange: Mercury. Communication, travel.
- Red: Mars. Passion, will, strategy.
- Green: Venus. Love, esteem, receptivity.
- Royal blue: Jupiter. Influence, wisdom, wealth.
- Black: Saturn. Protection, boundaries, restriction.

When building a foundation to your practice, the other secret is that you advance through the basics themselves. Like any muscle, the psychic muscle gets stronger with exercise. The best way to commit yourself to a devotional practice in a Witchcraft framework is to have some form of daily practice.

The best advice for this, if you don't want to develop a quick ten to fifteen-minute rite, is to incorporate small acts of magic into regular tasks you already do as part of your routine. For me, the daily ritual is my spiritual check-in and a time to address my spirits with thanks. Simply lighting a candle or burning incense or a specific holy herb will release your desired intention. This could take the form of a personal cleansing, protection spell, or wearing a protective talisman or charm you have constructed for that daily purpose. All simple acts link to the chain of our connection. Having small magical rites or charms throughout the day not only helps us live magic as a lifestyle, but also allows us to build deeper spiritual relationships with ourselves. Aside from showing gratitude, daily practice is the best time to implement a routine of basic psychic hygiene.

Wherever you are led, this journey is not about the destination, but experiencing the journey as a full human being. As Witches, we often tend to bring up the topic of doing things "the right way." The only thing I have concerning my insecurities in this matter has been a wise saying from a friend: "The work will teach you how to do the work." Witchcraft may not be for everyone, but it *is* for those who have the willingness to do it. If you find the thrill in night flights through the woods and ecstatic dances around the fire, magic may come to you easier than you ever expected. This effort is the first step of the seeker. *Dare* to take that step. *Know* you have the power buried within you. Use your *will* to bring that power into existence. Keep that extraordinary power *silent*, so it may be guarded as the treasure it is.

CHAPTER ELEVEN

INSTRUMENTS OF THE ARTE, TOOLS OF THE TRADE

The greatest tool of the Witch is the mind. As such, our personhood is all needed to work powerful magic, but having physical tools helps. (That's why they are called tools.) There is a profound psychological effect in working with the instruments we naturally associate with the Craft. They act as reminders and profound symbols unto the practitioner of the power they wield. Each tool has a unique spirit that the practitioner places within every working object, whether this is by the artistic design of the tool or the prescribed formula given by a tradition of how a tool should be obtained. Both ultimately result in the tool becoming dedicated to a specific current of magic worked and feeding the indwelling spirit within. Over time, the Witch connects with the symbolism, meaning, and virtue that each item carries, progressing them further into the Mysteries the tools have for their owner.

The tools of the Craft carry long histories of their esoteric meanings and, importantly, why and how they are to be used once they find their home in the hands of the Witch. Each time we use a tool, it has information to share with us. It could be the way it feels in our hands or the way it appeals to our aesthetics. Its charm could simply be in the story behind how we found a certain ritual item. When a tool is found or, more often, when the tool finds its way to us, we consecrate or *hallow* that tool to the purpose of its nature and metaphysical virtue.[183] The instructions given to the tool in the hallowing rite it as a magical object. The tool then becomes

---

183 Hallowing is just another term for consecration.

a conduit for the practitioner as the instrument's inner symbolism is awoken to manifest as an extension of the practitioner's energy in an act of magical consecration. In this way, the object transforms, becoming not just a tool but a *touchstone* or a key to the otherworld.

Tools are extensions and tokens of our magical power, making it easier to feel the power flowing through and out of us. More importantly, the tools make it easier to direct the power raised and show the power exactly what needs to happen and where it needs to go. These tools of the trade don't need to be anything expensive, but they do need to be durable and composed of a natural element. Therefore, plastics and synthetic materials are not ideal. This is not a preference or aesthetic choice for me. Artificial energies are ineffective for most because they have no natural resonance from the natural world. If we want to raise and direct magical energies properly, we have to use conduits and touchstones that are going to be effective. An easy way to keep this accessible is by visiting thrift shops or taking the time to go into the natural landscape and source items that can easily become a tool once you creatively build or personalize them as your own.

THE ALTAR

The altar is a living icon and a mirror of the magician's world as they desire to sculpt it in their divine images. The altar is the central focal point for practice and a place of power that can be a temporary or growing collection. It can also be a fixture, cabinet, or table that you regularly tend to and use as the symbolic representation of the Witchcraft you practice. An altar that is consistently in use is sometimes referred to as the *working altar*. Building an altar is an act of artistry and self-care, as we decide to set aside time and a place within our homes to make room for the self, magic, and spirit. It houses all our tools and working materials, keeping them protected and honored as sacred objects. How we treat an item will often influence how we respond to the item once we use it. In Witchcraft, this is a very animistic relationship we hold with the tool by putting it in a place of respect and only using it for magical purposes, nothing else.

The altar gives space set aside as sacred for items and even the spirits we evoke. Even when not in use, the altar is the dwelling place for the relationships we hold with the otherworld. It is as pleasing to our spiritual company as it is pleasing to us. When reading other books on the Craft, you may find particular placements or requirements for the altar. This makes sense when it concerns a particular tradition or coven-oriented group working, which is for the sake of group organization, practicality, and safety so that no Witch catches on fire from the altar candles.

The altar, for me, is mainly a place of gathering. It is a gathering place for community, inspiration, power, and the spirits. Even if not literally, all of these things are summoned and gathered in the heart before a ritual or meditation. At the altar, settling takes place within the mind where one can come into the presence of magic and divinity. This spirit or presence is an inviting energy that calls us to claim a place of connection, study, sorcery, or rest. It acts as the microcosm of our world, representing what we are and the powers we hold.

Although there are no specific rules to setting up your altar, it is traditional that you use intentional placement that corresponds with symbology. I suggest that everything on the altar has a purpose and serves the rite. Furthermore, the altar is traditionally at the hearth or the main location of activity within the home. This is not ideal for everyone, so setting up your altar in a personal space where it can be enjoyed and engaged is just as appropriate.

THE TOOLS

"Thus, said the daimon: the Divine Artist must listen and obey the tabu, dictated by the ancestral and totem familiars, he must learn the way of preparing the sacred instruments. Failure to observe their secret laws is the proof of unworthiness to walk upon the path of the art magical."[184]

Making or personalizing your tools not only builds a personal connection with them, but by creating, you are imbuing magical focus and putting a piece of yourself into whatever you're making. This is not only a spell, but also the most direct way to build a connection to converse with a magical object. Witchcraft, as the Craft of all crafts, has a place for every trade and skill. Traditional skills like blacksmithing, weaving, and art all play an especially prominent role for Witches, as these skills have the natural ability to produce a magical material.

---

184 Chumbley, Andrew D. "The Sacred Instruments." *The Azoetia: A Grimoire of the Sabbatic Craft.* Xoanon Publishers, 1992, p. 16.

THE BOOK OF ARTE

In my opinion, this should be the first tool acquired for journaling, collecting information, and taking inspiration to construct your rites and spells. This is one of the most immediate ways you can advance from the basics in Traditional Witchcraft. The Book of Arte is the tool for personal growth, development, and chronicling your magical career, and is sometimes also called a *Book of Shadows* or *Book of Mysteries*. This is essentially an all-in-one formulary and journal of personal reflection. It is the Witch's journal, scrapbook, diary, research log, liturgy and ritual recorder, and collection of recipes, spells, prayers, artistic recordings, and visions of trance and dream. It has a bit of a mixed history in terms of its representation in pop culture and media, which can add to some confusion about different Witchcraft tradition's practices and how a Witch should keep their book.

In the founding of the modern Witchcraft movement, Gerald Gardner kept a working diary that became known as *Ye Book of The Art Magical* or *The Book of Shadows*.[185] Its contents are still kept secret today among initiates to preserve this particular form of Witchcraft. However, because it is a system passed from person to person in sacred spaces along with the oaths of secrecy, it is continually added to with personal additions, reflections, and methods. It is equally liturgical and an evolving working system. It is meant to be a book recording what works and what does not as a praxis. Nothing is truly set in stone for your personal work, yet a tradition preserves itself, so it remains a passable tradition. This means it still evolves and is added to from generation to generation, but the core material and practice remain.

The book you keep becomes an amazing time capsule of what you believed at a given moment, in the same way this book preserves my authorial voice, which will probably change as time goes on. This is part of the magical resonance all writing carries with it. The pen is the wand as we take the invisible language of the aether and transmute it into the symbols of words. Therefore, the Witch's book has its own spirit as a tool. Perhaps one day, you will pass it to your students, initiates, children, and downline of those to follow suit.

---

185 Howard, Michael. *Modern Wicca: A History from Gerald Gardner to the Present*. Llewellyn Worldwide, 2010.

The Blade

This is the main tool and spiritual weapon. It is called several different things depending on the tradition you are from. Known as an athame, arthame, or dagger, this tool commands and projects all facets of the Witch's power. This usage of the inner fire is channeled through the blade in all manner of sorcery and casting. The blade was forged in fire, so as such, it's ruled by that specific elemental property. It can represent the first flash of lightning that came from the Gods, an inner dwelling Mystery of the fallen ones, or the forge of the Gods.

The blade most recognizable in Wica is derived from the traditional black-handled knife from *The Key of Solomon*.[186] Today, it's most commonly used for consecrations, projecting power, and exorcizing or banishing anything not wanted in the space. This tool is used in every circle casting, setting the boundary and creating the spherical portal where we can travel to that liminal working place and meet the Gods halfway between the worlds. It is probably the most forceful tool as a tool of command. Therefore, it shines with the virtues of willpower and determination of the person wielding it. A knife is a very distinct symbol, and if you're not careful with it, you can cut yourself, so be aware while you use it.

The Wand

The wand is the implement used to make the calls to the otherworld to send forth the Witch's magic. This tool is often used to summon and beckon what we seek into our space. Unlike the blade, the wand is an inviting and gentler tool. It tends to be used in interactions with deities, spirits, and healing, and can direct any power to your specific spell or ritual. As an extension of oneself, it can be seen as an exaggerated pointed Witch's finger. Traditionally, the wand is made of wood, and it will amplify the wood's given magical properties, mingling with its natural virtues. The wood of the wand still maintains a part of the life and the spirit of the tree it came from, giving a direct link to the Earth and the indwelling spirit of the *dryad*, or "tree spirit."

---

186 MacGregor Mathers, S.L. et. al. *The Greater Key of Solomon: The Grimoire of Solomon.* 1888.

Certain woods make for better wands than others. There is a specificity to how they work, depending on the wood's magical properties. For instance, willow, hazel, and rowan would all be outstanding options for all types of beginner magical work. Willow is particularly wonderful for healing, while rowan is known to be one of the magical trees of Europe. However, woods like yew and blackthorn are specific to blasting and baneful work. The traditional measurement of the wand is from the base of the elbow down to the tip of the index finger. It should feel comfortable in your hand and vibrate, still humming with residual power while it's not in use. As it is from a tree that has spent its life cycle reaching towards the sky and blowing in the breeze, its elemental property is that of Air. Communication, mindset, and intellect are the main virtues of Air that assist the wand in calling out to the otherworld and projecting our thoughts, hopes, and desires.

Sometimes, the wand is called the *conjuring stick* or the *scepter*. The scepters once used by kings and queens were cultural signs of status and a symbol of their own divine rule as the representatives of the Gods on Earth. In military affairs, the wand was a tool of command on the battlefield to direct the armed troops where to go. This sense of pointing, commanding, and moving forces by the direction or gesturing of the wand is exactly how we still engage with the tool today. Just like an orchestra's conductor uses their baton to tell the orchestra how to play under their direction, the Witch executes the same thing with the invisible orchestra of the Mighty Ones.

THE PATEN/HEARTHSTONE

Whether it is a metal disc, a stone, or even made out of sculpted wax, the paten is the altar's foundation. This round disc often sits at the center of the altar or is accessible enough to be a focal point where you set your working objects as you conjure and enchant them. This is where the magic, blessings, and concentrations are performed on the altar or at the foot of the stang. As the foundation, it has a strong Earth Elemental correspondence ruling over it. It often acts as a direct portal or passageway for the forces we seek to come through.

The paten or *hearthstone* can be viewed as a generator of magical power that stores excess energy within it as a vessel. This stored energy can then be used when the atmosphere or the magical fuel for a spell is lacking.

A sign—traditionally either a pentagram or pentacle—is often inscribed upon it as the Witch's symbol, providing protection and balance. This can be your own design, or you can find a traditional symbolic design that speaks to you. Some traditions inscribe several symbols inscribed, and it remains just a blank slab of stone, metal, or wood in others, yet they work in the same way.

The plate can also serve a purpose in conjurations, divinations, and invocations, but it's most common for the paten to hold the offerings of cake during the libation of a traditional circle.[187] That's because we feast on cake or slices of bread to ground ourselves at that point in the ritual. As we eat the blessed cakes or bread, we remember the Earth that bore us the grain. Serving the cakes on the paten is symbolic of taking from the Earth, but always giving her the first share as we say thanks in return.

The hearthstone is an open gate to the land of the Gods and all that upholds the practitioner or working coven. By touching the stone, your mind has the brief ability to glimpse directly into the twilight of the otherworld. As an emblem of the home and the magical family within, it remains a tradition to keep a hearthstone in several lineages of the Craft.

The Chalice

The chalice holds all the Witch's libations of ritual wine or juice. Within this vessel, all fluids are made sacred and enchanted with the blessings of the Gods. This consecrated fluid is offered to the Gods, then drunk and taken into the self to ingest the blessings of the circle, the land, and the folk into the self. It is the mystery of the sangreal and a representation of the chaotic fluidity brought into order by the artistry of the Goddess. The cup, a sacred container, can also stand as the very traditional representation of the womb of the Great Goddess figure. Out of the cup of life flows the power we weave and the power we breathe. Within the chalice, you may brew your potions and fluid condensers of the Arte. The chalice is also the symbol used in the most solemn rites in initiatory Craft and serves in the Traditional Witch's rite of the Housle and the Necromantic rite of the Red Meal.

---

187 Generally, the offering is of either cakes and wine or cakes and ale.

Each ritual provides a completely different experience from the chalice. For those partaking in the rite, there is deeper context for the meanings held evident in the chalice's symbolism, bridging several branches of the Craft. The symbolism of the chalice is twofold: the Mysteries of fertility and sacrifice. In contemporary Witchcraft, the emphasis is often on the fertility blessing. This type of blessing often pairs the chalice with the blade as its projective counterpart, as the chalice is a tool synonymous with receptivity. Its receptiveness is often believed to be symbolic of the Goddess in her role as a mother and a benevolent giver. When the blade is ceremoniously used to consecrate the fluid inside, this is a fertility blessing. While it is often not specific to literal fertility in human life, it does represent the fertility of the mind and the spirit's pursuit of happiness. The coven and the Gods bless this brew together to spiritually nourish those who drink its contents. This is how the Mystery of the holy cup is consumed, bringing us into a Witch's Eucharist with the Old Gods.

The fertility aspect of the chalice is significant to the folklore of the divine marriage between the sovereign king and the Goddess of the land herself. At specific times of spiritual peak during the seasonal shift, there was the belief that the Gods came together in a mystical sexual union, promoting and regenerating the powers of the land through the spiritual fertility and fulfillment of the people. This is recorded as one of the deeper origins of Greek myth and considered the ritual prototype for the fertility rites of the Ancient Mediterranean known as the *Hieros Gamos,* meaning "Divine marriage."[188] Within some magical practices, namely Wica, there is homage paid to the mythos of a polarity in which two things come together and often magically complement each other. The symbolism tends to be highly sexually charged but truly is about the push and pull that exists between two energies. Like the complimentary pairings of the Sun and the Moon or the lover and beloved, the bounds of polarity know no limits. Even within Christian thought, there's a polarity or specific form of Divine marriage represented by the shared union between Christ and the Church, termed the *sponsus et sponsa.*[189]

---

188 Nissinen, Martti and Risto Uro. *Sacred Marriages the Divine-Human Sexual Metaphor from Sumer to Early Christianity.* Eisenbrauns, 2008.

189 Jung, Carl. *Memories, Dreams, Reflections.* Vintage Books, 1989, p. 395.

In the rites of the Housle or the Necromantic operative working of the Red Meal, the chalice serves in its same role along with the blade as a remembrance of *sacrifice* rather than fertility. Instead of blessing the cup, the blade symbolically swipes or "cuts" the top of the chalice, as if the Witch is cutting the neck of something. The cup spills out wine, representing the blood spilled upon the Earth and the idea that everything that is taken is given, and what is given is also taken. We drink the blood of the Gods and spirits imbued in the chalice in remembrance and in celebration of that which gives so we are sustained. The grapes must be harvested and crushed to make the wine. Death gives unto life as life gives unto death.

THE STANG

The stang is the traditional Witch's portable altar, walking staff, and tool identified as the ultimate Godhead by passage through the Horned One of Witches of Old. The word *stang* comes from an old Nordic word meaning "pole." It's often a "y"-shaped staff or pole with antlers or horns fixed to the top of it.[190] It draws power up from the land and holds its power in connection with the Witch that wields it. Those awakening the Witchblood should soon come into possession of one, as it is often a traditional sign of the spirits (or, specifically, the Horned God himself as Keeper of the Witchblood) bringing one into the Craft. The Horned God invites you to *raise the stang* or, in other words, it's time to roll up your sleeves and get dirty because there is Witchcraft to be done!

The stang is a living icon holding the Godheads and the egregore of the working group or person using it. Its spirit works with us as a companion and guide upon the astral and physical roads that we tread with it in hand. The stang protects, summons, and connects us to the worlds below, center, and above. It can be seen as the World Tree or *Tree of Yggdrasil*, connecting all the worlds as the axis mundi. (These are traditional cosmologies held by Witches connecting the realms of Earth, sea, and sky.)

---

190 Pearson, Nigel G. *Treading the Mill: Workings in Traditional Witchcraft.* Troy Books, 2017, p. 22.

When used in rites of fascination or entering trance by focusing upon a singular object, the stang can become a tool we use to perform astral travel and journeying work. As a tool of night flight, it's common to see Witches in the European woodcuts riding upon forked stangs and pitchforks, as these are also versions of a stang. The shape represents the horns of the Horned One and the "v" or vaginal opening from where life emerges, a stark representation of unity in the figures of the Witch Gods.

Between the horns of the stang, where the base of the staff meets the two prongs, sits an illuminated candle. The light that "shines betwixt the horns" is the symbol of the spark of life that inspired all consciousness and shines the power of the Witch's Truth: the lightning that fell from the heavens and the fire from the Gods used to illuminate the lonely and wild places.[191] The light from the stang is there to guide and teach all gnosis of magic as a source of the unnamed, unknown, and the shapeless. Sometimes, this force is visualized as a serpent or a power from the northern pole star itself, serving the Witch in information of wisdom and discernment. It also often takes the form of Lucifer or, as Robert Cochrane coined, "the star-crossed serpent."[192]

At times, the stang may become the physical incarnation of the Horned One and treated and decorated by the practitioners in such a way. It may be used in oracular workings to gain insight and danced around to summon his presence into the forked staff so it becomes his vessel. For me, the stang serves as an altar with all the representations I need imbued into its symbolism. When erected in the ground at an outdoor working site, the other few immediate working tools, along with an offering of bread and a bottle of stiff drink, are easily placed at the foot of the stang. My stang is made of oak, the tree known as the "king of the woods." It is my companion to walk the land with, a holder of my power, and a gate to dance with the Old One himself.

---

191 "The light betwixt the horns" is a Traditional Craft saying, acknowledging the power of the Horned One and the working candle that's set between the horns on the stang during the working.

192 Oates, Shani and Jones, Evan John. *The Star Crossed Serpent*. Mandrake of Oxford, 2012.

The Broomstick

The broomstick, or the *besom,* still makes us think of the simplicity of the Village Witch. It is common for it to be hung around the home as a protective charm, placed over a doorway or standing upright with the broom brushes facing up in a corner by an entranceway. The broomstick holds its virtue as the symbolic marker of boundaries, flight, and, naturally, as a tool of cleansing and banishment. Essentially, it functions as a Witch's wand with a phallic handle covered by the receptivity of the brushes, creating a potent fertility symbol.

As a tool, you may use it to cross over to hidden places you make mental journeys to. For instance, in some traditions, the broom and sword are liminal markers of space and dimension. They are laid across each other to create an X at the edge of the Traditional Witch's compass or circle. This creates a liminal gateway, over which Witches and entities may step across to gain access to the sacred ground. Traditionally, the broom is made up of the three sacred woods: an ash handle, birch brushes, and bound with willow. These represent the Mysteries of rebirth and the symbol of the night flight Goddess. This is the Witch Mother in her aspect of the Dark Mother. In its most practical use of cleaning the hearth and home, the broom sweeps away and banishes any dirt and unclean energy. Sweeping, which is already a rhythmic action, can sometimes be a trance-inducing tool on its own. When done mindfully, and with the help of an added charm or a repeated mantra, a sweeping exercise over oneself or space is an excellent way to clear out any energies that are no longer serving.

The Icons

Icons or *fetishes* are representations and vessels for the powers you may invite to occupy these ornate pieces of statuary and art. I've seen everything from clay sculptures to dolls and herbal bundles used as icons. The important thing is that it provides a comfortable dwelling for a spirit to reside in, and that its image evokes the same energy of the entity as you commune with it. Idolatry is part of the artistic venture of the Craft that allows the practitioner to find dwellings of spirits in anything. My first set of icons was a quartz crystal sphere resembling the Moon and a small deer horn representing the Horned One. There are beautiful statues, wall plaques, ceramic vessels, and wood sculptures available for sale from your local metaphysical shop and the vast array of websites.[193]

Hallowing an icon is more of an involved affair than hallowing a tool. The idol is not just a tool of concentration but acts as the body of the spirit made present in their working relationship with you. either a set period or for as long as the vessel remains taken care of. A broken statue just won't hold in the same way, in my experience of housing and creating fetishes and icons. Regularly feeding an icon is part of the responsibility of housing it. This could be in the form of prayers, offerings, or clear directions of what you need and what your expectations are from that being. Essentially, the icon is invoked and the indwelling spirit lives within for a while, where it is then ritually re-invoked every time it is held in congress with the spirit by summoning them directly.

Having an in-depth knowledge about the spirit you're housing is an obvious good rule of thumb. By hallowing an icon, you are taking on the responsibilities of housing that spirit since you are the one who ultimately is responsible for its manifestation in the physical realm. Never make an oath or a deal you can't keep. A great example would be if you say as part of your contract that every Friday night, your idol of Aphrodite is going to receive an offering of incense, rosewater, and champagne. These are all great offerings, but then you are going to have to provide these goods every Friday night or break your deal. Not for nothing, but that's a lot of money over time. When I do my budgets, I include a small amount of money to feed my spirits and the general spending that comes with being a Witch. Some spirits can be pretty understanding, but always be true to your word because we are dealing with invisible and often powerful companies.

The more time and effort you project into the same image or icon, the more power it will collect. This will make communication more effective and easier to do. Offerings of incense and candle flames to represent pure light are the most basic offerings I can usually provide as part of my daily practice. Some like to make ritual waters and perfumes for their icons and ritually bathe and cleanse them as part of their devotion. Others will anoint specific parts of the idol with oils; offer necklaces, flowers, and coins; and speak to the statue daily. The most basic traditional custom is greeting them daily, for they are a guest in your home.

---

193 When looking for a statue, Enchanted and Pentagram Shoppe in Salem, Massachusetts are two of my favorite options.

The Cord

The cord or *Witch's Girdle* is both practical and symbolic. On a magical level, this is an easy go-to tool for spell casting. Each cord is unique to the tradition that uses it, and it is usually dedicated by the practitioner at the beginning of their path. This represents not just their identity but their direct link to the powers they work with. In this sense, it is the umbilical or astral cord to the spirits, and, more specifically, to the Witch Mother figure. The cord can be any color or woven together with different colors to create specific correspondences. These could be planetary or inspired from mythology, like the red thread of Ariadne used to help Theseus find his way through the Labyrinth. My cord is woven with red, black, and white, representing the blood, the power, and the sacred, which are the three keys or virtues of my folkloric work.

The cord can be used for working weather magic, but also holds the same significance as cords used in Masonic and Solomonic techniques. One of the key components of its symbolism was much darker. It was the remembrance of the old rule that if anyone should betray themselves, their oaths, or their people, the cord could become the noose of the hangman, echoing the victims found in the bogs of Ireland with braided cords left around their necks as sacrifices for these early communities.

In some cases, the cord is worn as a halter around the neck. Ritually, this is a symbol of importance to the literal ties we hold to the Witch Goddess in her role as the Dame of the Witch Covenant. It can also be worn as a cincture around the waist. Some groups will use it as a symbol of rank, or as a symbolic representation of all the ideas mentioned that also serves practically, holding tools and the general function of the robe. In spell work, you can use the cord to tie knots of power and store certain intentions in the cord itself. Nine knots in the cord is the most common number, but this is entirely up to the practitioner.

The cord also has a naturally magically potent binding or tying effect. As such, it is used over the representations of your enemies, or you can bind blessings over those you wish to help and heal. During hallowing, the cord is the best tool to have on hand. It can unlock other tools by tying certain frequencies and powers into your objects, making them bound to you for life. To help you erect the Witches' circle, the cord can be pre-cut to your desired radius to quickly and accurately measure out your circle.

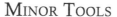

MINOR TOOLS

There are many other tools Witches use, like candles and a miscellaneous collection of bowls, ash pots, and incense thuribles. Make sure you are ready with offerings like fresh flowers and wine. Have charcoal tablets for loose incense and spare jars for herbs on hand, and you can never have enough candle holders! Witchcraft can easily become a collector's dream or a hoarder's nightmare. I think this depends on your organizational skills and the reality of how much you use versus just collect. This is a common trap. Tools that are not used just become stagnant with energy and add to the clutter, which is a frustrating block for power. There's nothing wrong with having stuff, but if it becomes a crutch, it defeats the purpose of the magic we use to enhance our lives.

The trick to avoid clutter is for the practitioner to collect techniques or items that stimulate the part of us that finds its way into the Witching headspace. All these tools can play their part in ritual and workings. Their place of rest will be on the altar, working alongside you. I have evolved with what tools I employ on my altar, as every item serves a purpose. Some of my smaller touchstones have become more permanent than others. Others have been surrendered on the sides of nature trails, offered in the cracks of mountains, and drowned in the waters of flowing rivers.

HALLOWING

Hallowing removes any energetic residue that may still be upon an object you have chosen for the Arte. All tools and objects must first be purified, neutralizing the item and making it ready to be filled with a new spirit. It is then charged or given clear directions of what and how it will perform.

The way a tool is hallowed depends on its natural correspondence and virtues. The practitioner summons the virtue of the tool and made one with themselves by crafting it as the extension of self and the magical double it is. By the rite of being hallowed by the powers of the Elemental realms, it will always serve a correct use. It will serve by the breath and the Witch-fire you grant to it by words of the spell, touch of the hands, breath from the lips, and the projection of your inner sight.

A tool may be consecrated with a secret alphabet or a personal sigil and then placed aside, only to be used when the rites were underway. For wands and staffs, they could be hollowed out, creating a tube-like shaft down the tool where a mixture of potions, oils, and herbs would be stuffed inside the tool. Then it would be blessed in the Elements and sealed up with solid wax, forever keeping the spirit inside and working with the flow of the Witch's pulse. This is done by repeating special words of power, binding the tool to the one who speaks or births it into existence. This object would then become identified as part of the spiritual body of the Witch using the secret tool of the Witch's red-handled knife or *burin*. In this case, a single drop of Witchblood would be used to anoint the tool. Blood is the life force, and so by the extension of it, the Witch is making a small sacrifice that awakens the spiritual life in all things. (You can read more about blood work in Chapter Fifteen.)

Purifying the tool, personalizing it, and giving directions on what you need from it are the best points to keep in mind as you consecrate these special items. Part of the benefit of working with tools comes in time as we learn to speak their subtle languages. We listen for when they need routine purification and an extra boost of power. Setting my tools in moonlight always gives them an extra charge of Witch power. Even submerging them in a flowing stream of water or wrapping them in cloth and burying them in the Earth for a few nights is a great way to give them empowerment. All of these techniques employ a deepening our relationship by understanding the physical responses from working in symbol and skill with the tools of the wise.

MAKING YOUR CORD

Pick three colors that coordinate with the intentions and correspondences of what you want to project into the world. For example, if you wanted to enhance your power as a Witch, you could use red for the Witchblood, white for purity, and black for protection. However, the important thing is how you weave these cords together. This weaving enchants the process of braiding by using rhythm and focus, treating the creation of the cord as a spell. Each wrap of the strands encapsulates the words you say when you weave together the cord. Notice the textures in your hands and feel them merge with the rhythm or speed at which you weave the braid. You may formulate your spell off the top of your head or use the following.

Cord of the Mother! Moriae I receive!
Magic be summoned by the cord I weave!
Cord of enchantment, Cord of the Maid!
Cord of my blood! I fashion, I braid!

When it is finished, sleep with your cord under your pillow for one Moon cycle, keeping it as close to your person as possible and allowing it to become a part of your astral body. You can also consecrate your tool using a combination of incense and holy water. Some may leave it on the altar, hearthstone, or mantle for a set time to collect power from that chosen place.

HALLOWING INCENSE

- 2 parts Dragonsblood resin
- 1 part mugwort
- 1 part vervain
- ½ part rose petals
- 1 pinch of angelica root powder
- 4 drops of hyssop oil
- 4 drops of cinnamon oil
- Optional: camphor (just a pinch goes a long way)

In a mortar and pestle, crush the resin until lightly chunky, not completely powdered. Add the pulverized herbs and petals before adding your hyssop and cinnamon oil. Stir generously after each drop. Allow it to cure together for a few days before use.

HALLOWING WASH

- 4–6 cups of spring water
- 1 handful of sea salt
- Mugwort (as much as you feel is correct)
- 1 lemon, sliced
- Small palm full of cloves
- Pulverized meadowsweet

This brew is not to be ingested! It is only meant to wash the tools that are being hallowed and feed them extra purification qualities.

Bring your cauldron to a boil with 4–6 cups of natural spring water or water you have collected from a living body of water. Add salt and stir until completely dissolved. Next, add your lemon slices and cloves, and let simmer for a few minutes while taking the time to stir. By stirring up the wash, you are making a conscious movement to direct the energy within the pot. Often, this is *deosil*, which means "with the Sun's natural direction" or "clockwise," to bring forth, invoke, and work harmonious magic. *Widdershins,* or stirring counterclockwise, may be used when communicating with the Witch Gods or performing banishing work. You can also coordinate your stirring movements by the moon phase at your precise time and location: widdershins for a waning and new moon or deosil for a waxing moon phase.

Next, add your herbs and allow to simmer until the potion becomes yellow-tinted. Bottle and use immediately. This can also be bottled in a spray bottle and used as a spray to mist over your tools and space.

Sealing Oil for Consecration and Protection

- Base oil of olive, grapeseed, or jojoba
- 4–5 drops of myrrh essential oil
- 4–5 drops of rue essential oil
- 2–3 drops of cedarwood essential oil
- 2–3 drops of rosemary essential oil
- 1 solid resin to preserve your sealing oil (like a small chunk of frankincense, myrrh, or copal)
- 1 small chunk of calamus root
- 1 juniper berry

Take any size vial you desire and fill it halfway with a carrier oil of your choice. Enchant the calamus root by calling upon it to strengthen your oil and add its virtues of command to your oil of sealing and protection. Next, add your essential oils drop by drop, taking time to connect with the pure extracts of the plants. Connect with each herbal spirit and empower them to do your bidding. Drop by drop, with your exhale of conscious breath, release power into the oil.

Add a chunk of solid resin (to preserve your oil) and the juniper berry. Don't forget to date and label your bottle. Amber or blue-colored bottles are best as they help protect your oils from sunlight, and keep your bottles stored in a dry and dark place. Some Witches will take the time to heat a small cauldron with tealights and warm the oils, allowing them to fumigate and merge. This also pulls in the practice of rhythmic stirring and concentration as you bring the oil into its natural power.

The Rite of Hallowing

This rite is best performed at midnight, twilight, dusk, or twilight, the times of liminality. Have a stable working place set up either by itself or at a formal altar, with a durable clack cloth set up with the following:

- Witch's cord
- Bowl of salt
- Bowl of water
- Hallowing incense
- Sealing oil
- Red candle

First, take the bowls of salt and water and place them on either side of you. Pick up one bowl in your right hand and the other in your left. Ensure your incense is burning in the center before you light your red candle. You may add your own symbol or sigil series to add further personalization to your candle, as the red candle represents the pulse of your Witchblood flowing.

Take up the bowl of salt, hold it towards the North, and speak its holy charge.

Charge of the Salt

I conjure you, oh salts made pure as ye are!
By trees and shores of the standing stones
By the strength of Gods and mortal bones!
I exercise all within ye, the minerals of magic and the salt of
the Earth!
So Mote It Be!

Combine the holy salt with the bowl of water and speak the Conjuration of the Waters of life over the bowl while mixing the salt until dissolved.

Conjuration of the Waters

I summon and stir ye up as the Holy Waters.
For within the veins of the Gods, you bubble and flow,
May all powers and virtues of the scared now show!
In the name of the spirits and Gods that dwell within
This spell of creation betwixt now to begin!
So Mote It Be!

You may make a holy symbol over the now-transformed waters, whether this be a pentacle, triquetra, or Celtic cross. Spirit may even give you a clear visual of an unfamiliar symbol or sigil to use. This symbol just allows you to make the gesture of sealing and completing your work. Oftentimes, these symbols tie together the powers of the Elements and are then energetically placed within.

Next, hold your hands over the fumes of burning incense and speak the charge to awaken the smoke of purification so that all you seek may be carried upon the fumes of air to the stars above.

Charge of the Incense

Holy smoke! Holy smoke! Perfumed skies are now awoke!
Fuel this place and all that reside here within this scared bower
To cast all worries to the fates and raise the Witch's power!
Stretch to the stars that it may carry all desire
upon thy clouds of air and the heat of enchanted fire!
So Mote It Be!

Similarly, hold the right hand over the flame of the working candle and say the Invocation of the Flame. Know that in speaking this charge, you are addressing the spirit of the Fire as a friend and working companion.

Invocation of the Flame

Holy Fire! Holy flame!
I summon thee in the Old One's name
Fires of the stars, Fires of Earth below
Fires of the dust, and fires of the coal.

Work and illuminate this Hallowed rite
Blessings upon this the torch bearer's light.
Harken to the hidden company of all the fallen Suns
Ignited and remembered by the presence of the infinite ones.

Now, the working substances are enchanted and ready for the hallowing of your tool. Bind the tool with your cord by wrapping it slowly and methodically around the item, visualizing your power merging into the object.

Next, sprinkle the holy water on your tool. Place it over the incense burner so the object can become immersed in incense smoke, then hold your tool by the burning presence of the working candle and visualize yourself as if you were a giant standing over the Earth, speaking face to face with the brilliantly colored planets. Hold up your tool, presenting it to the power of the Council of the Old Gods, and say:

I, (your chosen name), do call upon the powers of this place to create and empower this (state tool type). May it be imbued with all the virtues that it must have to serve me well. By the blood that flows and quickens within me, I call this tool into the court of my power that no other power may change or challenge it. I summon the powers of the land, the winds, and the familiar into this holy tool. This tool is hallowed! So Mote It Be!

Unwrap your tool from your cord and anoint it with a few drops of sealing oil. You now have a properly blessed and consecrated tool.

CHAPTER TWELVE

TRANCEWORK

Using trancework as a gateway point for communication and interaction with unseen forces is one of the oldest keys in magical paths. Trance may be performed by means other than techniques of meditation, as it's also encountered in techniques using hypnosis, drugs and intoxicants, sensory deprivation, ritual fasting, and sight deprivation. In time, you will find a system that allows you to comfortably alter your mental state and retain the messages, symbols, and ability to further build the right relationship with Spirit. For me, I use a repeated script in my head over and over again until I know I'm *elsewhere*. I've also used a blindfold to block out any light, a sensory deprivation technique to assist retreating within the self. I set myself up with soft drumming in the background and begin a slow rocking from my core while connected to the ground. This could go on for minutes, up to an hour, as I slowly build faster and faster until my body has lost sensation in the swaying, but my mind can wander free to make a journey. I highly recommend customizing your own trance induction script, incorporating the symbolism and images of your specific spiritual landmarks. This is a great creative exercise and a way to figure out the certain keywords that trigger your focus into a trance.

Trance ranges from an internal meditative journey to a full-blown spiritual intercession where the spirit or Gods take over the mind and body of a practitioner. This is *trance possession*, falling into the category of ecstatic practices. These are the high vibrational activities performed by practitioners that provoke a meaningful experience by the stimulation of ecstasy or a state of sudden and overpowering emotion. *Ecstasy* does mean an overwhelming feeling of joy and happiness, but its true meaning is closer to "free from flesh."[194] This often takes the form of ecstatic dance with intense drumming holding a trance-inducing beat. In conjunction with a directed conjuration or invocation to a specific spirit and the protocols granted for that specific being, a full-on possession *might* occur.

The combination of dance, music, incense, and community can all lead to a wild frenzy of the satyrs or a revelation of wisdom from a familiar spirit of the working coven. Not all trance involves the cultural association of possession, and this is an important point to keep in mind as you further your research. In trance possession, the body may make unusual gestures, movements, and sounds. The possession involves the temporary departure of the trance worker's soul to make room for the spirits and deities to speak through. Unlike lighter states of trance, this requires full surrender, and there is often no memory or cognition of what is happening during the time you are *ridden* or possessed. Spirit mediumship, for instance, is considered by some to be a special kind of possession because the possessed person is participating as an intermediary between the human and the supernatural worlds.

Trance is the mind and the body's reaction to an environment that is diminished or changed purely from the environment or from certain energies evoked. What you see, hear, and feel out of the trance is going to impact the awareness you hold moving forward. Trance and meditation share two sides of the same goal of the practice. The distinction between the two, however, is that trance is often a much deeper state of altered brain waves, but the internal or external experiences are more visceral to the practitioner. Like a light state of meditation, it's normal to lose focus or fall asleep the first couple of tries. Once you work past the overwhelming relaxation and get used to the fuzzy headspace, you'll find that your awareness does not diminish or wander off.

The goal of the trance in a ritual or magical operation is for the powers that the Witch conjures speak directly through the body of the trance worker. With each round of practice, the practitioner will not just learn to recognize these magical states of flow but will also be able to test their limits. This comes from the repetition of practice. For Witches, there must be an exploration of how these different states of breathing, body posture,

194 Penczak, Christopher. *The Gates of Witchcraft: Twelve Paths of Power, Trance & Gnosis.* Copper Cauldron Publishing, 2012, pp. 20.

atmosphere, and sense of place all work together to achieve different levels of trance. Everyone's way of receiving information is going to vary, as everyone is wired differently. Some people are highly imaginative, skillful in memorization, and make excellent oracles in trance-related activities. Others are more auditory and great with vocabulary, able to simply open their mouths and let the Gods do the talking.

TRANCE TECHNIQUE OVERVIEW

There are common misunderstandings that to do trance, or any form of journeying, means to empty the mind and be still and relaxed so that you cannot *possibly* be distracted by any outside influence. This is one method of several techniques, but if trance is something new to you, I would not recommend that approach with your first trance adventure. These techniques branch into three distinct pathways, each unique and centered on different focuses in the body and the breath: *inhibitory, exhibitory,* and *partnered* techniques.[195]

Partnered techniques rely on the comfort and trust level between two working practitioners who can use the energetic push and pull between them to take turns counting the other partner into a trance. This is the safest pathway, as it guarantees you have a spotter to make sure nothing goes sour. The other person is there to support you as you enter your trance state, and to call you back to your normal state of mind when it's time to return. The partner system also allows the pair to have someone act as a scribe, recording what phenomena may occur while the other person is tranced out. Often, there is safety and comfort in numbers, so having someone to offer their support is always the best way to start if possible.

The next path is the inhibitory technique. This is what we're thinking of when we imagine those silent and still meditations. These are the techniques that set out to quiet the mind, rest the body, and bring a feeling of deep rest and calm. Inhibitory techniques direct the focus inward on the internal world or the inner eye. Silent meditation, isolation, using a blindfold or oracular cloak to block out all physical vision, and silent concentration upon a fixed point known as *fascination* are all examples of inhibitory trance work.

---

195 Penczak, Christopher. *The Gates of Witchcraft: Twelve Paths of Power, Trance & Gnosis.* Copper Cauldron Publishing, 2012, pp. 20.

The last technique encountered is the exhibitory pathway. These are techniques like dancing, loud chanting, sexual activity, and jumping. Given the name *exhibitory,* this path drives the inward focus to outward stimuli in the physical, sensory, and external world. These are often fast and high energy techniques that use the entire body, excitement, and what would best be described as quick and sustained motions. These controlled movements and gestures are often taught to practitioners in hopes of being a foundation of movement or sacred dance. A true exhibitory technique should make the user feel as if they have exalted or separated from the physical body or separated from normal consciousness. The best imagery to illustrate this is the idea of a waterpipe that slowly builds pressure until it bursts, propelling the water in the same way as we become propelled into another mental state during trancework.

TRANCEWORK AND WITCHBLOOD

Unlike many mainstream religions with a pulpit to the congregation, Witchcraft uses no intermediaries between us and the worlds of the spiritual. With tools like divination and trance, we communicate *directly* with the spirits of the sacred for ourselves. This is part of what makes the Witch unique as a conduit able to work on behalf of their communities. The Witchblood holds its specialty in direct connection to the otherworld by the rites and rituals we do, the powers we claim unto ourselves, and the most sacred rites of initiation and elevations. According to our mythos, if we are truly direct descendants of the forces of Gods and spirits, then our blood connection is naturally going to come into play. Blood flow is a crucial piece to how we enter trance, as by lowering the heart rate with relaxation and breath, we alter the way our blood moves.

Notice your pulse rate in your veins and use your breath to guide you through those channels within is a place to start. As mystical as it is, it works. As a visualization technique, apply pressure on different pressure points, holding them down with your fingers and then releasing pressure. Note the rushes and differences you may feel in the flow.

- Exhibitory (quick breath, high energy): notice your blood boil.
- Inhibitory (slowed breath, relaxed): notice your blood simmer.
- Any pathway: notice your blood change.

BODY POSTURES

This research into and the practices of posture techniques would not have been possible without the groundbreaking work of Dr. Felicitas D. Goodman. Dr. Goodman's discoveries started as the phenomenon of speaking in tongues, evolving into the discovery of ecstatic trance and altered states by holding of ritual body postures found throughout the ancient world and Indigenous peoples of the American Southwest. The evocative recreation of holding a specific sacred body pose would lead the holder into states of mystical experience. Different poses stimulate very specific effects in the person, so the poses are placed in several categories of mystical experience. This was all published in her 1989 book, *Where Spirits Ride The Wind: Trance Journeys and Other Ecstatic Experiences.*[196] Dr. Nicholas E. Brink, author of *The Power Of Ecstatic Trance: Practices for Healing, Spiritual Growth, and Accessing the Universal Mind,* he had collaborated with Dr. Goodman to determine a series of seven categories of trance postures.[197] These were the poses of healing, spirit journeys, living myths, celebration, initiation, metamorphosis, and divination. There are probably several more to be discovered as we take inspiration from the poses that capture our spiritual senses.

The spirit catches us in fifteen minutes of repetition of sound and holding of the pose or posture. The reason most of these postures are considered "religious" is the fact that they bring about interaction and union with the spirit world, and hence are out of our secular reality. Holding ritual tools and wearing ritual masks may also be incorporated into the poses you develop and experiment with. The art of imitation not only mimics what has come before us but is also a natural impulse of magic in our bodies. We can think of it as a hardwired impulse within the brain, the body working *sympathetic magic,* which is the philosophy that like attracts like. If we dance like satyrs, working at imitating the dance of a goat with our legs bent up on the balls of our feet—if we give into the experience—we *become* the satyrs. Imitation itself is a very powerful magical tool, and it's one of the best-kept mystical teachings of

---

196 Goodman, Felicitas D. and Gerhard Binder. *Where the Spirits Ride the Wind: Trance Journeys and Other Ecstatic Experiences.* Indiana University Press, 1989.
197 Brink, Nicholas E. *The Power of Ecstatic Trance: Practices for Healing, Spiritual Growth, and Accessing the Universal Mind.* Bear & Co., 2013.

the Arte. Charles Fort, an American writer who used scientific methods to evaluate anomalies, once wrote: "The theologians have recognized that the ideal is the imitation of God. If we are a part of such an organic thing, this thing is God to us, as I am God to the cells that compose me."[198] When placed in a Witchcraft context, this quote suggests that we can become one with the Gods, as we are of the same mystical cells.

Felicitas D. Goodman discovered a six-step protocol that makes for effective and transformative trance work. I've included and adapted her guide for my practice and include it here.

1. The person needs an open mind to fully immerse themselves in the experience of trance. You will need to make yourself fully relaxed to induce an altered state of consciousness.

2. There should be a sacred space with a clear boundary setting apart the mundane headspace from the sacred. The space should have a clear boundary line, and all spirits that you find helpful to the work should be invited into the space.

3. Use a technique to quiet the analytical brain. This is the rational and analytical part of the brain that, when shut off, often leads to those pleasurable meditative headspaces of connection and inspiration. This could be counting the breath, fascination upon a single point, or a meditation exercise. I recommend using a simple grounding and centering exercise for this.

4. Rhythmic stimulation and noisemaking activate the blood and the nervous system. The suggested speed is 200 beats per minute using drums, rattles, or other percussive instruments. You could also employ the practice of chanting and other forms of intonation using the voice to drone out the analytical brain. This results in slowing your heart rate and dilating blood vessels. Stimulate the Witchblood bringing it to power by the drumbeat.

5. This is when the practitioner would incorporate the use of ritual body postures and hold them for at least fifteen minutes. Inspired by Hindu and Buddhist *Mudras*,[199] Goodman believed in the possibilities of the body guiding and evoking

---

198 Fort, Charles. *Wild Talents.* Baen Books, 1932.

199 *Mudra* means "mark" or "gesture" and is a symbolic pose, gesture, or hand sign.

a spiritual experience of ecstasy on its own just as effectively as the brain and any religious structure can.

6.   Return to yourself. The returning of everyday consciousness once back from a trance always requires aftercare. You may experience a drop in blood sugar levels, so having a snack and juice is helpful to ground yourself afterwards. Spiritual aftercare and check-ins with ourselves are vital to maintaining a healthy practice. Spiritual aftercare consists of making sure you are safe, secure, and, in a group setting, that everyone is back to themselves. It is grounding, hydrating, and being able to record what experiences you may have had so they can be reflected on later. The key here is *processing time*—and having enough of it. Through reflection, you can use your trance experience to fuel future projects and express the same energies felt through art, poetry, dance, and storytelling rituals.

Focus sharply on maintaining the pose for fifteen minutes or longer. At the same time, allow the etheric body to spiritually hold the space, allowing the whole self to merge with the image held in the mind's eye. Holding the space and the pose itself provides an intense emotional experience. It humbles me that we are using the same postures used by our ancestors to access the otherworld. As if by holding by imitation, we too become one with these ancestral spirits and, by extension, become one with the Divine forces. By the imagery we are drawing from, we too become icons and Gods.

BOUNDARIES AND RECALLS

Setting boundaries for yourself before you undertake trance work is important and should always be a preliminary preparation. There's an element of risk at play when altering perception and changing reality. Trance is not meant as escapism but as a tool for self-fulfillment, so certain boundaries are important for us. For example, I try to be in a neutral headspace so as not to allow my conflicts to leak into the work that I'm doing. Trance work can be a scary thing if undertaken while dealing with unresolved conflict, anger, or grief. While in your trance, there may be otherworldly experiences that take you back, and not in a nice way. The rules of this world don't apply there, making things occasionally mind-boggling and frightening.

Know these three rules: you can always leave the trance, you can always say no, and you can always change your mind and change directions. Everyone, from Druids to Witches, and Spiritualists, has said that not all gifts from the otherworld are gifts, all spirits are not always wise and benevolent, and anytime you are offered to take food or drink, don't! It's not for us. This is one of the major taboos I've found myself and other Witches still subscribing to.

The next piece of safety you may want to implement for yourself is what's known as a "recall." This can take the form of a change in drumbeat or music, the stopping of your vocalization, or a pre-determined safe word or phrase to ease yourself back into your normal consciousness. My word for calling myself back is simple. Through repetition, I've trained my brain to respond to the word *cauliflower*. Humorous? Yes. Effective? Absolutely!

A recall is implemented because, for some (myself included), trance can be sticky to get out of. Sometimes it feels too comfortable, or like there is more to be said in the vision even though that energy has passed. For some, it's the conscious decision to stand up slowly and move around until they feel fully present again. My usual routine involves re-engaging the physical senses and taking time to do some deep stretching after holding the same position for a certain amount of time.

THE SPECTER, EYE, AND CORD

The specter is the Witch's *other* body, sometimes coined *the double*.[200] The term is used to reference the self you envision interacting in the dimensions of the spirit world. Essentially, it is the astral body of the Witch. This is where the Witch's soul projects outwards. The double can travel to other dimensions and work magic in that trance-journey state. This is seen using the screen of the mind, or simply the Witch's inner eye. Visualizations, imagery, and being able to spontaneously imagine will be some of your greatest assets in trance work.

Visualization provides the secret symbols of the Arcane that the Witch receives from the rites of ingress, congress, and egress, whereby the discernment from spiritual contact is transmuted and made incarnate within the body by the hand of the Witch. These visualizations are specific

---

200 Lecouteux, Claude. *Witches, Werewolves, and Fairies: Shapeshifters and Astral Doubles in the Middle Ages.* Inner Traditions, 2003.

and symbolic because they give us a direction or road map to travel along so we are not bombarded with too much spiritual information or blankly lost in the journey. Sometimes there are specific colors, symbols, landscapes, or mythological characters that make up a specific scripted journey known as a *pathworking*.

Suggested imagery or the symbols of the Arte rely upon where the Witch wants to go. For Witches, we use the valleys of forests, the hollowed trees, the sacred wells, and the spiral staircases to make our way to the lower worlds or castles in the sky that spin. Symbols of the full moon, astral temples, geometric symbols, or sigils all play a role in these spaces. These symbols or scripts we play out to ourselves are the same places of folk memory that provide a road map for us to travel along safely. Language is visualization, and the inner sight is the tool that allows us to utilize that language. All this allows the Witch's double to function when this part of our multi-layered soul is awakened.

One of the specific symbols of trance is the imagery of the silver cord. It is often seen as a silver light that connects the person to their physical body, most commonly connected to the belly button and seen as the astral umbilical cord. The silver cord is visualized and maintained during the journey while a Witch is astrally traveling. The cord is also a great callback to regular consciousness as the image is clear and allows for an immediate grounding channel as we work through different levels of trance.

ALLIES AND ORACULAR EXPERIENCE

Spirit communication—visions of people, places, or events that are yet to come—are not uncommon among Witches who do trance. There are spirits all around us. We fashion ourselves into something like a radio dial by using a trance, tuning our frequencies up or down so we are in a mental state where we can perceive these entities. You may acquire different symbols, tools, or wisdom from these spectral meetings, which happen while holding trance- or dreamwork-related rites. With all this information, it's a good idea to seek the protection of spirit allies before doing trance work. These are the entities that connect across realms and boundaries. For instance, a psychopomp or gatekeeper is an approachable figure to explore your spiritual relationships.

The oracular experience can come in many different ways. This could take the form of a person in a trance spontaneously describing what they are experiencing or related imagery out loud. There is also the magical skill of sketching or drawing your visions in ways similar to automatic writing.[201] On the other hand, this could be a full-out trance-possession. In trance-possession, someone else is in your body's driver's seat and you are completely elsewhere. While occupied by Spirit, your body may speak, describe, teach, move around the space, dance, grunt, make noises, or ask for offerings or favors. (It's often very recognizable when someone is faking.) The goal of trance-possession is to completely surrender. Surrendering to the spirit creates the humbling experience of merging with something completely foreign and outside of oneself. This is why *ecstatic* is used here, as we free ourselves from flesh, and Spirit becomes incarnate upon the body of the chosen worker. Some may speak languages they have never studied; others may have an altered physical stance or facial movements. If working in a group setting consistently with the same entities, these miniature changes in the person will become like code words to the group, showing if the possession has occurred *correctly*.

SEIÐR AND SEETHING

In the Old North, *seiðr* was a type of magic that was practiced during the late Scandinavian Iron Age.[202] *Seiðr* was believed to be connected to the reshaping or weaving of the future and practices of divination and is prophetic by nature. Pronounced as "seeth," it is held in balance with the Germanic magic of *galdr*, or magic concerning the use of the runes often vocalized or sung as an invocation, in many Scandinavian practices.[203] Culturally, *seiðr* was considered a darker and more dangerous affair of magic taught by the All-father Odin. Although Odin taught the practice, *seiðr* was a skill associated with femininity, so it was often deemed a skill for women and queer men. In an interesting parallel with the Luciferian mythos of Azazel teaching the Arts considered taboo unto the daughters of the men of renown, here we have Odin teaching

201 This is considered another form of trance, as the repetitive movement of the pen/pencil induces a state where spirits are free to write through the conduit of the person wielding the pen.
202 Penczak, Christopher. "Seidr." *The Gates of Witchcraft: Twelve Paths of Power, Trance & Gnosis.* Copper Cauldron Publishing, 2012, pp. 136–136.
203 Ibid.

the magick of *seiðr* to predominantly women, although we know there were several groups who resisted that categorization, with men known as *Seimard* and women as *Aeidkona*.[204] It may have been considered a name for all magics that were not runic or guarded closely like those in the passing of spoken charms, songs, and sung invocations.

When people are talking about *seiðr*, they are often referring to the trance technique known as *seething*. Many modern followers of Heathenry and Nordic-inspired paths are performing this type of work and using it for a myriad of magical and ritual operations. Diana Paxson is one of the best-known authorities on these types of trance techniques, and she has introduced the term *Oracular Seidr* to describe the practices of journeying through the nine realms of *Yggdrasil* and prophetically allowing the spirits of Hel to speak through the body.[205]

According to Dr. Eldar Heide, *seiðr* appears to mean "thread, cord, snare, [or] halter."[206] Dr. Heide is one of the most respected academics in the field of researching Nordic magic and Viking religion, and he made his mark on the field in 2006 on *seiðr*. In his doctoral thesis, *"Gand, seid og åndevind"* (translated as *"Gand, seid,* and spirit-wind"), he goes into great depth on the etymology and philosophies concerning the tradition of *seiðr*.[207] He points out that practitioners would have been able to send their mind forth in spiritual form to do tasks outside of the body, reinforcing the relationship magic was thought to have in the ancient worlds with the winds or powers manifesting as a wind, associating the spiritual rites with a thread or spinning and with the breath. This is very close to the depictions of Nordic Völva with a large distaff, using the act of spinning and weaving as a trance induction method.[208] (This is one of the reasons that distaffs have also been used as wands.) Practitioners also

204 Penczak, Christopher. "Seidr." *The Gates of Witchcraft: Twelve Paths of Power, Trance & Gnosis.* Copper Cauldron Publishing, 2012, pp. 136–136.

205 Paxson, Diana L. *The Way of the Oracle: Recovering the Practices of the Past to Find the Answers Today.* Red Wheel/Weiser, 2012.

206 Heide, Eladar. "Spinning seiðr." *Old Norse Religion in Long-Term Perspectives: Origins, Changes, and Interactions.* Nordic Academic Press, 2004, pp. 164–170.

207 Heide, Eladar. *Gand, seid og åndevind.* Diss. Bergen. University of Bergen, 2006.

208 Heide, Eladar. "Spinning seiðr." *Old Norse religion in long-term perspectives. Origins, changes, and interactions.* 2004. Vägar till Midgård 8. Lund: Nordic Academic Press. pp. 164–170.

probably had a symbolic staff, much more ornate to identify themselves as a Priestess, with which to wield their magic.

It has been said that by *wyrdworking* or entering a trance by seething, one can see and determine their fate. Heide also shares that, according to his research, *seiðr* was probably a practice in which the practitioner used spinning to conjure spirits in conjunction with movement and breath or vocalization: "Seiðr (initially) seems to be all about the spinning, and sending of, and attraction with, and manipulation by, a spirit cord."[209] This is very reminiscent of the universal image of the silver cord mentioned earlier. He also points out that the spinning served to deploy of the person's mind, or what he calls a *mind-in-shape emissary.*[210] This is the individual's spirit visualized as a cord or line of thread, which is animated to perform various tasks of Witchery, healing, psychic information, or journeying work. Based on the meaning of *snare, seiðr* is contingent upon its meaning as the symbol of a rope or cord. As he says in his thesis, "Binding is not very characteristic of seiðr. However, with a cord, one can not only bind but also attract things, and this is characteristic of seiðr."[211]

Movements that imitate spinning motions, like literal spinning, rocking, shaking, swaying, or shivering, can all be used to manipulate the physical senses by raising the power within the self to enter trance. In Witchcraft, this practice of spinning can be recognized in the rite of walking widdershins around a fixed axis point within the magic circle. This rite is called "Treading the Mill" in Traditional Witchcraft. A stang stands in the center as a fixed axis point while the coven circles around the stang, taking its place as the effigy of the Horned One.

For a modern seething practice, you have to be grounded and ready to break a sweat. Your hydration will also impact the experience of seething, so make sure that you are well hydrated. For many, water is a powerful conduit for spirits to travel through. By being well hydrated, we are making ourselves an easier channel for spirits to slip through if oracular work is the goal.

You can prepare yourself for seething by standing with a loose posture and slightly bent knees. After a few grounding breaths, you are going to

---

209 Heide, Eladar. "Spinning seiðr." *Old Norse religion in long-term perspectives. Origins, changes, and interactions.* 2004. Vägar till Midgård 8. Lund: Nordic Academic Press. pp. 164–170.

210 Ibid.

211 Heide, Eladar. *Gand, seid og åndevind.* Diss. University of Bergen, 2006.

start vigorously shaking and trembling the arms and legs with all your might while also trying to bounce on the balls of your feet. Build these motions up to a faster pace, hold it, and allow the body to speed itself up and down at your will. Some will try this kneeling or seated by rocking until a frenzy is induced. You are going to do this until exhaustion or until you feel the power you are building come to a peak. Many use the visualization of bringing a cauldron to boil, slowly up to a raging boil. Drop to the ground if you must, and then pay attention to how your outside surroundings feel.

Do things feel closer or farther away? Do you feel the attention of spirits, or are you completely alone in the space?

INGRESS:
A Trance Induction

I recommend recording yourself reading this so you can listen to it as an aid in your trance work. (*Ingress* refers to using trance to go to the inner world of the Witch.) This induction utilizes simplistic imagery and four-fold or square breathing:

> *Relax the body, ease the spine*
> *Surrender the ego now to align.*
> *From your eyes to your feet*
> *Your self to meet*
> *With spirits, you'll greet*
> *For now to repeat*
> *In yourself to retreat*
> *The blessings sour, the blessings sweet!*
> *By the count of ten, breathe in for four.*
> *One…two…three…four…and holding for one…two…three…four…*
> *Out for one…two…three…four… and holding empty for one…two…*
> *three…four…By the breath of the four, I open the hidden door!*
> *(One…two…three…four…repeated for a full round)*

Take time to breathe fully and deeply, feeling your lungs expand in your belly with each breath. Allow this breath to bring you deeper and deeper into the right headspace. Regulate your breathing in and out at your desired pace until it becomes automatic.

By nine, you see your body fully relax.

By eight, you relax your eyes and eyelids, and you unclench your jaw and fingertips.

By seven, you feel a pulse of energy surge up from the bottoms of your feet to the crown of your head.

By six, you visualize a bright, brilliant ball of light that will lead you to the gates of your most inner self that is correct and of the deepest embers of the Witch-fire burning within you.

By five, you allow yourself to bring a small path in the forest into your field of vision using your Witch's eye, not the physical eyes. Allow each subtle twitch, outside noise, and disturbance to just be a quiet and subtle reminder of the stillness and the quiet you hold within your body at this moment.

By four, follow the path and notice what trees, plants, or creatures you may see, until you find yourself coming to a portal. This could be any portal: a swirling vortex, a door, gates, or a staircase. Decide to either pass through the portal or keep journeying where you are between the selves.

By two, use the breath to direct your focus to your desired place, question, or imagery. Fully project that internally in a trance, as if to clearly state your intention, bring it up to your portal, and know you will use this as your place of return when you're done.

By one, take the step through the portal and, using your mind's inner voice, count down from thirteen to zero to yourself so you may operate on a clearer and more accurate level, bringing yourself to where you need to be.

When you are ready, use your callback technique or mentally journey back through your portal by counting up from zero to thirteen. Take your time going back down the same forest trail and floating slowly into your body. According to many accounts in folklore, you must always return the same way you came in.

CHAPTER THIRTEEN

RAISING POWER: TECHNIQUES TO QUICKEN THE WITCHBLOOD

RAISING POWER

Everything in the universe vibrates on a frequency. These frequencies are commonly known as *energy*. By speaking, clapping, or making contact with another surface, you release a small and often unnoticed amount of energy. Feeling energy could look like feeling the temperature difference, a tingling sensation like static, or numbness in the hand. The energy that's picked up on a psychic level is often sensed through visualization or paying close attention to the voice in our stream of consciousness. These are the most common ways energy is discussed among practitioners, and we often perceive or label energies in terms of feelings and emotions.

Whether these waves of energy are of the four Elements, a monument of the land, or any spirit, the power the Witch uses comes from the discipline of focus and the effort exerted in contact with the magical phenomena. Some may experience this power in martial arts, such as *chi*. Others relate it to the force of *prana*, or "sacred breath." The effort of what is exhausted and exorcized also appears in the quality of the results. In the process of expending energy, we draw from the land, the cosmos, and ourselves to create magic.

Magical power flows. It is made up of a continuum of practitioners creating a current. This magical current makes itself known through the secrets of the traditions and in the shared experiences of the wider magical communities. The person's will acts as a catalyst for the desired results, allowing a practitioner to perform. Ultimately, even in covens, it is up to the user alone to raise power in a way that is most effective for the transformation of self beyond the rite. Using practices that are ancestral, divinely inspired, and spontaneous, we can weave together the chosen mechanics that allow us to pulsate with Witchblood.

With practice and discovering techniques, you will learn the freedom of allowing this current of Witchcraft to catch you! It'll sweep you off your feet and, instead of moving through ritual, you can allow ritual to move through you, where speaking from the heart creates a new rhythm to the ritual and allows all your impulses to become a part of the ritual. Some of the best examples of finding what worked for me were the spontaneous moments when I allowed the ritual to inspire me on the fly.

One of my biggest pet peeves when reading and researching rites and rituals was the part in so many books that stated to do X, Y, and Z, then it would be time to "raise energy" or "raise a cone of power," and that would be the end of it. This was understandably frustrating for me as a beginner because the literature I found never really explained the "how to" part. Yes, I carried a lot of local and family folk magic with me into my practice, but power raising? I was a little lost and more than a little overwhelmed with the options. Not only was it so much work for me to remember the directions and what I wanted to communicate, but now I had to come up with ways to stimulate the atmosphere around me? This seemed like an overwhelming series of trials and errors. It is for these reasons that this chapter was created, so that you may get a taste of different techniques, serving as inspiration for you to develop the practice that speaks to you.

Everything from healing to banishing can be directed according to the Witch's desire and skill set, as long as there is fuel for the fire. Simply put, we cannot give what we don't have. Magic needs fuel, direction, and a deliberate release to be effective. This being said, I stress the importance of replenishing your energy by grounding, taking breaks, and fueling your body with nutrition so you have more than enough energy to dispense. Knowing your emotional headspace is also vital before a spell is performed. A healthy mental check-in with yourself is a part of my coven's pre-ritual ritual. Depending on our circumstances and where we are mentally, there may be certain rites and spells that we may not be in the best headspace to participate in, and this is more than okay. Part of carrying power is knowing when to take a step back and allow ourselves to take that necessary processing time.

Knowing when to step back is vital. In a coven setting, sometimes we can add to the energy by simply sitting quietly and holding space for those physically working the power in the circle. Those sitting out still contribute to the raising of power by mentally focusing the energy upwards within the sacred space. This is one way someone can hold space for others energetically. In many ways, we fuel our spirits, spells, and circles with our mere desire to show up and do the work. Presence lends itself to presence. Spirits will often acknowledge we've made the space and effort, and oftentimes time they thank us for this work in the ways of signs, omens, and synchronicity.

QUICKENING THE WITCHBLOOD

"Thus, by those adepts of alchemy who both dissolves and combines element within element, this heart advice may be applied as a subtle means to behold manifest form and character as other [supernatural] modalities of the single power which each and every substance holds in hypostate."

—Andrew D. Chumbley[212]

Magical currents and energy are most commonly identified through what is *felt*. Our psyche often communicates information about what is in our environment through emotions. Learning to feel with the body in addition to the emotions is part of the learning curve of the Craft. Emotions that are the most controlled yet intense are the most powerful conduits of magical power production because they hit our core beliefs and whole perceptions of self. Thinking about passion and what makes one passionate is at the core of awakening the blood. By finding what makes you tick, you can find the modalities and expressions of power that naturally stimulate the blood that flows within. When we get excited, passionate, and intense, our heart rate speeds up. This is the body's natural response to the powers and energies around us that speak to our Witch-soul. When we summon and arouse that emotion, both mentally and physically within the body, the blood responds, quickening. Gerald

212 Chumbley, Andrew D. *The Azoetia: A Grimoire of the Sabbatic Craft.* Xoanon Publishers, 1992.

Gardner writes, "Remember this: you will never advance if your blood is not stirred and quickened, for truly 'the Blood is the Life'."[213] Quickening the blood releases magical power, and the more we build the intensity of the technique, the more power is raised toward that desired goal. The more power raised, the more exhausted one becomes, but the likelihood of getting results is that much more.

"There is no magic without arousal."[214] Arousal is also an especially powerful word when thinking about magic. This could be direct as sexually generated power or merely the arousal of specific emotions, visual cues, trance triggers, and physical impulses. Arousal is not a dirty word, nor is power, nor sex. When we are drawing up the energy to sustain ourselves in a grounding exercise, we are enticing and arousing the spirit of the ground we are standing upon to engage with our energetic field. We often visualize this magnetic energy as a large tutelar force in the shape of a red serpent, also known as *The Red Dragon*, coiling up from the ground to empower workings. This is the spiritual blood of the Earth, or the ley lines of the land personified.

DIRECTING THE WITCHBLOOD

Power raised means nothing if it's not used properly. There are loads of energy raised around us all the time, from concerts to mega-churches. The key difference is that Witches do this with conscious purposefulness and are directing it towards a specific purpose, into a specific object, or towards a specific location.

Once raised and gathered to a peak, power must be directed with willpower. Behind the will of each worker is what Witches might call *intention* to a desired and specific outcome directed under the power of the Witch's dominion. This direction or command is *the spell*. Directing power can also be part of the technique used to build power. For instance, chanting a few lines stating the specific goal is an incantation you are using to not only raise the necessary energy but give the direct command of what you need it to do. In addition to using

213 Gardner, Gerald. *"Recapitulation." Witchcraft Today.* Citadel Press, 2004.
214 "Book of Shadows." Salem. Written by Brannon Braga, Adam Simon, and Joe Menosky, created by Adam Simon, Fox 21 Television Studios, 2015.

symbols, tools, herbs, and all the correspondences you can coordinate together, the more direction it is for the universe to carry out your bidding. It is important to have a written spell either written as part of the collective work of the ritual itself or beforehand. Making your incantations as specific and simplistic as possible will be your greatest asset in charging your magical implements.

RELEASING THE POWER

The first thing to determine in releasing power is when the raised power is at its peak. This is a practice of being able to sense when the energy has reached its climax or pinnacle point. It's ideal to release the power being raised that has already been continuously directed or charged throughout the working when the peak is reached. This release is usually left to the High Priestess or the coven Seer to oversee. Their job is to sense this spiritual climax, add to the power, and feel how much fuel is needed for the work to be effective. When they feel enough energy has been dispensed, they will signal to the group to stop immediately. This is done either by all members dropping to the ground, raising arms in the air, making a noticeable gesture, or shouting a certain word of power as a group that completes the spell. Some will use peak as the time to shout out the command of the spell. If you are raising energy to heal your neighbor Patty, for example, at the peak you might raise your hands to the sky and shout, "Patty is healed! Patty is healthy! Patty is healed!" or a simple "Health!" while directing the focus into a photograph of Patty on the altar.

This type of release could also be done as part of directing magical power to its desired destination. For example, some of the best techniques I've seen have the group drop the energy into a specific image or icon, towards a specific quarter direction of where your magical target resides, or simply up towards the cosmos.

Afterward, there will be a noticeable change in the atmosphere. Temperature changes are the most common as circles and temples become full of heat after successful work, even when outdoors. Heat, after all, is the most common form of energy. Taking time after this to let the Earth absorb the excess energy is always a good practice. This excess energy that has been raised can also be directed into the hearthstone for future energy of blessings unto the coven and the self.

THE CONE OF POWER

The cone of power is the most well-known working technique and piece of Traditional Wican practice that has become an absolute staple for the casting, direction, and releasing of magical power. This is a natural shape that collects upwards when energy is performed in a space. Even several of my non-Witch friends and practitioners of other paths have noticed the cone of power. Its imagery is crucial to understanding the function it plays on the practical and metaphysical levels of the circle. It could also be seen as a pyramid, a tall mill-like building structure, or a balloon that expands to a point and then pops.

As we discussed earlier, the magic circle is cast not only to protect all of those participating within the circle but to contain all of that energy raised so it can be gathered to the point of an explosive climax. When this magical energy is produced, it builds upon itself, spiraling with the direction that the working group is moving in. In Traditional Wica, this is most often deosil. As the technique is worked at a pace that allows the rhythm to build faster and faster, the magical currents sometimes visualize the threads forming a conical shape. This tall, towering structure spins up to a peak or pyramid-like shape until, like a volcano, it is catapulted into the world. Some like to use the imagery of a rotating slingshot, the kind that is spun in a circle over the head until enough momentum is built up for a stone to be released to hit its target. The cone serves this same function, right down to the circular movement that we know from seething. Any moments that mimic revolving and spinning are immediate trance inducers and conduits of power.

Even though the cone of power was popularized by Gerald Gardner, its origins could very well be before him with his predecessors of the mythical New Forest Coven. These were a group of Co-Masons, Rosicrucians, and, by chance, Witches! They introduced Gardner to Witchcraft and initiated him into their system, which he then expanded and added upon, creating the Gardnerian Tradition. This was the first incarnation of Wica and the original system worked in the contemporary era in terms of what is considered "core ritual," including practices like circle casting, calling quarters, and rites like Drawing Down the Moon.

Gardner also had his own beliefs when it came to the way Witches naturally produced energy. For him, his belief was firmly rooted in the idea that energy is exerted outward from the body itself. Therefore, wearing clothing and unconsecrated jewelry would block the flow of this natural power emanating from the Witch's body. In his writings, this is part of the reason that he is insistent that Witches work magic *skyclad* (nude).[215] Working this way has its benefits and is my personal preference as an individual. However, the wearing of clothes doesn't actually seem to inhibit the power flow in any way, so it is only a matter of one's tradition and the consent and choice that always goes along with that, keeping in mind we are all spiritually autonomous adults.

THE TECHNIQUES

Some techniques of blood quickening and raising power have already been explored in depth like the use of trance and seething-related work in Chapter Twelve. It is also important to note that the acts themselves are pathways of raising the blood merely by their performance and the effort it takes to execute these workings. This is part of what Witchcraft rituals are designed to do, as they build with magical resonance as they are shared amongst folk throughout time. In understanding energy work, physical effort will release energy from our bodies. The power is in the courage of the performance!

SACRED DANCE: MOVEMENT AND GESTURES

"The great lords of the upper sky know the steps
of their dance too well for that."[216]

When we feel the ecstatic rush of passion and power, we can't help but dance! Sacred dance is by far one of the oldest artistic and religious expressions of the sacred embodied since we were early humankind. We clap to show gratitude as an audience and we leap for joy at weddings; why should we not then continue to dance for the ecstasy of self? Why should we stifle our impulse to spin and shake into communion with the Gods? Unfortunately, many Western religions have made religion itself lose its sparks of celebration by divorcing it from the personal

---

215 Gardner, Gerald. *The Meaning of Witchcraft.* Red Wheel/Weiser, 2004.
216 Lewis, C. S. "The Dwarf Tells of Prince Caspian." *Prince Caspian.* Harper-Collins, 1951, pp. 49–50.

religious expression of dance. A communal Witch's dance is an even I will truly never pass up on because of the awesome power it raises and how quickly it spikes!

When a Witch dances, it is a dance by imitation in the image of the Divine Creator of your deep mind. It clears the mind and purifies the body of all and any psychic debris, emptying your physical self so the work of the *Magna Mater* can move through you. The body channels the thoughts and expressions of the mind with a series of controlled movements, either rehearsed or spontaneous. Each movement and gesture of the dance works together to create a spell and release of Witch-power from the physical body by getting the Witchblood pumping. These dances are those that call back the postures and steps of our ancestors, allowing them and their legacies to continue incarnate through us as the descendants of the Witchblood. These steps all build up into the atmosphere. Each step you take will be energetically active, as the energy will naturally end up marking out the shape you craft by making a sigil through the geometric design of your footsteps. A dance is much like anything else in art. It tells a story and communicates something from the primitive part of our Witch soul. The shapes and the gestures danced all communicate the message of the dancer to the audience, coven, and spirits. By dancing, you are using movement and gesture to send off this physical power exerted out of the body along with your sweat-like words, prayers, and, most importantly, spells themselves. Many Witches who enjoy this pathway of power have taken the time, effort, and inspiration to develop skills in other schools of dance.

Dance should connect you with your body and the connection we hold with other people when movement is shared. There are several dances that Witches can explore and investigate. It is worth noting that most custom folk dances are also aligned with the holidays, seasons, and celebrations of the people. Several Witches' dances are taken out of local folk customs or a specific culture. Morris dancing, the regional festivities of the Hobby Horse of Bromley, and the sword dance of the British Isles are some favorites of my fellow Witches. The Abbots Bromley Horn Dance, the May Pole Dance, and the Sword Dance are all dances with Pagan roots that are featured in 1973's film *The Wicker Man*.[217]

---

217 *The Wickerman*. Directed by Robin Hardy, performances by Christopher Lee, Edward Woodward, and Britt Ekland. British Lion Films, 1973.

Coven Dances

The Serpent Reel

This is essentially a variation of the spiral dance that was popularized by Starhawk of the Reclaiming Tradition of Witchcraft in northern California. The group is led by one person in a circle, all holding hands, starting slow and gradually picking up the pace. Coordinating a song or a chant with this dance is ideal, as it helps the collective focus on the rhythmic pacing. When the leader decides the time is right, they will split off from the circle and, still holding the hand of the person to their left, lead the entire group in a wild snake-like pattern. This random series of serpentine pathways will become faster and faster, further apart and closer. The leader is purposefully whipping the group around corners and edges like a snake's tail until everyone is fully exhausted. The benefit of the Serpent's Reel is it allows energy to be raised, slowed, and then raised again. It is not a dance that needs to be set in the imagery of a cone of power, as it's more about waking up the land and getting the attention of helpful spirits. The mimicking of the snake acts as an invitation. It raises beautiful energy and can easily be employed in any Pagan festival setting.

The Traditional Circle Dance

The traditional circle dance is a grapevine step, starting with the right foot in a circle deosil. The grapevine is a step out to the side with your right foot, then crossing your left foot over the right leg, and then stepping out with the right foot again. Then, cross the left leg behind the right and continue to follow through the step by stepping out with your right, alternating crossing in the front and back each time. The group holds hands or stands alone in a circle, starting slow and then picking up the pace until reaching a full run, dropping to the ground at the end when power is felt at its peak.

Whipping The Steed

Horses are intensely magical creatures. They have been honored and worked with as sacred animals since the beginning and are associated with several spirits and deities. The Horse Whispers were a magical fraternity or guild of men who worked with horses and pursued the mysteries of initiation by learning the guild's deepest secrets of magically commanding and calming the horses in their care. This dance is in honor of those cunning men and these magical fraternities of old.

This dance is akin to shapeshifting, as the dancer will begin a meditative walk while internally summoning the horse spirit that lives in the collective spirit of the Witchblood. All animals connect with the lower soul of the Witch. By summoning their impulses, movements, and grace into the walk, we will slowly pick up pace as the horse. This is best achieved by holding a stance that mimics the bent back of the horse, slightly hunched over and using fists as hooves. You may notice your neck stiffening and your human awareness fading as it becomes gradually integrated with the horse. The walk will build up to a running gallop as Witches circle the border of the space, raising energy and building speed. For me, this dance is most comfortable to do in my solo practice, as there is no fear or inhibitions that can come with being observed by others.

In a coven setting, this can be just as effective with support of having others do this with you adding both moral and magical support. To increase the intensity of the dance and to further arouse the horse spirit to manifest, a Witch may be chosen as the *Spirit-Whipper*. This is done by using one member who playfully goes around the circle and taps those galloping around, as if to wake up the horse inside and increase the speed of the dancing.

CHANTING: MUSIC AND VOCALIZATION

Music comes from the Greek *mousikē*, which directly translates to "the art of the Muses."[218] By the grace of the Goddess herself, music is classically related to the voice's ability to enchant, persuade, entice, and even strike fear. The voice is what vibrates the sacred names and the words of power. It's in the voice's natural music that the Witch speaks an incantation and makes these crafted words manifest in reality. Music becomes the medium that weaves together the collective story of humanity, forever evoking memory, emotion, and truth. When we use a conscious sound in line with our intention and will, we too become like the Gods as we create with our breath and emotion behind the sound. Music is the other

---

218 Rouget, Gilbert. *Music and Trance. A Theory of the Relations Between Music and Possession*. University of Chicago Press, 1985, p. 213.

universal language we speak, as it sings directly to all the senses because of music's universally felt, deeply emotive experience.

Sacred instrumentations have been something honored in nearly all ancient religions, from primitive percussive instruments to the lyre of ancient Greece.[219] Rhythm and altered states go hand in hand, so having music and the freedom of the voice is the second most direct pathway of power and is an even easier way to incorporate the words necessary to guide the power by using the voice's command to charge the work with your desired outcome. The words the Witch speaks in their circle creates, and when they sing, even the spirits can't resist stopping and listening.

By using any sort of magical vocalization and speaking to existence the silent thoughts of the inner mind with guttural sound and held concentrated notes, we grant words that much more energy. We know words have power, and as such, they are the tools to change the world. If we speak something over and over again, it becomes a spell. There are the physical muscle movements of working the breath and producing the sounds, as well as the chosen words themselves. Any sort of music works with the union of the element of Air as sound and vibrations fill the atmosphere. Healthy singing and the production of sacred sounds depends only on the breath control and the conscious direction of the sound from each practitioner.

There is the popular Middle Age Witch-lore of that Witches are able to use their voices to conjure up storms. This notion of "whistling up the wind" is famous and consistent amongst the cross-cultural practices of Witches and their relationship to the winds.[220] This is one of the pieces of magic that famously propelled the Scottish Witch Hunts, as women became accused of involvement in an underground network of Witches led by Agnes Sampson in 1590.[221] The coven accused of being in league with the Devil tried to kill the king's bride at sea by conjuring up storms to drown the ship. This was the inciting incident that started the Scottish Witch Hunt led under King James VI.[222]

219 Rouget, Gilbert. *Music and Trance. A Theory of the Relations Between Music and Possession.* University of Chicago Press, 1985, p. 213..

220 Pepper, Elizabeth. *Witches All: A Treasury from Past Editions of the Witches' Almanac,* 1977, p. 25.

221 Levack, Brian P. "The Trial of Agnes Sampson, 1591." *The Witchcraft Sourcebook.* Routledge, 2015.

222 Ibid.

It is true that some of the best chants, charms, and incantations are sung. It is these secret songs that are never to be uttered unless it is in the proper time and place. When these songs are unleashed, the frequencies released by the vocal cords will alter the environment. I also love experimenting with magical music by singing a few songs that go along with the spellwork I'm performing or the celebration of the Sabbat that exudes the same mythos and seasonal celebration.

The benefit of singing a group chant is that not only do we drone each other out to dismiss any nervous energy, but also that when everyone uses the same rhythm, they can root themselves into the natural rhythm of the land by vocalizing as a collective, so the chant and the movement of the energy becomes far easier. You can feed off each other's energy as a chain reaction moves its way throughout the circle. The rhythm of instruments or clapping transforms into a sung chant as the meter of the words keeps the beat. This pulse is the same pulse of the spirit of the land that we are tapping into and mimicking on this plane. Even deeper still is the heartbeat of the Great Mother, the songs of the Witch waking her from her sleep.

CLAPPING UP THE CONE

Rhythm is the first foundational skill to have in your toolkit if you want to work effective magic using techniques of vibration and vocalization. Not only does this help when combined with the technique of dance, but it helps Witches align their internal pulse to the pulse of nature's rhythms. Start by taking a few deep breaths, clear your headspace, and set the intention to use the energy of your claps to create a rhythm that will build into a cone shape. This energy, once raised, can be directed to the cosmos or into any given spell.

Start by building a steady rhythm by rocking or humming slowly. When you are ready, begin to clap in an intentional rhythm. You can coordinate the claps with your breath, rocking motion, or intensity of the hum. Build this up organically until you feel you have transformed the atmosphere around you. Take time to see if you can sense the shape of the cone. Turn to your skill of visualizing, or simply put your hands out in front of you and see if you notice any changes through your hands. Focus your intention and shout a one-word statement of intent that will act as the word of power to send off the energy you have summoned.

You can repeat this as often as needed. This is a quick modification to the full coven operation in a Witch's properly prepared circle.

Chanting uses a simple two- to three-line piece that rhymes and uses a few easy notes. Write the chant's lyrics in a way so the chant can be easy to memorize and straight to the point. Rhyming is best but not a requirement, as long as the chant communicates its intentions precisely.

Intonation is a long and drawn-out droning sound, usually vibrating sacred names or vowels. Use a belly full of breath and allow the sound to pour out of you with the breath until you are empty and need to come up again for air. This is an intense exercise of raising energy very slowly so that focus on the intended target can be fully engaged. Some will use intonation as a grounding and centering exercise, while others will use it for the effects it has in working magic. If you want to increase the difficulty, you can use this as a harmonizing exercise. Harmonies are the pleasant cross tones of frequencies aligning into a choral sound. It is especially amazing to tap into the energy of the group as you must listen to each other and sense the energy of the entire group. Some masterpieces of songwork and chanting have been birthed out of harmonization.

Sacred Performing: Theatre and Drama

This is my favorite technique to work with as an actor and performance artist, as it allows me to call upon all the skills I already use. (As such, I offer an in-person class and lecture series called *Arte of The Icon* that delves into this topic.) The amazing thing is just how much the roles of actor and Witch serves the same purposes. The first is the transformation of the atmosphere and environment that transports the audience to another story or world. The second job of the actor or the ritual leader is to evoke emotion in the participants of the experience. Storytelling through drama or a Mystery play is one way that spirits can be given an embodied form. Theatre also works in necromantic fashion, as the voices of playwrights long dead are resurrected and brought to life with each performance. We employ the theatrical arts as part of our liturgy and as a way of preserving our legends, mythology, and folklore. For me, a good ritual is always good theatre. Ritual not only tells the story or animates the unbelievable, but ritual also creates the story we wish to tell using magic. Theatre preserves teachings and carries the legacies of the characters we idolize. Storytelling becomes interactive and alive as both ritual and theatre become the world mirror that reflects the best and worst parts of humanity.

As a teaching device, theatre offers another memorable way to ritualistically pass wisdom. The more theatrical, the better! As the relationship between performer and observer, power becomes a dynamic presence in the space. This power or presence that is raised occurs because of the emotions stirred in the realization of the deeper truth of the performance, as fantasy transcends reality when we fully lose ourselves in the performance. This is why we still pass on our best of legends, myths, stories, and performances.

Costume, props, acting, and story are all extra levels of enhancing your magical practice. These additions alter consciousness because they bring the imagination to life and give a specific form to the spirits in the body of the actor or the Witch. Ultimately, ritual tells a story. Rituals are continuations of the oral and folk traditions. They share a mystical learning that is usually only attained by experience. Presentation, theatrics, and the magical persona play a key role in a good ritual. All acts of performance also act as core offerings and rites of passage to the Gods and spirits. Our presence in our rites is the most important, as sometimes it is better to become part of the audience and observe.

SILENCE: RESTRICTION AND STILLNESS

Using silence, constriction, or difficult movements that bear some gravity is an ancient technique and one that is often associated with Witches. It requires self-knowledge, personal risk, and patience to endure this kind of inhibitory work. In restriction of movement, food, sleep, or the physical body, sensory deprivation can allow the mind to overcome the body's physical needs. The energy that is normally dedicated to those needs is then able to be directed towards a desired intent. This is an excellent tool for creating very potent mental power and physical sweat that can be directed and raised through the employment of sacred postures, gestures, focal points, and symbols to fixate upon. Very clear and focused energy is often the result of rituals of silence. Silence has been said to allow the inner ears to listen to the small mutterings of the spirit world. In silence, there is also the ability to withhold emotion and expression, as if to allow it to build internally

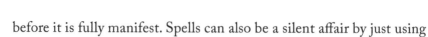
before it is fully manifest. Spells can also be a silent affair by just using our power of stillness and hyperfocus.

Restriction is an uncomfortable technique, but it is through the discomfort of restricted movement, tense muscles, and the challenge to get through these experiences that there is power raised in achievement and applying a slight strain to the body. Restricted movement lends itself to lots of psychic and physical energy being exerted off the practitioner, as well as the symbolism behind the movement, pose, or restriction of a chosen sense that directs energy and blood flow towards a specific function. During the Inquisition, there was a device used to punish accused Witches and heretics that became known as "The Witches' Cradle."[223]

When modern Witches learned about this punishment, they experimented with it themselves. They found that this form of sensory deprivation and the confusion of senses induced hallucinatory experiences. The cradle takes the form of a cloth or bag that is hoisted off the ground. This then allows the participant to swing gently in the darkened center of the cradle; the motion of the swing exaggerates the slightest movements of the participant. Profoundly altered states have been reported from the experience of restricted swinging. This involves hallucinatory visions and sensations, often taking place after fifteen to twenty minutes in the cradle, distorting time and space.

GREEN AIDES

We know that drugs and alcohol alter our perceptions and awareness. Herbs and plants consumed or smoked work as an aid in the techniques of altering consciousness and raising power. Smells and sensory input from rising incense smoke composed of herbs gathered at midnight creates a hazy room, which plays a role in contributing to the summoning of Witch power.

This power touches on the even larger category of herbalism and the Witch. The two have forever been linked. The magical use of herbs is in

---

223 Penczak, Christopher. "The Witch's Cradle." *The Gates of Witchcraft: Twelve Paths of Power, Trance & Gnosis.* Copper Cauldron Publishing, 2012, pp. 171–172.

line with the laws of correspondence: the virtues of the green world are identified by the herb's coloring, shape, and natural vibration. For instance, mugwort has silver leaves, often in small crescent shapes resembling the Moon. As such, its virtues are linked in practice with psychic ability, dreamwork, and spirit work.

Taking time to get to know herbs and speak their language will aid the Witch in all manners of work. Incense, oils, salves, and ointments are all in the Witch's repertoire. Consider using or making your own tinctures, fluid condensers, washes, and magical perfumes. The point of using substances is to give the etheric body a small push from the spirit or influence of the plant, placing one into a trance state.

Pre-Ritual Witch's Brew

- 1 tablespoon black tea
- 1 tablespoon mugwort
- ½ tablespoon powdered jasmine
- 1 pinch of rose hips
- 1 slice of raw ginger root

Add 1–2 tablespoons of the brew per every 8–10 oz of boiling water and allow to steep for five minutes. Add cream, milk, and honey to taste if desired.

A Witch's Sacred Smoking Blend

- For relaxation and grounding within the body.
- 2 parts cannabis of choice
- 1 part dried mugwort (food grade)
- ½ part dried damiana leaf

Grind together until blended and smoke using a blessed pipe set aside for spiritual work. *Disclaimer*: This may stop dreams. If dream work is important to you, do not attempt it. Smoking is a health risk. It's also not legal to smoke or possess cannabis in several parts of the world today, so be advised of your local laws if you decide to create and use this blend.

PLEASURE: SEXUALITY AND SENSORY

Sex is sacred. It's vital to natural expression, continuation, and the love of life itself. Witches tend to be very sex-positive and open-minded when it comes to different sexual expressions and lifestyles. There is a large crossover between the Occult and Witchcraft community and the kink community. Many Witches who work sex magic are also well-versed in tantra and other schools that include sex and pleasure as a spiritual rite.

Partnered or solo, sexual power is raw magical energy. Lust, passion, and physical connection are all powerful energies that are naturally a part of sex. The polarity between people and exploring power exchange occurs in the same way during sex as they do in magic. Power is raised through masturbation or sexual activity. You can release this energy when the mood is right or, best, at the moment of orgasm. In the same way that you would visualize or shout your desire as you build power, climax is used to direct this sexual energy to your specific goal.

THE TABOO: PAINS AND PILGRIMAGE

Testing limits and working past obstacles are at the heart of the technique of pain. Pain is probably the least used of these techniques for obvious reasons. However, wisdom is sought out equally from the pleasures and the pains, as there must always be balance. Pain is often known to Witches as *an ordeal*. Some practices are reminiscent of the medieval Flagellants, a Catholic sect of monks who used floggers and whips as a way to detach oneself from the body for the sake of forgiveness of sins from God.[224]

Sacred body modification is altering the body for the symbolic dedication to a chosen path. This could take several forms like tattooing sacred art, symbols, and magical scripts, or body piercings to commemorate Witching experiences like dedications and initiations, as well as physically marking ourselves to the Gods. Tattoos are a way of personally furthering one's spiritual self-identity and making a sacrifice of ink and blood. Ordeals of nature and isolation are also common in

224 Nethersole, Scott. *Art and Violence in Early Renaissance Florence.* Yale University Press, 2018, p. 107.

initiatory experiences. Facing the elements like a rainstorm, navigating lost in the woods, and walking on hot coals have all been used as ritual testings of energetic power. By facing the things we fear in controlled and sacred settings, we can reframe our trauma responses and gain a sense of mastery over self-control.

Drawing Witchblood

Revered and feared
The wine in the grail
The offering to the Ancients
Pact made between the veil!
A flash of power erupts
If a scratch or cut is made.
Take care of the faery blood
It shall be a helpful aid!
This is the sacrifice of old
This is the blood made of gold.
This is the fluid that turns the mill
This is the water of my Will!

CHAPTER FOURTEEN

THE WITCH'S WORD: CHARMS OF POWER

All of creation began with the winds of change and the breath's metaphysical pact with the voice in the power of the Word. The Witch, like the Gods before them, knows that by speaking the most sacred names aloud, they hold power over all. The spirits speak in symbols, rhyme, and poetry. The charm, therefore, charms uses just as much as it enchants the spirits to do what we ask. This is why the charmer uses a truly poetic Craft, as it relies on soothsaying and finding the words that create the needed atmosphere.

When we truly value our language and the vernacular in which we speak our enchantments, we become the creator and destroyer of worlds. A charm could be a simple spoken verse said over an object to awaken the object's natural symbolism and animistic spirit within. Using horseshoes, a rabbit's foot, or a shiny penny for a good luck charm are just a few examples of how diverse and readily available these spells are for everyday use.

For Witch and cunning man Cecil Williamson, the most important methodology was the repetition of the charm when spoken. This is the first rule of thumb when using a charm and is a foundational technique shared by practitioners of the charming traditions today.[225] Williamson regularly worked charms by using wind and smoke from swinging incense, either at a simple altar set up or at the hearth where the chimney could be used. He would speak the charms into the fire or incense smoke,

---

225 There are specific traditions of magic that are rooted in the practice of giving and receiving charms from family members, personal tutors, or by the spirits themselves.

allowing the charm to be carried on the plumes to travel up the chimney and using this visualization as a way to propel the power of the spell into the world. Graham King also recorded in *The British Book of Charms and Spells* that Williamson would place himself in a swing he had built for himself with loads of incense burning beneath him. Then, using the repetitive motion of the swing itself to induce himself into a trance, he would charm in the haze of the fumigations.[226]

The repetition of the charm not only inducts the Witch into the correct state of mind but also raises and instructs the power simultaneously. This could be as simple as sitting down in a rocking chair and using the rhythm of the rocking to speak one word (such as love, health, or protect) repeatedly over the image of your intended target.

As society and cultures changed, so did the symbolism and wordings of the spells and charms used. This is why historical charms tend to be overtly Christian, and is where the relationship between the Church and the Craft must be reexamined. To quote from Graham King's book, "Much like old folk songs or antique furniture, they gather regional and personal variations of a patina that often improves with age. The literal meanings and pronunciation of words change, the ingredients, the saint's names, and the language all change, but over the years the magical essence of the spell survives."[227]

WORDS OF POWER

The words of power that a Witch may use in a charm are the sacred names of deities and ancestors. They could also be phrases, sayings, or mantras in a different language that exude the same feeling and tone as the mood you're trying to generate. Latin vernacular naturally calls up magical rituals seen in the Medieval period and portrayed to us in Hollywood. There is power in the languages we may not be fluent in, but take time to learn how to incorporate the language properly to craft a charm that will succeed in its communication.

Barbarous words of power are the most well-known of the words spoken. These are funny or off-sounding words that evoke a sense of cryptic magic

226 King, Graham. *The British Book of Spells & Charms: A Compilation of Traditional Folk Magic*. Llewellyn Worldwide, 2020, p. 23.
227 Ibid, p. 25.

but have no real meaning or translation. Despite this, they have been used by magicians and Witches throughout time, so these words have built up a mystical power from their repeated usage. Magician Aleister Crowley even stressed the resonance barbarous words carry with them when used as a proper way to break down the mental barriers of the practitioner. He describes them as "long strings of formidable words which roar and moan through so many conjurations have a real effect in exalting the consciousness of the magician to the proper pitch."[228] They appear frequently in the Grimoire tradition of the Renaissance and the Greco-Egyptian Magical Papyri.[229] Most consider the Enochian script and language provided by Dr. John Dee and Edward Kelley to be the most famous barbarous language.[230]

One theory behind magical words goes along with the idea of finding the words in trance from the spirits directly. The experienced magicians would have made up certain barbarous words without regard to proper translations or the language itself. They were spontaneously speaking the words as if just to open their senses and allow the sounds to be derived from the inner mind. Words that were either mistranslated, misheard, or just flat-out made-up have all survived as part of the charms in the magical canon today.

EXAMPLES OF BARBAROUS WORDS[231]

- Abracadabra
- Apheiboe'o'
- Eko, Eko
- Thoathoe'Thatho-oythaetho'usthoaithithe'thointho

---

228 Crowley, Aleister. *Magic in Theory and Practice.* Dover Publications, 1929.

229 Dieter Betz, Hans (ed.). *The Greek Magical Papyri in Translation, Including the Demotic Spells, Volume 1.* University of Chicago Press, 1986.

230 Laycock, Donald C. *The Complete Enochian Dictionary: A Dictionary of the Angelic Language as Revealed to Dr. John Dee and Edward Kelley.* Red Wheel Weiser, 2023.

231 Deerman, Dixie and Steve Rasmussen. *The Goodly Spellbook: Olde Spells for Modern Problems.* Sterling Publishing Co., 2008, pp. 183–192.

AMULETS AND TALISMANS

Amulets and talismans are probably the most popular methods to come out of charming and spell working. The terms are often used interchangeably, but they do have specific connotations. An *amulet* is specific to a charm of protection, not only the physical protection of the person who would own it but also the protection of their wealth, their luck, and their health in general. These are all forms of protection, but an amulet's function is to preserve and protect the owner in all these various intents.

A *talisman*, on the other hand, works as a charm of *empowerment* and as a further gift of power to the person who uses it. It is a charm that brings the intended person extra skill and power from the outside or heightens that which already exists within them. Whether they are a simple or intricate design, an object or jewelry, they are for the Witch to wield.

Charm bags are a popular way to incorporate multiple items into a charm spell that requires a set of physical components. Depending on the region, a charm bag could also be used in box form, known as a *wishing box* or *bounty box*. A basic charm bag contains a mixture of herbs with different objects that carry meaning called *curios*. These, as well as stones and symbols written on parchment, are charged and charmed before they are placed inside the bag. The bag is then regularly ritually charged and empowered by anointing the bag with oils, alcohols, and brews. To continue feeding the bag is to continue feeding the working.

Written seals, signs, and petitions all have made their way into the Craft as charms in their own right as well. The personal symbols a Witch creates are the inspiration of their artistic desire, sometimes called a *sigil*. This sigil magically operates as a symbol representing the profoundly artistic symbology of the Witch. It could create a contract or statement of intent with the universe or spirits; we address these as petitions. Sigils or symbols known as *seals* specifically act as the symbolic doorway that conjures the spirit and specific virtue we seek.

RHYME AND REASON

Spontaneous rhyming is one of the best skill sets of the traditional charmer, as many believe rhyme is the easiest language to speak with spirits. Rhyme has a natural musical quality, is often poetic, and is easy to memorize because of the rhymes themselves. Words of power are often easy to incorporate into rhyme. As a poet will use rhyme to weave together a narrative, the Witch can paint the imagery of the spell in rhyme. You can improvise words based on sheer need, performing these words in a style that has long been attributed to bards and skilled wordsmiths who were believed to be touched with the gift of soothsaying from the Gods themselves.

PRACTICAL CHARMS

HEALTH

While visualizing the person and holding a strong mental link with the person in your inner eye or while holding physical artifacts that belong to the person, say the following:

May (name) be well, May (name) be whole.
From physical body to within the soul.
Form muscle to tissue, blood to vein
Shall (name) now be made whole again!

WEALTH

Speak aloud to empower any money magic or when extra cash is needed:

Money I want, Money I need
Money I ask, So Mote It Be!

PROTECTION

Speak the charm whenever needed as many times as necessary:

Protection of mine be upon thine,
by command of the word and the eye of the divine!

A WEATHER WORKING CHARM

To begin, find a stone or boulder half in the Earth and half above ground. This stone provides a liminal spot between the world above and below. Sometimes, this rock is called a hideaway stone or a knock rock. Take a wet rag and slap it upon the chosen stone to create a rhythm while speaking the following charm:

Winds of the air I now proclaim!
To blacken the skies in Witchcraft's name!
To fall the waters and weep the Dame
To bring the rain! To bring the rain!

THE MILL CHANT (ABRIDGED)

Air breathe, and air blow
…
Fire flame and fire burn
…
Water steam and water boil
…
Earth without and Earth within–
Make the mill of magic spin!
Work the Will for which we pray!
Io, dia, ha, he-yay![232]

CHARM TO RAISE POWER

Tread the mill, tread the mill!
With the spirits of good will.
The Wild Hunt is off to kill
Eat, drink, and have your fill!
For magic works tonight!

---

232 Deerman, Dixie and Steve Rasmussen. *The Goodly Spellbook: Olde Spells for Modern Problems*. Sterling Publishing Co., 2008, p. 232.

A Witch's Evening Charm

Now journey into realms of sleep
For now, my soul rises to leap.
Over the veil and into desire
To seek wisdom of the Sabbatic fire!
May I wander to the dream's den
Until dawn shall I return again.
To wake refreshed from the council I've held
With spirits of Gods in this spell!

SPIRIT CHARMS

For Divination

This charm is to be spoken over any divination tool or equipment. You can incorporate this into the asking of any divinatory question to enhance spiritual contact.

Oh, Mystical tides! Now Foretell
Prophecy flows by this spell
Speak your truth
Speak it well!

For Ancestral Blessings

This charm is best if spoken in a cemetery or place that is charged with the ancestral current of power.

In Blood and Bone, by Heaven's Throne
Under the Earthly Stone: I do remember you.
Names forgotten, long since dead
For all you've given, for the blood you shed
Grant me a path so I may see
The mystery of all I am and am yet to be!

FOR SECRET KNOWLEDGE TO BE REVEALED

Utter the following charm under your breath in a relaxed, meditative state until you are sleepy. Repeat for six consecutive nights before bed, focusing on the specific area of the knowledge you would like revelation in.

Audi, Vide, Tace. Ad Astra, Ad meliora. Altius! Compos mentis!

FINDING MEANING

Some charms are found in nursery rhymes and children's fairy tales. The old stories carried with them the folk customs of our Pagan ancestors. Mother Goose, in particular, is the reimagined Dame Holda flying upon her goose, leading the souls of the ancestors.[233] Magister Robert Cochrane found much mystical meaning in the nursery rhyme *The House That Jack Built*, which ends with the following image:

That hides a maze.
That is worth a light.
And into the castle that Jack built.[234]

LOVER CHARMS

ATTRACTION CHARM

Take a small square of lace you can easily conceal. Using red ink, make a small dot or heart in the center, then fold the lace square towards you three times, turning the square to the right with each fold. This creates three folds in total, applying the charmed number. Next, scent this lace with a magical perfume or love oil composed of herbal scents

---

233 Studebaker, Jeri. *Breaking the Mother Goose Code: How a Fairy-Tale Character Fooled the World for 300 Years.* Collective Ink, 2015.

234 "The House That Jack Built." *People of Goda, the Clan of Tubal Cain,* June 24, 2019. clantubalcain.com/2013/06/30/the-house-that-jack-built/.

of rosewater or lily of the valley. While you make each fold, say the following charm each time:

Beauty and glamor I cast with the folds of lace.
For as long as I should possess it
All Good (men, women, people, or desired type of person)
shall notice my face!

Keep this in a secret place or carry it with you daily.

Lover Revealed to Me

It's best to perform this charm on a Friday, the day of Venus. Start with a freshly cut rose. Take time to breathe, and pluck off the petals while reciting the following charm:

By this rose and by the thorn
Reveal my love to me
Who am alone and forlorn!

Seduction

Light a taper or other candle on a Friday. Anoint your candle with an appropriate oil or magical aroma, then carve or trace a septagram (seven-pointed star) into the candle. Speak this charm aloud seven times over the candle:

Spirits of bubbling passions
Spirits of the flame!
Bring a partner in the Old One's name.
By all arousal of touch and kiss
I cast this by the Sevenfold star of bliss!

CHAPTER FIFTEEN

THE DEDICATION OF THE WITCHBLOOD

This rite summons and stirs the Witch within *you*. It's a rite that allows the seeker to have their first brush with the Gods, magic, and a sense of the spirit of Witchcraft itself. Dedication is not the same as an initiation. An initiation is a specific event within a specific tradition's framework. Some traditions are older than others, but what matters is your connection to the work. Dedication and initiation are both considered very important rituals of rebirth. As a rite of passage, it anchors us to the change we are about to experience within our bodies and lifestyles.

Every tradition has different protocols and ways of doing this. Dedication, on the other hand, is the claiming of yourself to pursue your magical path. Think of dedication as setting intention and making space to begin the pursuit of a spiritual lifestyle. Initiation is the commitment to the priesthood of the Craft, and that is a huge role of responsibility. Initiation's essence is in becoming connected as part of the larger "family tree" of that particular tradition and all practitioners within it. The reason for this is called *lineage*, as a way for people to trace their tradition back to the founders. For Gardnerians, this is to Gerald Gardner; for Alexandrians, this traces to Alex Saunders.

The Craft has changed a great deal since the 1950s, not just up until the 80s, when it was seen as a completely closed practice. It was nearly impossible to be considered a valid Witch without an initiation. This is because the only public Witches were part of these closed practices birthed from the British Traditional Witchcraft movement. As time went on, there was more interest in the Craft than there were initiators to go around. As a result, other groups, traditions, and ways of making magic started emerging. Usually with the trope that what they were doing was a more valid, older, and traditional form of Witchcraft. Even when you look at the fine details, it's clear all these groups are drawing from the same source materials and collective ideas of Witchcraft at that time. All these different groups evolved and began presenting the world with different takes, on different histories and different interpretations.

Doreen Valiente was brilliant and very outspoken on the topic of self-initiation. She was interviewed for a small documentary called *Earth Magic* in 1988, viewable online. In it, an interviewer asks her a question that is still being asked in the community today: "can somebody initiate themselves as a Witch?" Doreen simply states that there is no need to ask for someone's permission to follow the Gods. As long as one is sincere, they will be on their path and be able to learn their magic just the same. It may be different or take more time if one is working alone, but her best line is "a Witch, is Witch, is a Witch."[235]

RITUAL OF DEDICATION[236]

This ritual is to be performed alone in the most private place possible. Prepare an altar with the following, knowing some of these are optional:

- Athame
- Salt[237]
- Water
- Anointing oil of choice
- Incense of choice[238]

---

235 Earth Magic Video (1988). *Alexandrian Witchcraft Timeline and Archive.* https://alexandrianwitchcraft.org/earth-magic-video/.

236 I have given a basic structure for Circle casting in this chapter for you to follow. It can be applied and adapted to any work if you wish to work within the paradigm of the circle. There are several ways of creating sacred space, and the circle is just one of many methods.

237 I prefer Kosher salt as an Earth-based salt.

238 I recommend pure Dragon's blood resin burnt on a charcoal disc in a thurible. Stick incense will also do just fine.

- A chalice with wine or juice
- Two altar candles
- Witch's cord
- An offering of fresh flowers[239]
- A black journal

If you have not acquired your tools yet, the power of your hand will do. The power of gestures and movement reminds us that we are the main conduit of magic. This ritual should be performed as close to midnight as possible, under either the waxing or the full moon.

Mark out a five- to seven-foot-wide circle. You can create the barrier line by using cornmeal, flour, cornstarch, or even salt. It should be big enough for you and your altar, even if you need to cast through walls and doors. Take a ritual bath with salt and red rose petals. Allow yourself to enter ritual headspace. You can include atmospheric music, incense, and special gestures as part of your bath as a pre-rite warmup, and may perform this ritual either skyclad or robed.

Once you are ready, take time to sit in front of the altar without jewelry, makeup, or distracting clothing. You want to be as close to *the natural you* as possible. First, light your candles and incense to set the space. It is best to anoint your candles with your anointing oil before their first use.

Breathe deeply and envision your energetic field expanding around you. Using your breath, visualize your blood flowing through your veins. Imagine you are speeding up the flow, causing energy to rise and expand outwards from your body, with each breath. Firmly fix in your mind that this is the night that you shall claim the Witchblood.

Remind yourself of the hidden company around you, your ancestors, and the lost stories of Gods and fallen angels. If you wish to acknowledge the nature spirits and the wildness of your fetch, use it as a guide. Feel it in your gut, rising into your head. When you feel fully alive and the spirit feels correct in the atmosphere, you are ready to begin. Ground, center, and align yourself with the work you are about to perform.

Move your focus to the blessing and consecration of each of the Elemental representatives back into their "purest" forms, constructing the world within the world. These are the blessings of the salt (Earth),

---

239 Roses and lilies are most appropriate.

Water, incense (Air), and working candles (Fire). Each element is usually placed on the Peyton, the acting symbol of Earth, which is the center of the altar where the power of the circle is directed.

Salt Charge

Creature of Earth, holy salt from land and sea
Banish be all evil and malignity
Purify all by this rite of the appointed place
Cleanse and purify by thy purest face!
So Mote It Be!

Water Charge

Oh thou Waters of life, I do stir and conjure you by that which is
most sacred, I consecrate in the names of the God and Goddess of
creation where so I bless thee.
So Mote It Be!

Add three to nine pinches of salt into the water, stirring to combine, and focus the power through your athame to create the waters of life.

Incense Charge

Behold this perfumed offering of air on the rising smoke!
All hidden and of spirit now awoke!
I charge this incense by fire and by air
To welcome the old ones, by the scent so fair!
So Mote It Be!

Candle Charge

Blessed Be fire and flame!
Blessed be thy holy name!
Quicken the blood, the soul within
Now and forever may magic begin!
So Mote It Be!

Casting

Once all the charges have been said, the Elements are ready for use once the casting is complete. Now, casting the circle can begin. With attention to your athame, allow the internal power of self to fill you up. Visualize yourself projecting out a flame of Witch-fire to mark the circle, allowing your tool to act as an extension of your magic like a lightning rod. The circle charge can be as simple as:

I cast this circle. The circle is cast!

You can also speak more elaborate circle charges if you wish. No matter the level of simplicity, this is to be spoken out loud, as you are speaking the circle into existence.

The Circle Charge

I cast and conjure this magic circle, by the power of my will and by the power of my heart. I cast this place as a place between all time and space, as the wood between the worlds and a meeting place between the worlds. May this circle protect me, may this circle contain all my power, may this circle be now, as it was and as it always will be! So Mote It Be!

First, cast the circle with Water, since all creation started with the sea. You can start sprinkling around the circle the same number of times you cast it with your blade. Three times around the circle is always best. After the water, bless the circle with the incense, making the same rotation around the circle to purify and fill it with the blessings you wish to have. The circle is then cast!

Invoking the Four

The four watchers or guardian powers of the directions are ready to be welcomed to the outside of the circle's edge to protect and aid their eyes to the rite. This creates an anchoring effect to the circle's direction and suspends the circle in time by the gaze of the quarters.

Starting at the North or the East, hold up your chosen instrument of the Arte to salute the direction. Envision that guardian coming towards you. This makes a bold statement of welcome and affirmation to each of the directions. Many Witches like to hold up their hands, draw an invocation symbol in the air, or bow as a gesture of greeting and humility towards the spirits of the mighty four.[240]

I (name) call upon the spirits and keeper of the (North/East/South/ West), powers of (Earth/Air/Fire/Water), to stand with me and keep watch over this sacred space! I welcome you and bid you greetings to this Rite! So Mote It Be!

INVOKING THE SPIRIT

A simple method to invoke Spirit is through a formal invocation or song, or the act of lighting a prepared candle or oil lamp to symbolize their presence. Once that candle is lit as the invocation begins, it will be radiating that Spirit in the purest form of light, staying until you dismiss them.

INVOCATION TO THE HORNED GOD

First, raise the right hand in a gesture of welcome.

I call to the mighty Horned Lord of the worlds between
Guardian and Keeper of the Arcane!
Answer my call by thy immortal name.
Be here oh Great God of the Witches of old
I invoke thee to cross the sacred threshold!
Stag, ram, goat, and bull-horned God of starry night!
Be present and pay witness to the Witching rite!
You are welcome to this hallowed place!
So Mote It Be!

---

240 *Elemental Pentagrams:* Invoking or banishing pentagram at each point according to its elemental ruling, and when you are invoking or banishing at these specific points, any consistent symbol of power can be used for this. I've found these spirits respond no matter what sign is made.

INVOCATION TO THE GREAT GODDESS

Raise the left hand in a gesture of welcome.

> *Mistress of magic, Queen of the cosmos, Mother of all!*
> *Great Goddess of the Witches, answer this call!*
> *I do honor and invoke thee, with the holy flames*
> *Goddess of infinite faces and 10,000 names!*
> *Be present to this rite, walk, and speak!*
> *For you are the wisdom that all seek.*
> *She of beauty and strength, the bright lunar-eyed*
> *Come to the dance, by winds of fate you ride!*
> *So Mote It Be!*

Begin to walk the circle widdershins slowly and deliberately. Use the sensation of walking round and round to focus on releasing and banishing all previous influences in your life that may be holding you back. This is the walk of renewal. Walk until the atmosphere is thick with energy. You may have the feeling you are not entirely alone. Dip your index and middle finger into the blessed water and anoint your forehead (the third eye), the back of your neck, wrists, and the bottom of your feet.

> *I bless myself that I may hold the power of this space, to claim the rite*
> *of the Witch and walk the hollowed round. By the Water pure, I am.*

Take up a vial of anointing oil and anoint the same spots.

> *By the oil, from the feet to the head.*
> *Between the worlds of the quick and the dead,*
> *I anoint in the names of the Ancient ones!*

Take up your Witch's cord and pull it taught, holding it high above your head, and pronounce:

> *I pull a cord on the loom of fate*
> *I have come to claim mine!*
> *By the trails I've walked*
> *by the sign of the star*

Most darksome and divine!
I have followed the quest for the Lady of Enchantment
She the crescent lunar shine.
I am held in the Old One's honor
I have discovered this cunning of mine.
As my ancestors before me
stretching back to the beginning of time.
I charge the blood with the powers of the Witch
by this spoken tutelic rhyme!
Awaken the blood! Awaken the blood! Awaken the blood!
Summon! Stir! In the sight of spirits
Those of hidden standing stones.
Stir my soul, my hands, mine eyes
Stir my blood, my belly, my bones!
I profess I be a Witch! I am a Witch! I am a Witch!

Tie the cord tightly around your waist. Now, sit in front of the altar and quietly meditate on what being a Witch means to you. Envision a golden stream of light from the Gods above and a radiating ruby light shining from the ground below. Allow the light to fill your body, inspire your mind, and drive your ambition. Stand up and move to the northeast portion of the circle, declaring:

I am of the stars, of the woods, and the fields!
I am of the roads, of the springs, and the sea.
I am the crafter, I am the seer
I am of Gods and they are of me!

Now, using any technique you resonate with, open up to the atmosphere. You are going to raise power. Surrender to the spirit and allow yourself to let go in full submission to the power that moves you. When the peak is reached, or at full exhaustion, drop to the ground. Speak into the Earth's ground and say:

By this my most sacred of rites in the Old One's name!

Collect yourself and re-ground. Take up your chalice and make a toast to the spirits of old by holding your cup up to the sky.

> *May my spirit serve the craft as the craft serves me*
> *Whatever is given is also shared back to thee*
> *For nothing is a gift*
> *Without taking*
> *For taking is nothing*
> *Without the gift*
> *May I remember this rite of truth in love*
> *May I remember this rite of becoming.*
> *To the Old Ones of the Witchblood!*

Pour a libation on the ground or in an offering bowl first. The spirits always get the first share. Then you may proceed to drink. Next, place your left hand over your left eye and hold your right hand over your groin area. If you can, stand up on one leg and incant the following.

> *Blinded but all-seeing*
> *Shaper and Former*
> *Wielder and Guide*
> *A power upon thyself!*
> *By the sign of the one-foot God*
> *By the Fires of gnosis fallen from sky,*
> *I am a Witch!*

Take up your blank black book. This will be your Book of the Arte, where you will record all future spells, rites, experiences, and information.

> *In days of old, it was said that it was the Devil who made us sign his book.*
> *By the pacts and contracts of the Witches of old, I too shall sign my name*
> *in a black book of the Arte. Unlike the times of persecution and torture,*
> *we are free to love. Ours is to bliss in the ecstasy of the Great Queen and*
> *the Horned hunter of the dark and light! I sign my name unto myself*
> *and in the presence of the hidden company gathered here. So Mote it be!*

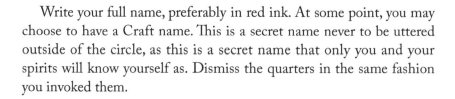

Write your full name, preferably in red ink. At some point, you may choose to have a Craft name. This is a secret name never to be uttered outside of the circle, as this is a secret name that only you and your spirits will know yourself as. Dismiss the quarters in the same fashion you invoked them.

I give you my thanks for the protection you have afforded my circle, may you be blessed and now return to your realm in the name of the old one!

If the presence does not leave right away, you can clap your hands vigorously while chanting:

Hekas! Hekas! Hekas!

To uncast the circle, walk around the edge of the circle widdershins while chanting:

Oh, mill of power cast round by three
Now go to ground into stone and tree.
Within and without what I see
In the name of the Holy Mystery.
This circle is uncast by me!
So it is! So mote it be!

CHAPTER SIXTEEN

BLOOD MOTHER, BLOOD KEEPER: HONORING THE WITCH GODS

The Blood Mother is just one of the many guises the Goddess may take, the abstract space that holds all creation and pure consciousness. The Blood Mother is a Goddess of what I would term *pure consciousness*. She is the creative urgency to be made manifest in all things, and through these creations she is present, disguising herself within all thought forms and physical matter. She holds this matter, carrying it as scaffolding. As a shapeshifter, she creates new forms for her desire. Like a snake sheds its skin, so the Blood Mother sheds the power of knowledge and bliss wherever she is in all forms and regardless of the guise she takes. Whether she is dark and vengeful or loving and nurturing, she is always shedding the power of ecstasy.[241]

She is known by many names. Her Mystery is that she is the embodiment of the ceaseless frequency of creation. She is the ecstasy of fate's spinning and the drive for us to evolve, as our desire for happiness is very much a part of that evolution. She is the one who has our back, after all; she is the space that supports all matter from behind us. You can use anything to represent her. My relationship with her deeply relates to the Mysteries of the cauldron, dance, and the red woman with the fire in the belly.

---

241 "Meeting the Goddess of Consciousness, Sally Kempton." *YouTube*, YouTube, 11 Feb. 2016, www.youtube.com/watch?v=MPYhEyIjFrM.

Her particular interest is in liberation, so the world may know the ultimate truth and, on a more personal level, so we can be Gods ourselves. This is what often wakes us and allows us to then be truly conscious. As a result, we can never un-know information once it has been revealed. This is where her severity may come in. It is only through us, as the creations, that she can view the world. Therefore, we don't get to truly wake up to our consciousness until it is she who wakes us and sees the world through us first.

The Blood Keeper is also known as "the Man in Black" or the trickster side of the Horned God. It is he who records our journey and keeps us empowered with a fierce will. He also rules the idea of discipline for the sake of humility after the rites of initiation and dedication. He acts as a guide and a guardian by making his presence known by the sound of trotting hooves around the energetic barrier of the woods. He is the gray-eyed rider of the northern winds as winter comes, truly the shadow twin or alter-ego of the Horned God of light and Sun.

He holds the Black Book with the records of all Witches who have signed their names, and his mind holds the secrets of worlds below and the transformation of death to rebirth, for he is also a force of death and the Mysteries of the places unknown. As such, he is a comforter and a bringer of peace, despite his misunderstood nature.

As a consort figure, he is quite an androgynous figure, half-animal and half-man. His Mysteries are not linear and, like the Pied Piper, Witches follow his lead on the winding path. He is the pause (and sometimes the frustration), but like a plow, it is he who turns up the ground so seeds can be planted. We call upon him to open the gates to the other side. Therefore, he is the protector of virtue as he dispenses the magic of blessings on those who answer the call of his hunting horn.

PREPARATIONS

Set up an altar and your sacred space as you see fit. This is written as a traditional rite to be done outside with the stang erected in the ground. The stang will act as the representation of the Old Ones and will be the altar at its base. This is a rite of honor, connection, and offering. Magic can be worked depending on your need but will not be included here. The effects of the rite are cleansing and inspiring, and often help us align to our higher self, which is the sleeping God within.

Materials you will need include:

- A stang
- Blade/athame
- Flowers
- Whiskey or red wine
- Fruits, bread, and honey
- Bowl or cauldron with blessed water
- Shiny coin or crystal
- Anointing oil
- Fires of Azazel incense (cedarwood, juniper twigs, and sandalwood)
- Incense thurible and charcoal disc
- One red candle (the candle of the Blood Mother)
- One white candle (the candle of the Mysteries known and unknown)
- One black candle (the candle of crossroads, the meeting place between the worlds)
- Bottle opener
- Matches

Create a drawing or personal representation of how you view the Blood Mother and Keeper. I have used everything from a seashell to a small, handmade clay figure. She is elusive, so the simpler the icon, the more we can communicate her liminal and changeable nature to our psyche. For the Blood Keeper, he is the dark reflection of the shining Horned God. Any animal antler/horn is an excellent representation, as well as a fire poker, representing his weapon of office. After all, it's he who assists the forge in the Witch's fires of the first blacksmith, the fires of Azazel.

CANDLE PREP

Using a toothpick or carving tool, you are going to carve a small pentacle on the red candle and anoint it with your anointing oil. On the white candle, you are going to carve a symbol to represent the secrets not yet known, the unfathomable Mysteries, with a simple circle. Lastly, carve the black candle whereby its light you shall be able to provide a light to the spirits and Witches of the crossroads with a simple X.

RAISING THE STANG

Clear away any leaves and, if you desire, mark out a big enough circle with dead branches. (A circle is not necessary for this.) Raise the stang, ensuring your stang has been *shod*, especially if you are consistently working outside.[242] Your stang will be most grateful. If the ground is too hard, you can use a tree stand or a flowerpot filled with dirt or soil. Many Witches like to decorate and adorn their stang with garlands, flowers, symbols, and pendants depending on the occasion. Some may tie arrows representing Diana's hunt in an X shape, which also signifies the crossroads and the four-quarter ways where we meet. Once you have raised the stang, lay out your working tools as a simple altar at its foot.

A RITE TO THE BLOOD MOTHER AND THE BLOOD KEEPER

Hold your arms up to the sky and proclaim to the spirits and shades of where you stand:

> *I (Your Name) come by the round*
> *I (Your Name) do summon the mound!*

Then stomp your right foot three times:

> *Three knocks upon the floor*
> *Three knocks on the Lady's door.*
> *From the valley deep and the water's shore*
> *I bring you offerings for me to pour!*

Light your incense and your candles:

> *Blessed be the fires and flame*
> *I charge you in the Old One's name*
> *To work and aid the rite I do*

---

242 *Shod* refers to a process where magic is imbued into the stang, and then metal or lead is used to seal up the bottom base of the stang so the power stays within and does not leak out of the staff.

Until the Gods are to come through.
I offer the light, I offer the smoke
Burneth bright by which I evoke!

Now, take your blade and go to each of the four directions. Take your time to address each of the spirit roads and ask them for their protection. Hold your blade up in a salute of acknowledgment. While chanting, use your blade to open the gates for spirits to come through by making a slicing motion down, as if you were cutting a part in a curtain.

Coniuro spiritum! Conjuro Spiritum!
Conjuro Spiritum genii locorum!
I conjure the spirit! I conjure the spirit!
I conjure the spirits of this place!

Take up your burning incense to fumigate the working area and waft some big plumes of incense towards each of the directions. Then, take up your anointing oil and make a dot on your third eye. Hold your hands out in front of you, palms facing up, and take a few deep cleansing breaths. Sitting or standing, take time to ground and center and turn your awareness to your surroundings. Does it feel as if the woods are closer to or farther away from you? Does it feel like you've sufficiently gathered in the hidden company?

Hum for this section and gently rock or walk deosil. This is done to generate power but is also used like a walking meditation to ease yourself into a headspace where you can effectively invoke. Take up the whiskey and, continuing to walk in a circle deosil, pour out the contents on the Earth while saying:

I call to the Horned One by his face of the dreaded night!
I call to the God of the Witches by candles red, black, and white!
I summon you by this favored offering that I pour
Oh, the ancient Keeper of the gates!
Come step through the hidden door.
That with you, I may learn the secrets yet to be.
May the gates be open hence by thee!
I offer my love and my thanks for all that you are
I summon and invoke you by the sign of the star!

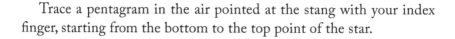
Trace a pentagram in the air pointed at the stang with your index finger, starting from the bottom to the top point of the star.

> *Come and dance, may this space be free!*
> *May you be amongst the woods,*
> *Be present in the fetish tree!*
> *By the stag, two-horned, by velvet green,*
> *For God's Light burns there in between!*

Go to the stang and waft more incense as an offering. Chant and dance widdershins if desired. Feel the presence of the Keeper and speak with him as desired.

> *Ballimach! Ballimach! Ballimach!*
> *Evo Evo Sol antak!*
> *Annawil dee a-dak!*[243]

Next, take up the bowl of water and hold the crystal. Using your breath blow onto the crystal slowly and deliberately to bless it. Then using your spit make an equal-armed cross on the crystal and drop it in the center of the bowl. Raise the bowl to the moon and then down again to the ground. If you can manage to catch the reflection of the moon in the water, this is what you need. If you can't manage this, allow the crystal in the bowl to be your focal point as you address the Blood Mother.

Place your focus into the bowl, allowing the water's reflection to ease you into a meditative headspace, breathing deeply. With each breath, slowly bring your awareness to the heart. Take the palm of your hand placing it over the chest and see if you can breathe into the space behind the heart. With this, place your awareness behind you and sense the Mother. She who is always there, who has always been holding us from behind.

> *Beloved and Sacred Lady*
> *Goddess of the Witch's Blood.*
> *Descend upon this place of meeting*

---

243 These are Barbarous words of power, but they have the frequency and music in them desired.

By the power of the flower's bud.
For you are the force of nature's beauty
That grows and blossoms in the spring.
You are the holder of all creation
Of every single living thing!
I invoke the Goddess of the Ancients.

Trace a pentagram in the air pointed at the stang with your index finger, starting from the bottom to the top point of the star. While you do this, say:

Goddess of the Hidden Arte.
Accept these my humble offerings!
Given with a loving heart!

Now dig a small hole in the earth to bury the rest of the offerings. Stomp upon the spot three times and say:

I honor the Gods with blessings
As they have strengthened me.
I honor these powers from me to thee!
May It Be So!

If you have a desire to work magic, this would be the time. Take up the bowl once more, holding it up to the sky. With the utmost intent, say:

Goddess of the nameless! Goddess before the time
I give my thanks to you and your powers sublime!
Depart now from this place, So I may take my leave.
Blessed Be oh my beloved Blood Mother
By all the magic that you weave!

Take out the crystal and pour the water on the ground. Once the water has been emptied, simply say:

So Mote It Be!

Turn to face the stang and extinguish the white and black candles. Take the lit red one in your right hand and say, addressing the Keeper:

By the light of the blood for the Horned King's reign
I give my thanks, may you now depart from this domain!
Close the gates! All now depart!
In thy name of the nameless Arte!
So Be It!

Now, pick up your blade and go to the four spirit roads once more. See the cut you made earlier in your mind's eye and, using the blade, swipe across and envision that portal you opened in each direction now closing like curtains. Simply bow and say:

Depello Spiritum! Depello Spiritum! Depello Spiritum!
Hinc itur ad astra!
I release the spirits! I release the spirits! I release the spirits!
From here the way leads to the stars!

Hold your arms outstretched and declare:

This rite has now ended!

Stomp your foot three times and leave the area as you found it.

CHAPTER SEVENTEEN

HEALING THE BLOOD: RITE OF THE ANCESTORS

Generational curses are a tricky obstacle that many of us may encounter. When I first started working with the inner concepts of tapping into the Witchblood, I couldn't help but notice the direct link to things like genetic memory, genetic trauma, and the negative habits that are often learned from ancestors and our immediate environments. When we start communicating with the ancestral realm, whether in specific or very broad ways, the influence of those ancestors begins to offer the support we may need. However, past trauma, addictions, and emotional dysregulation are all something that I would recommend working through with a licensed therapist or counselor if you find yourself in this position.

I believe spirituality is a tool and not a Band-Aid. The balance of everyday mental health care and spirituality *must* work together to function at a healthy level. This is a rite of honoring our ancestors that's meant to be repeated or performed weekly as an offering of our time. You may never know which ancestor may come through, for they could be so far up the upline that we have no solid knowledge of who they once were. However, this rite opens the door and sends a signal to all the ancestors who can help us with the specific situation or problem we bring. This in itself is a working that takes a circumstance or situation to the ancestors for them to take on and transform.

The dead make the most excellent eyes and ears, which we as the living may not be able to fully infiltrate. Oftentimes, they experienced the same struggles in life experience, so they may have key pieces of wisdom, for the dead are everywhere, sometimes called the *silent audience.*

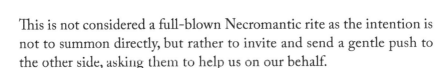

This is not considered a full-blown Necromantic rite as the intention is not to summon directly, but rather to invite and send a gentle push to the other side, asking them to help us on our behalf.

By working with the ancestors, we are working with ourselves and our link to the connection with those who have gone before. In my experience, once deceased we go to a place where we can still intercede, but we can also understand our mistakes and other important universal understandings as we return to the source of the Arcane.

THE RITE OF HEALING

What you will need for this rite includes:

- One white candle
- Offering of fresh water in a clear glass
- An offering of a favorite food or an item your Mighty Dead would appreciate
- A skull or representation of the Mighty Dead (These could also be pictures of specific loved ones.)
- A handful of dried wormwood
- A small cauldron for a fire (This can be achieved with alcohol and Epsom salt. You'll want enough for the salt to be saturated plus some extra, so the alcohol sits on top. Note that this has to be pure alcohol to achieve the proper effect.)
- A scrying tool: anything reflective that allows you to soften your gaze and maintain focus on your inner vision (The scrying mirror, crystal ball, or other tool will act as an amplifier and extra conduit for the ancestors to intercede during the rite.)

Inscribe the white candle with a word or symbol of your need. Light the candle and allow the peace of the flame to absorb and surround you. While seated, allow your arms to rest on your knees with the palms facing up. Take three deep cleansing breaths, filling your belly with the fuel of the breath to move the fire of the will. Once you are filled with breath, bring your attention to the ground and the underneath.

Envision the Earth opening and allow your consciousness to follow the cavern getting wider and wider, allowing you to walk through, down, and around into the below. Notice the roots of all trees and plants interlocking and sending messages to each other through the roots. See the vast expanse of mycelium as the world of fungi feeds and nurtures the land now above you.

Work your way deeper still, feeling the sense of gently descending past crystals, stones, and bones long forgotten, hidden in the deep Earth. Feel the temperature get cooler and cooler until you come to the bottom. Sense yourself feeling the deepest part of the mud and allow your feet to spread their energetic roots to the very bottom of this earthy cavern in the world below. Anchor yourself to this place and, in your head, project the message that the roots will serve you in this rite. These roots will be your grounding and a direct line of communication for the blessed ancestors to follow. Envision this like a thread for them to follow up to the world above, where we honor their spirits.

Now, turn your attention back up to the world above where your physical body sits and awaits your return in trance. Allow yourself to rise with your roots propelling you back up to the body, rising faster and faster past the stones and the bones, past the mycelium and tree roots, further back through the expansive cavern until you rise through the floor and gently allow your consciousness to come back to you. Move your feet, wiggle your hands, and allow yourself to hold the presence you have just brought up from the world below. When you are ready, open your eyes and prepare the offerings.

Hold the clear glass of water up to your ancestral representation and say:

> *I come before the spirits of the Mighty Dead!*
> *I open the way for their intercession!*
> *By the blood shared, by the blood chosen, by the blood inspired!*
> *I give you my ego for this time together*
> *May I surrender my pride from the land of the quick.*
> *To listen and learn better from the land of the Mighty Ones.*
> *I invite you to come and sit with me now*
> *For there is nothing but the now.*
> *Nothing but the continuum of the I am*
> *For you are I and I am you*
> *Ancestors beloved I honor this rite to the spirit's view.*

Take a moment and softly blow a stream of breath onto the surface of the water in the glass, imbuing it with all your emotions, will, and needs. This is part of your breath of life being offered through the water to feed and fuel the ancestors. (This breath of life is part of what helps animate them in our daily relationship with our ancestral practice.)

Set this beside your representation, and offer the food or other item while chanting or singing:

> *You who have weeped!*
> *You who have reaped!*
> *You who toiled and fought*
> *You who nurtured and taught.*
> *Eeeee ohhhhh ahhhhhh*
> *Ancestors of mine!*
> *Eeeee ohhhhh ahhhhhh*
> *Ancestor's shine!*
> *Eeeee ohhhhh ahhhhhh*
> *To follow the rooted line!*
> *Come, oh Blessed Dead!*
> *Come by Spirits white, black, and red*
> *The obstacle I offer is for it to be shed!*
> *Within me the truth, for you to embed.*

Light your cauldron fire and meditate upon your obstacle. Allow yourself to release all worries and emotions into the fire. Pour your prayers and calls for guidance into the burning presence. Envision your words entering the fire as a thick smog being swallowed up, consuming all of the worries and obstacles you face and transforming this energy, where the power arises anew, clean, and fresh. This renewal brings us new creative energy and opens a way for our ancestors to bless us with helpful information through inspiration. These spirits offer us wisdom for our highest good, as we are continuations of them, and they are all parts of us.

Pick up your dried wormwood and feel the power of the plant spirit. Connect with your senses and observe what you feel from this ally. When you have connected with wormwood, speak this charge:

> *With the power of this green friend,*
> *Power of the plant I now hold.*
> *Work for me a hundredfold!*
> *Hundreds upon hundreds*
> *Blessings of all that should*
> *Work for me now ally of wormwood!*
> *For the virtue of dead man's advice*
> *Shall heal me to an internal paradise!*

Toss your wormwood in the cauldron fire and allow it to be consumed in the flames. When this is complete, take as much time as you can with your scrying device. See if you can receive or feel any instinctual messages. When you feel like the connection drops and the energy starts to dispense, simply tap the skull or representation nine times to close the gates. Take a moment to sit and let the experience settle before snuffing out your candle flame until the next time you hold a conference with your dead. When you are fully back in your body, clap your hands together and make a strong audible exhale out of your mouth. Afterward, ground, settle, and do any necessary spiritual aftercare. I recommend a strong cup of coffee or tea for this.

This rite has ended, the gates are closed! Back to the world I know!

CHAPTER EIGHTEEN

FLIGHT OF THE WITCH

The place where Great Ones continue to dance
Where Witches of the world now work in trance.
For the ability to slide out of the bodily suit
To journey to the Sabbath in spectral pursuit.
To convene with others like them work fire.
Those near and far fuel flames of desire.
Traveling past cycles, a reunion with the dead.
Lightly hovering above the feathered bed!
Dreaming deeply, in the sky, we float.
By rite of Witch-flight! This skill I devote!

FLYING

The image of a woman flying across a full moon sky on a broomstick is the first thing people think of when asked to imagine a Witch. However, spirit flight is an integral part of the continuation of Traditional Witchcraft. For those who partake in the fires of the Sabbat, it is a rite of freedom and ecstasy that allows the soul to be unleashed from the weight of the physical body.

From the late medieval to early modern period, the belief that Witches flew to attend a diabolical Sabbath, tended to by the Devil himself, was the climax of Witch-hunting propaganda and was the foundational knowledge that people of all classes would have had of Witchcraft. These tales became more embellished with time, as stories of the supernatural often do, growing in popularity compounded by the panic stirred by the Catholic Church's accusations of Witchcraft for anyone who went against conventional society. This fear, rebellion, and social contagion were part of what produced a lot of profoundly impactful folklore.

From commoners to the aristocracy, folks told tales of those who held nocturnal convocations with demons and nymphs. This imagery beautifully combines the horrible and the erotic, and this sensationalism of the grotesque has always been popular because sensationalism sells. This idea of the Witches' Sabbath combined with the imagery of Christian heresy and Pagan folklore was a masterful scheme, and no one was unaffected by such propaganda.

Spirit flight is recorded with a great diversity of practice. Witches could be mounted on the backs of animals; the Sabbatic goat is the favorite accusation from the Church. However, they could ride on any household object, such as a broom, pitchfork, or staff, to the assistance of other nocturnal spirits. A great example of this comes out of the Sicilian Trials that took place in Palermo from 1579–1651 where a total of sixty-five people fell victim to the Witch-craze.[244] There is a report from 1588, known as the Fisherwife of Palermo, in which the wife of a local fisherman stated that she and her child could fly through the air with fellow Witches, riding on goats to the meeting place of Benevento, Italy. According to her tale, this was the cause of the fairy folk or elven folk known for spirit-knapping certain people in flights of astral projection.[245] In Germany, Witches were recorded confessing several times to manifest in the form of orbs of lights, traveling upon the passageways of troops of the dead.[246]

From the records of a self-appointed Witch-finder, Chonrad Stoeckhlin, he encountered a woman by the name of Anne Erizenberegin in 1586. The accusation was based solely on a local shepherd, who reported to have information directly from the leader of the phantom trails. Under torture and interrogation, she confessed that she was indeed able to travel

244 Christ, Rachel. "The 17th Century World of Witchcraft." *Salem Witch Museum*, 23 Aug. 2022, salemwitchmuseum.com/2021/12/17/the-17th-century-world-of-witchcraft/.

245 Ibid.

246 Ginzburg, Carlo. *The Night Battles: Witchcraft & Agrarian Cults in the Sixteenth & Seventeenth Centuries*. Routledge, 2015.

through the air in spirit form but was not one of the Witches seen. So began the Witch hysteria of Oberstdorf. Stoeckhlin soon fell victim to the same fate, under the same accusation no less, for overstepping his power and acting in the position of the local bishop. Erizenberegin claimed she had learned her powers from Stoekhlin's mother, most likely out of vengeance while imprisoned. Since Stoeckhlin was seen as a Witch-finder by the community, it was easy to say he knew about Witches because he was one of them.[247]

Another example of the Witch being accused of flight appears in Gerald Gardner's *The Meaning of Witchcraft.* This is the case of Margaret Ine Quane and her son, also accused, who was burned at the stake in 1617 in Castletown on the Isle of Man.[248] Her crime was that she possessed a phallic caved broom handle, which she would straddle and fly through the fields to ensure their growth.[249]

Historically, the use of trance techniques takes a person into other realms. There was a separation between the world of dreams, memory, and normal consciousness, and the world of dreams was the world of the spirits. Many of these practices are described in the same style and approach, yet they are similar to other techniques that are Indigenous to various regions and labeled as Shamanic throughout the world. This idea of sleeping deeply to navigate the spiritual body into the dreamworld was recorded by the historian and friar Venerable Bede. He wrote once about an Irish priest who was able to perform what we would call flight. As he writes, the priest "died one night and came back to life the next morning," and then was able to give a detailed account of where he had been and what he saw.[250] This sleep like death is one of the most commonly repeated accounts, and if there is a salve, balm, or ointment involved, there is undoubtedly a reason for this coma-like sleep. (See the section *The Ungentum Sabbati: Flying Ointment*).

247 Howard, Michael. "Stoeckhlin." *By Moonlight and Spirit Flight: The Praxis of the Otherworldly Journey to the Witches' Sabbath,* Three Hands Press, 2019, pp. 33–34.

248 Gardner, Gerald. *The Meaning of Witchcraft.* Weiser Books, 2004.

249 Howard, Michael. *Modern Wicca: A History from Gerald Gardner to the Present.* Llewellyn Worldwide, 2010, p. 102.

250 *Bede the Venerable Saint. Ecclesiastical History of the English People; with Bede's Letter to Egbert.* Penguin, 1990.

All classes of European society were under the rule of both the church and state, as the two were generally seen as the same. They held the belief Witches were those who knew how to send their spirit bodies outwards, causing all manner of ill will, while the physical body laid in a sleep or coma-like trance. English author Reginald Scott, in his book *Discoverie of Witchcraft,* describes challenging a self-professed Witch to fly. She took him up on it and sequestered herself alone in a locked room.[251] Unbeknownst to her, Scott was spying on her through the keyhole.[252] Here, he saw her smear an ointment on her body and then drop to the floor losing consciousness. Despite their efforts to wake her, she would not wake. When she finally did, after several hours, she began to describe to Scott all of the other lands she had traveled to. In today's world, we may sometimes refer to this as an out-of-body experience or as "remote viewing." In these states of dream and trance, it's the Witch's double, or the spiritual body, that flies conscious and aware as the physical body is entranced in its sleep. Once detached, the double makes a journey to attend rituals, hold meetings, and converse with the otherworld.

By understanding we are of the Witchblood, we exercise its quality to journey to places out of time. In the deepest recesses of the mind, there is an ability to travel to worlds beyond our imagination. These are the hazy, dream-like fairy landscapes of mountain tops and wooded glens where the Witches of past, present, and future congregate at the Eternal Sabbath. We seek our way through the mental journey to find this vivid Oneiric realm where we may join our kinfolk of the Witchblood. This liminal place is where the eternal flame of Witch-fire is kept burning at the macrocosmic center of the world. This is tended by the generations of those who have journeyed to the spark of the Sabbath. It is a place my Witchcraft takes me frequently.

It is at the crossroads between the waking and dreaming state of mind that the Witch-flight is found. All these levels of consciousness can be achieved by the Witch, which is why the figure was so feared. The Witch could spell you without their physical presence, simply sending forth their astral double to do their bidding.

---

251 Scot, Reginald. *Discoverie of Witchcraft.* Dover Publications, 1989.

252 An ironic link with the Greek belief that the Gods could enter the bed-room at night through the keyhole while the person slept.

THE ELABORATED THEORY OF WITCHCRAFT:
A HERETICAL HISTORY

Understanding the way flight works for Witches today requires time to unpack the history and the folklore surrounding the reimagined image of the Witch from the Middle Ages to the late modern era. This period is what scholars have coined "The Elaborated Theory of Witchcraft."[253] The Elaborated Theory of Witchcraft was the notion that was shaped and shared amongst theologians, inquisitors, philosophers, and jurists of the period (those being the men in power, making it so these myths and fear tactics would trickle down throughout all classes of society). It was generally believed that Satan had started a worldwide conspiracy to recruit mainly women to his war against God. By selling their souls to him, he would give them magic, riches, and power if they would perform the most heretical and horrible acts against human nature. This period was hyper-focused on examining the nature of Witches and what they supposedly practiced. When looking at the theory today, it's easy to realize how much of the popular imagery of the Witch originated in pre-Christianity and was reinvented by the Church to its advantage. Many of these tropes and concepts have been reclaimed and reworked by modern Witches.

This image later appears on a fifteenth-century woodcut portraying the Witch's flight on a broom and wearing of animal heads or possibly masks.[254] It's been recognized by most that much of what we know that the beliefs and practices of a Witches' Sabbath are partial fictions from the Christian Church in its long span of persecution and anti-rhetoric against non-Christians, including Jewish, Muslim, heretical, disabled, and impoverished people. When looking at the history of the claims made by many under torture, we start to see the same tropes and ideas of apostasy and heretics bleed into each other.

The Witch flew, rode on an animal's back, or spiritually transported themselves to the Sabbath in a dream-like state. The Sabbath was seen as

---

253 Sledge, Justin. "Witchcraft - the Witch Flight to the Sabbat - from Inquisitional Myth to Psychedelic Flying Ointment." *Esoterica*, YouTube, 22 Oct. 2021, www.youtube.com/watch?v=1CaLMJgYVuk.

254 Peters, Edward and Alan Charles Kors (eds.). *Witchcraft in Europe, 400–1700: A Documentary History*. University of Pennsylvania Press, 2001, p. 35.

a nocturnal meeting and congregation of demons, ghosts, and Witches. This is a ceremony where all matters of horrible evils would be carried out, from infanticide to sexual taboo, such as kissing the Devil's asshole.[255] It was preached from the pulpit that this was the Devil's army on Earth to bring disease, misfortune, and, above all, death. Witches were the ones held responsible for the dying of cattle, the failure of crops, and any malignity that could not be rationally explained.

At the Sabbath, the Devil would teach his followers how to poison and curse his enemies by the droves. These followers were mainly women, although we know there are several men accused among the numbers of the European Witch-hunts of old. The meetings were presided over by the Devil himself, and would also include dancing, feasting, and orgiastic sex among those present. Everything in the Witch's ritual was seen as a reversal and perversion of the Christian religion.

Flight was one of the central themes of the Sabbat but was one of the last pieces of Witch-lore incorporated into the mythical imagery of the Sabbath by theologians. Even though the flight was brought up by some of the earliest accused, its evidence is fragmentary until the first wave of the European Witch panic hits in the fifteenth and sixteenth centuries.[256] The idea of flight is brought up by the accused themselves near the beginning of the first wave. Here we see the emerging parallels between folk practices, Christianity, popular belief, and torture. Under torture, the accused would have had to say anything. An alarming point about the confessions of the Sabbath was the sheer number of those accused of being in league with the Devil alongside anywhere from fifty to thousands of other fellow Witches, depending on the individual and degree of torture. The inquisitors needed names of those also in attendance, so as a result, the geography of the Witch-panic grew.

Ultimately, the Church had to go as far as to re-establish canonical law to explain the supernatural phenomenon reported, even though original dogma wrote off spirit flight as a delusion and impossible. As a result, we see the Church recycling what I call the "stock sins." These are crimes, sins, and accusations that were historically applied to all oppressed and marginalized people from the medieval to the early

---

255 Called the *Osculum infame* (the kiss of shame).
256 Levack, Brian P. *The Witch-Hunt in Early Modern Europe.* Taylor and Francis, 2013.

modern era: infanticide, cannibalism, desecration, incest…the list goes on and on. This is why history slowly starts to merge groups of the oppressed and marginalized; all of this vernacular turns into one great conspiracy of Witches.

Mountains or a dream landscape often appear in the reports of the Sabbath as well. Central Europe had accounts of Witches who would travel to Venusberg Mountain to meet the Queen of the faery realm and the otherworld's Mater, Dame Venus.[257] These flights show physical and spiritual meeting places; whether they are on a hill or in a dream, there is a link, as these locations specifically symbolize the center or meeting points of this world and the other world. The landscape features of vast fields, mountains, and groves also line up with what was believed to be the realm of the faeries in the surviving pre-Christian faery lore. The meeting places described do reflect the belief in both real and nonreality spaces where spirits and Witches would ride.

HOW WITCHES TRAVEL

Beliefs of Witch travel to the Sabbath take the form of Witches being able to project their astral double into the form of their totemic animal or familiar self. This is the primal connection the practitioner maintains to further the expression and love of the animalistic view of self. The *fetch* is the bestial self, able to travel to realms we may not be able to go to in human form. This was seen throughout Britain and Germany, also known as the *fylgia*, a practitioner's animal specific to their personality or character qualities as a double or "follower" of the Witch in a spectral form.[258] Oftentimes, this is in the guise of their familiar spirit, which shares a similar character with the fetch.

The fetch takes form to whatever essence the Witch's temperament and personality attracts. The fetch chooses you and is with you upon the time of your birth. When one taps into the essence of the fetch, one can use this primal energy of the primitive to project the soul by the force of animalistic energy.

---

257 Levack, Brian P. *Demonology, Religion, and Witchcraft: New Perspectives on Witchcraft, Magic, and Demonology.* Taylor and Francis, 2001, p. 88.

258 De Vries, Eric. *Hedge-Rider: Witches and the Underworld.* Pendraig Publishing, 2008, pp. 106–108.

One example in history of the shapeshifting is seen in Italy. During the Middle Ages, it was believed that a Strega transformed into a screech owl at night to prey upon children and harvest their blood to drink.[259] The idea of the malevolent Witch stalking their prey would become a very well-known myth in regions of southern Europe. This is where we get the depictions in history of Witches in the form of birds, werewolves, or mounted upon a wild animal. As the *Canon Episcopi* would agree, we are the folks who mount the backs of the animals to roam with Diana on her wild hunts with her phantom armies.[260]

THE *UNGENTUM SABBATI:*
FLYING OINTMENT

The use of flying or lifting ointment makes an appearance in the historical record more often than the broom. This is essentially a hallucinogenic salve or lardy fat that would have been smeared and rubbed into the body, creating effects of flying, weightlessness, delirium, visions, and visitations from all manner of spirits. The records of twelfth century Solerno, Italy, have more examples of the widespread usage of this kind of ointment, as it was a common one for recreational and possibly ritual use. This information was published in a series of three volumes concerning women's health called *The Trotula*.[261]

Examples of the use of the ointment are often sensationalized but abundant. One famous historical example includes the trial of the aristocrat Dame Alice Kyteler in 1324 Ireland.[262] She was discovered with a vial of ointment, which she supposedly smeared over herself with a wooden staff, before then leaping and jumping in a frenzy-like ecstatic state.

Flying ointment is a taboo subject throughout history (and even today) because of the nature of working with baneful plants and herbs.

259 Rabinovitch, Shelley and James Lewis. *The Encyclopedia of Modern Witchcraft and Neo-paganism*. Kensington Publishing Corporation, 2004, p. 262.

260 Guiley, Rosemary. *The Encyclopedia of Witches, Witchcraft and Wicca*. Facts On File, 2010, p. 50.

261 Gilmore, David D. *The Trotula: A Medieval Compendium of Women's Medicine*. University of Pennsylvania Press, 2001.

262 Seymour, John. "1324 Dame Alice Kyteler, the Sorceress of Kilkenny." *Irish Witchcraft and Demonology*. 1913.

Entheogens are the chemicals released that cause these flight states, and they play an important role in several cultures and religions as a way to make contact with the wider spiritual universe.[263] Entheogen translates in Greek to "the God within" or "God generated from within."[264] This translation grants us a peek at the importance of the plant spirit allies and how the chemical is used within a sacred context. Witches have long been the ones who possess the dangerous knowledge to administer these types of plants properly, notably those from the Nightshade or *Solanaceae* family. The plants remain allies today but practice safe use: they are still toxic and will kill in the wrong dose. The difference between a leaf and a twig can put you in the emergency room.

Although each ingredient in the salve varies depending on the recipe, most are not to be trusted. The hysteria of Witches and the Devil carries on from the late Middle Ages until the early modern era. These historical recipes were deliberately altered by inquisitors to stoke further inflammatory propaganda and outrage, including the most baneful and foul of ingredients, such as bat's blood and fat mashed from unbaptized babies. There is an interesting consideration to be made for the naming of the Witch's ingredients during the Middle Ages. Some of these ingredients are the folk names of the herbs used by actual practitioners taken literally and added to the pile of stock sins ("eye of newt," for example, is mustard seed). Other herbs, like datura, mandrake root, henbane, and belladonna, all became closely associated with the Devil's plants, most likely for their poisonous nature and associations with folk healers, instilling fear with tales of people's terrifying experiences on these psychoactive trips.

Based on the wide diversity of recipes, each salve may produce different effects based on its ingredients. We know certain salves act as stimulants while others are crafted as hypnotics or hallucinogens. The application often puts one in a very deep sleep for several hours while the person may experience traveling to different regions and engaging with all types of spirits and creatures.

---

263 Ruck, Carl A. P. and Mark Alwin Hoffman. *Entheogens, Myth, and Human Consciousness*. Ronin Publishing, 2012.

264 Taylor, Bron. *Encyclopedia of Religion and Nature*. Bloomsbury Publishing. 2008, p. 596.

THE RITE OF NIGHT-FLIGHT

Oneiric oracles are at the heart of spirit flight in search of wisdom. There are several ways to work with dreams and interpret them. Dream dictionaries and interpretations are wonderful complimentary tools to Witches' dreams and flight. These dream interpretations are great reflections from the pool of the collective consciousness of our world, speaking to us in symbols and omens.

To attempt flight, you will need a riding pole, staff, stang, or broom of personal choice. This will be the main instrument your focus will be directed upon to propel yourself into flight. It is also recommended (and very traditional) to use a flying ointment or an herbal aide for trancework and flying experiences. This could be a salve, tincture, ointment, tea, or anointing oil, and it works most effectively if applied before you begin the rite.

Make sure you have a large area of floor space to lay down (or just your unoccupied bed) that is as comfortable as possible. Ideally, you will want to be so relaxed that you could easily fall asleep. Have your magical journal and a glass of water on hand to record your experiences and hydrate afterward.

RITUAL SET UP

Have a sacred space set up with as many protections you can include. I prefer a magic circle for this because my physical body is left vulnerable as my spirit is out to do other work. If you wish, I recommend casting one around your bed. Some will draw inspiration from Eastern magical systems and use a magic carpet. There are many stories in folklore of Witches flying through the chimney to soar through the night air. Purposely put these images into our mind's eye as helpful tools to enforce the sense of weightlessness.

Have your carpet, bed, or space clearly marked as a protective boundary. Put an incense burner and a candle on a small stool or the nightstand, providing a small working altar for the incense to increase the atmospheric change. The last thing you will need is your instrument to ride upon, as you will be laying down with your tool as a sensory guide to your night visions as your mind hovers outside the physical sensorium.

The Rite

Settling the Mind: Fixing the Road

Light your incense or flame. Sit in a comfortable position with your legs crossed. Taking your besom or riding stick, place the handle in your lap with the stick standing straight and bristles upright. Breathe deeply and go into a light trance. Do this until your thoughts are only of calm and security in the work you are setting out to do. Rocking helps in this position, all the while holding and connecting with your tool of flight.

Notice how the tool supports itself and its symbolism and allow yourself to feel as if the broom can hover with you. Imagine the sense of weightlessness and allow yourself to sink into relaxation. Some will use a countdown system for this (I prefer to hum and rock myself into this headspace), all the while forming the idea of where you'd like to go. Could it be an underground mine, a glass hotel, or a floating castle in the sky that turns slowly by itself?

Releasing the Body: Surrendering the Outer

When you are ready, extinguish the flame and lay down with your broom next to you while remaining slightly entranced. As you lay, feel your muscles giving way and feel yourself sinking and slowly rising from where you lay. Surrender all and any bodily sensations, as these are also friendly reminders of the stillness and the relaxation you hold within. Allow that part of you that is within to rise into the air a few inches. Now you no longer actively hold this stillness but use your spiritual body to explore and express it. Visualize it and try with your mind's eye to see your spiritual body and the surroundings of your room.

Opening the Oneiric: Sleeping Sorcery

Be warned that, once you have reached this step and begin seeing outside of yourself, this is when most people startle themselves back into their physical bodies. The more you practice and can maintain outer connection, the easier this step will be to do. You may fall asleep the first few times, but practice is the key. Your spirit double calls out to the winds of flight and uses the feeling of the physical tool beside you to fall into a sleep-like state. You can use the following chant for grounding, muttering it under your breath while settling into sleep.

Ascend, Ascend, Ascend, Ascend!
To the Sabbat I attend!
I fly around the crooked bend
Until at waking is its end!

FLIGHT TINCTURE

Use a simple tincture of wormwood or mugwort together or separately. These herbs, known as *Artemisias,* are best for the workings of the moon, psychic work, and Witch-flight. They are named for Artemis due to the virtues of the herb carried from the lunar tide of power.

Choose a bottle or jar and fill it with dried herbs or the herbal combination of your choice. Cover the herbs with an alcohol that is at least 40 proof (though 80–100 proof alcohol is best). Be sure to cover the herbs completely by adding the fluid slowly. Add more of the herbs if needed. Leave it in a dry, dark place for six weeks, shaking it occasionally. You can coordinate this with the moon, waiting for two full cycles of the moon to pass.

FLIGHT INCENSE

You will need:

- 1 part Opoponax resin
- 1 part Benzoin resin
- 1 part Spearmint
- ½ part Feverfew
- ½ part Irish moss

CHAPTER NINETEEN

THE FIRST WITCH: A RITE OF VENERATION

Let us revisit the question: who initiated the first Witch? Before the time of recorded myth, there was magic, and magic lived within the body of humankind brought by she who was the first of Witches. This is a mythopoetic rite bringing in the elusive spirit of she who was the first to harness the winds and know the secret names. She holds a staff from the Tree of Knowledge, silver branched and glowing with blue light, her silhouette draped in black flowy fabric, and a torch firm in hand to light the way for the next generation. With her flowing black hair and a deep red mouth, her spirit wanders across time and place, for her job is rounding up the Witches of today back to the convening of the circle.

She finds those who have returned to this lifetime as Witches again, the people who have awakened in this incarnation, and the Witches who are yet to be. Make no mistake: she is not friendly, nor would we say she is nice. She may be known to you as the Witch of the Woods, the Gray Lady, The Woman in White, or the wailing *Bean Sidhe*.[265] Wherever there is a Witch story, the spirit of magic can't help but absorb into that landscape, leaving behind a spell, blessing, or cursing an entire bloodline or town that will still manifest after she is long gone.

Every town has its Witch stories. The Witch is one of our favorite characters to call up from the pool of memory. Growing up in Michigan,

---

265 Hutcheson, Corey T. "The Witch's Ghost- A Haunted Legacy of Magic." *New World Witchery: A Trove of North American Folk Magic*. Llewellyn Worldwide, 2021, pp. 377–390.

there was the legend of The Witch of Ada.[266] Ada Village is directly east of the city of Grand Rapids, founded in 1821 as a fur trading post and Kent County's first official settlement. The story takes place in the mid-1800s, when a woman in the village had become unfaithful to her husband. Her heart became lustful and so she began a dalliance with another man. She would go off into the woods (where Seidman Park is today) by the cover of night and meet with her lover in secret.

As time went on, her husband began to notice that his wife was not beside him in bed. Alarmed, he grew suspicious. His suspicions raised so much mental distress that some say he became noticeably changed. His skin grew pale, and his eyes were said to burn like red coals in his quiet rage. He formulated a plan to catch his wife in the act. While he was pretending to be asleep, she snuck out of bed and into the forest. He followed her, mind twisted from his jealousy.

There they were, half-undressed in an embrace upon a clearing, until the quiet of the forest was interrupted by the husband's brutal attack, first going after his unfaithful wife and killing her brutally. Then, the husband and the lover brawled. Both ended up killing each other from their extensive wounds. For generations afterward, people have experienced intense paranormal activity near what is Findlay Cemetery today, seeing a woman in a white dress wandering and wailing across the grounds. She is said to haunt in revenge for her murder. She still seeks her lost lover, and will take vengeance upon anyone in the woods, but only if you ask her to. She became a legend known as the Ada Witch as time moved on.

There are still traces of magic to follow from the mere suggestion of her. The Craft of the wise finds, catches, and sweeps us up into her domain. We can't help but be fascinated. Whether you have gone to her or she has sought you out, she offers you the gift of yourself and the liberation all that holds. Make no mistake, Witches are feared because we always have held power and influence by the very word "Witch." Whether these stories are the stuff of legend or urban myth, we find in the archetype of the First Witch, the First Teacher, and the First Initiator of the Mysteries. She is ours to claim as our guardian, guide, and patron saint of all Witches. Are you ready to meet her?

---

266 Eberle, Gary and John Layman. *Haunted Houses of Grand Rapids*. Silver Fox Publishing, 1994.

THE RITE OF THE FIRST WITCH

Acquire the following items:

- A shawl or veil: the spiritual mantle of the First Lady of Azazel (A mantle is the symbolic divine covering of our purpose, anointing, and calling to be one with the Gods. It is the bestowment of the gifts we hold as a token of our ancestral lineage tracing back to her.)
- A mask painted or designed to evoke your magical persona or inner animal under the guise of the First Witch
- Two altar candles
- Witch's cord
- Frankincense and myrrh resin incense
- Thurible and charcoal disc
- Stang
- Chalice of red wine
- Peyton or hearthstone
- Parchment paper with a declaration of "The Charge if The First Witch" written upon it in bold ink (making sure it's legible by candlelight)
- Wyitcha powder (See the recipe on page 236.)

Begin by carrying the stang. Use it to tap on the ground nine times to signify the beginning of the ritual. Place it firmly on the ground and draw up the power of the Red Serpent in Earth, the power of the land. Draw this up into the stang until the stang feels "full." Face the East and, holding the stang up in that direction, say:

I wander, I walk, I seek the One!
The one of the Night, the teacher of the many.
Grant me passage on the Eastern Road
So that the First of the covenant may come to this hallowed place!
By the Rites of the Witchblood!
So Mote It Be!

With stang still raised in hand, make your way to the South and say:

I tread, I dance, I seek the First of my kind!
The Sorceress of Legend, the Mother of kindred.
Grant me passage on the Southern Road
So that the first of the pact may come to this hallowed place!
By the rites of the Witchblood!
So Mote It Be!

Continue your progression, following through with the stang upraised to the West, say:

I step, I swim, I seek the initiator of the wise!
The brewer of secret, the root of a Pellar's power
Grant a passage on the Westward Road
So that the First of the Lightning may come to this hallowed place!
By the rites of the Witchblood!
So Mote It Be!

Walk to the North, holding up the stang, and say:

I climb, I saunter, I seek the Witch!
I Call the Witch! I awaken the Witch!
Magic's First Born, reveler in changeable delight!
Grant a passage on the North Wind's Road
So that the First of my line may come to this hallowed place!
By the rites of the Witchblood!
So Mote It Be!

Raise the stang and, once erected, make a slight bow of acknowledgment of gratitude.

Light your candles and incense to fumigate the working area with the smoke of the burning resin at each of the quarters. Take one of the candle tapers and pace around the working area in any direction you like. Loop around, zigzag, and walk restlessly, allowing yourself to fill

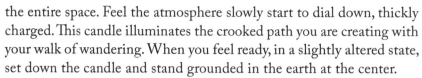
the entire space. Feel the atmosphere slowly start to dial down, thickly charged. This candle illuminates the crooked path you are creating with your walk of wandering. When you feel ready, in a slightly altered state, set down the candle and stand grounded in the earth at the center.

Place your hearthstone at the base of the stang. Take your shawl and Witch's cord. Start to wrap the cord tightly around the fabric, creating a winding effect. With each looping rotation, chant:

Loop around an' twist an' bend, Cloth I wrap, now transcend!

Take the cloth bundle wrapped with cord and make a bow knot. As you finish the tie, say:

May nothing be upon this cloth,
But the majesty of The Mantle of magic.
The threads become the music of the good folk.
The stitches become the crossways of power!
Cover and cloak me in the gifts of sorcery,
Anointed am I by ancestress's kiss,
Of all creation born out of the dark abyss.

Waft the bundle in incense smoke. Afterward, take up the mask you have fashioned and hold it up to your face, so the mask is looking back at you. Say:

Assembled am I who have been sworn to learn.
So by this mask, my spirit turns!

Untie the cloth and begin to get yourself into a very relaxed state of mind. Once you are relaxed, rock or sway steadily into a light trance. Music is recommended for this stage, as you are going to then wrap yourself in the mantle and don the mask. Allow yourself to lose yourself in the spirit of the First, what gifts she brings, and what stories she has to tell. Slowly feel yourself morphing into her image, aspecting into the spiritual form of her, with a total surrender of the ego, relaxing into the knowledge that her spirit now covers you completely and your physical senses are now, for a time, also of her own. Allow your mouth to open and her words to fall out. Vocalize and allow her to do the talking. If you feel the sensation, allow her to guide your steps. Do this until she is done with any messages, and then pick up the parchment with this charge to recite as you aspect her being.[267]

THE CHARGE OF THE FIRST WITCH

Behold Ye Shades and spirits of Earth!
For this time alone I return, as I have returned time before.
Feared and revered.
Long gone, but never dead.
I am the Witch in your head.
Old as time and forever alive
I am the Queen Bee of all hives.
From root to flower, and sky to rain
I give what you seek in the fire's name.
In the name of power, which none may know
By birch, ash, thorn, and willow!
I reside in the oaks with boughs touching down
Over my head a starry crown.
A covering of sacrifice, for the first I became.
As you too shall be, in these names…
Inanna! Ishtar! Lilitu!
These your greatest of grandmothers of mothers of mothers.
To the womb and tomb!
The Mystery am I! The Mystery are you!
This is my charge.
Send me home now child…

Slowly come back from the trance, feeling her presence leave you. Take as much time as you need to come back into your physical body.

---

267 *Aspecting* in trance means we are not fully giving up control to the spirit but can allow the spirit to guide our inner dialogue so we can exude the possession while not being completely taken over.

Take off your mask but continue to wear your mantle. Take your Wyitcha powder and say:

> *I claim the blood! I call the power back to me!*
> *In the name of the Greatest Mystery! (Throw a pinch of powder)*
> *I am the descent of hundreds upon hundreds.*
> *Witches, wise women, healers, and crones*
> *I descend from Watchers and giant's bones! (Throw another pinch)*
> *I call to the lineage of my most sacred self*
> *Of djinn, grigori, sídhe, and elf!*
> *The sons and daughters of men of renown*
> *Of mother and fathers in the ground.*
> *The powers I claim by the powder I cast*
> *From the First, and I who am last!*

Take up your chalice and pour out some red wine to offer, then make a toast to drink in silence. When you feel the energy has dissipated, pack up your altar and go forth with this renewed sense of self.

Wyitcha Powder

You will need the following ingredients to make Wyitcha powder:

- Powdered Dragon's blood resin
- Powdered patchouli leaf
- Powdered meadowsweet
- Powdered vervain
- Dust or dirt taken from a cemetery's entrance
- Crushed eggshells

This powder is used for banishing, to amplify when sprinkled or tossed over an open flame. It is best if this powder is created with a mortar and pestle, using the grinding rotations to imbue the herbals with magic. The crushing of the herbs is part of how I empower them with my charges and charms. Blend these ingredients in equal parts until combined and as fine as possible.

CHAPTER TWENTY

OPERATIVE MAGIC

HEALTHY POPPET SPELL

Create a poppet out of any type of orange, yellow, or white fabric. (Felt is my preference.) You can also use sculpted wax or clay with the oils and herbs pre-mixed. Another version of poppet making is baking flour, water, and the corresponding herbal mix to create a "bread" poppet, leaving an opening in the head where you can stuff the herbs and physical links to create an effective double of the person you are trying to affect. A link could be an artifact of that person's body, like hair, a fingernail, or a folded-up picture, their written name, date of birth, or the person's astrological sign traced on paper.

To create an herbal healing blend, you can mix the following herbs into a blend, using any amounts and proportions you feel drawn or guided to:

- Lavender
- Calendula
- St. John's wort
- White willow bark
- Eucalyptus
- Spearmint

Stuff your poppet with the herbal healing blend and seal the head shut. Devote it to become a magical double of the person by consecrating the doll with blessed water and oil. Dab a drop of these on the head, hands, feet, belly, and heart. Trace the sign of an equal-armed cross over the doll with your wand or finger, saying:

> *I consecrate you to become the body and*
> *the mind of (name of afflicted)*
> *May this poppet of cloth receive all the proper and*
> *necessary powers of healing*
> *As I work the spell!*

Using your hands, focus on your connection to the afflicted person. Project a warm or cool healing energy out of the palms of your hand. Let yourself see a golden light pouring out of your fingertips into the poppet and, thus, the person. If you don't know who they are, focus on the direction of their location. Some choose to only use magic on other people if they have permission from the person directly. Use this at your discretion, as good magic should bring good things. We work for the best result and the highest good.

Next using the wand, draw in the Solar energies of healing into the wand as you raise it towards the sky. Pull that into the poppet by tracing down to its feet, then tracing the arms to make the same cross shape. While doing this, say:

> *From head to toe, the illness goes!*
> *Healing pervades, and healing stays.*
> *(Name) is healthy for all their days!*

Light a loose incense composed of vervain, frankincense, and rosemary. Get the incense burning in a thurible or brazier with a charcoal disc. Now pick the poppet up gently, as it holds the person you are healing. Some Witches will sing to the poppet to soothe the person's energy. I employ using a rattle over the doll, visualizing the person doing activities they love to do while in the best shape of health. Hold the doll and start to rock yourself into a light trance. Repeat over and over again:

> *(Name) is healed!*

Use a diluted cinnamon oil to anoint the poppet on the part of the body that is ailing. Cinnamon is fiery and works quickly, as it is ruled by the Sun.[268]

In the name of Sol, the illuminating Sun!
By the balance within, this spell be done!
So Mote It Be!

Keep the poppet wrapped in silk or cloth to protect the spell and place it where it won't be found or disturbed. In one moon cycle, there should be a noticeable change in the person's health. When the spell is complete, wave your hand over it with a swiping motion as if you were sweeping away the magic that has done its job. (I like to think of this as wiping off a chalkboard.) Thank the poppet in a formal statement of intent, saying the charm below:

By rites that have ended and needed no more, return, return!
I thank thee for thy service now Depart! Depart! Depart!

Afterward, clap your hands together and shake off the energy like it's water.

THE WITCH BOTTLE

This was one of the most well-known spells of protection in Indo-European societies originating all over Europe and filtering into the British Isles. The bottle's oldest known purpose was for protection and counter-working baneful magic or to trap negative energies inside the bottle. Traditionally, its contents are iron nails or bent pins, salt, broken glass, and bodily fluids like urine or feces (only if you want to get down and dirty with it).[269]

---

268 You can also use the pin method by pinning the part of the body that needs to be healed, using the needle to drive the healing power into that specific part of the body.

269 Burns, William E. *They Believed That? A Cultural Encyclopedia of Superstitions and the Supernatural Around the World.* Bloomsbury Publishing, 2022, p. 83.

The bottle can be used to manifest several spells, depending on the intention and corresponding herbs, resins, fluids, and objects inside the bottle. The bottle would then be buried or kept in the walls of the home. A Witch's bottle lasts forever, or until its seal is broken!

First, you need to choose your bottle and its contents. Close the bottle and hold it with force, concentrating your power into the bottle as a corresponding brilliant-colored light . For example, a soft yellow or golden light is of the Sun and generates health. Red light is active, powerful, and used for protection, and green can help someone attract luck, love, or luxury. Next, clearly say your spell or prayer. Keep the bottle in a safe place where it will be undisturbed or, in the best case scenario, bury the bottle in the Earth.

Here are a few examples of Witch bottles for different situations:

- Neutralize Harm: write down the situation or name of the person causing the harm and add it to the jar, alongside herbs like lemongrass or sage. Make sure to bury it *off* your property and far away from you!
- Protection: write down what you are protecting, whether that be yourself or something valuable. Add pins, iron shavings, nails, or broken glass, and herbs like nettles, oak, black salt, or juniper berries. It's best to bury this bottle.
- Luck: write the matters you need a boost of luck in. Add herbs like clover, wormwood, and star anise.

To activate the bottle with your power, say:

> *A blessed bottle of magic's might*
> *I charge you with my power tonight!*
> *To grant me this thing, I ask, I pray*
> *By the Sun and Moon, I have my say!*
> *So Mote It Be!*

NAILS ON THE HEARTH

Acquire four large railway spikes or nails. Charge them with protection using your athame, saying:

Nails of Iron, nails I select
Protect! Protect! Protect! Protect!

Tie a red ribbon or thread around each nail. This is the virtue of Mars and its lively color of protection, will, and strength. As you tie the thread, say:

Power of Mars, iron red
Protect me from what lies ahead!

Plant the four nails at the four corners of your property line by driving them into the ground with a hammer. While you pound them into the ground one by one, feel and sense the energetic barrier around your home, and seal your spell with a simple statement:

So Be It!

FLAME AND NETTLES

All this spell requires is a candle, a thurible or cauldron, and a charcoal disc. Nettles sting, so be sure to wear gloves while handling them. Light your charcoal disc and allow it to heat up. Drop a handful of nettles on the charcoal and allow them to fumigate. Speak your spell into the smoke to bring in protection.

Next, inscribe any symbol of protection upon a black candle. This could be a pentacle or a design of your own making. Light the candle and allow the light to pierce the veil of the spirit world. As the candle burns, the spell takes hold.

Take the candlelight to windows, door frames, mirrors, and corners. These are the spots where energy will often stick or enter. Make sure these areas are touched by the light of the candle to seal up your home. Meditate upon the flame and see yourself being covered with protection, if this is for yourself, and pass the flame over your entire body (especially the eyes, ears, throat, and heart).

WITCH BALLS

Wards are specific protections that block the flow of malefic and baneful energies; the act of using wards is often called "warding." Wards have to be updated regularly and charged so they continue to work. The upkeep of the spiritual care of the wards is essential to the spiritual hygiene of the home. Wards can be symbols on a piece of paper that you post at certain points of the home and renew them with a freshly drawn symbol. Wards can also take the shape of any charmed object that is kept in the home to avert evil.

Witch balls are round glass spheres that are made from colored blown glass and have been used as wards since the seventeenth century.[270] They are hollow and hung in the home to avert the evil eye, reflect harm, and catch pesky and annoying spirits in the ball so they can't do any more mischief. One theory about how the ball works was that spirits would be enticed by the shiny color of the glass and be too distracted to do anything else. You can often find them today in garden centers, antique shops, and several Occult shops.

In American Ozark folk magic, the Witch ball takes a completely different form as a sinister working. Beeswax rolled in horse, dog, or black hair would be rolled into a pellet and used as a marble to throw at the intended target. This was said to bring misfortune, disease, and even death.[271]

MADAME MONEY'S MAGNET SPELL

Don't bother attempting money magic if you haven't done the practical work of applying to jobs, setting a budget, and making sure your approach is always with an attitude of gratitude to fill that hole of lack. This internal sense of worthiness is for you and nobody else, and is where prosperity

270 Davies, Owen and Ceri Houlbrook. *Building Magic: Ritual and Re-enchantment in Post-Medieval Structures.* Springer International Publishing, 2021, pp. 65–72.

271 Davies, Owen. *America Bewitched: The Story of Witchcraft After Salem.* Oxford University Press, 2013, pp. 31–33.

work truly starts. This spell, provided by my friend Thora, is an excellent prosperity spell she came up with for me to share here.

Madame Money is known by another name and that is Fortuna, the Goddess of wealth and fortune! You will need:

- Either a gold or green candle
- Two coins of your choice that are the same size
- Goldenseal
- Mustard seeds
- Cinquefoil

Goldenseal is expensive and often hard to come by in your local apothecaries or metaphysical shops. It has a rich earthy scent and resembles gold. Mustard seeds have long been used in magic for increasing and growing prosperity, but cinquefoil, also known by its folk name *five-finger grass,* is the main herb that makes this spell sing. The herb is shaped like a hand, so it acts as an extra hand to grab new opportunities of wealth your way.

Take a coin in each hand and raise them to the sky palms up, declaring to the Gods:

Oh Ye Providers and Watchers of old,
grant me riches and grant me gold
Touch the coins that they may attract!
To fill my need for this thing I lack!
May this be for the highest good of my life!
May the vaults of wealth be open!

Crush the herbs as finely as possible in a mortar and pestle while chanting the name of Fortuna, envisioning yourself what it would feel like to have that money. Use all of your senses: see the money, feel and taste the money. There is no need to inscribe or anoint the candle as you are going to be melting the wax. You can also melt down a crayon for this spell. Drip your candle wax on the coins while adding the herbal dust to it, building layer upon layer on each coin. Once they are completely coated in the wax, seal the two coins together so they become one. Add another layer of wax so they don't separate from each other. As you stick the coins together, say:

One is two, as the two are one
Bless this magnet for the wealth I've spun!
Coins of attraction, riches of the grove
Come to me now, a treasure trove!
In Fortuna's name, So Be It!

THE ENVELOPE PETITION

This was the first spell I remember learning. I use it very sparingly, as it has proven to work consistently every time for me. You will need the following:

- Sheet of paper
- Blue taper candle
- One shiny dime
- Peppermint oil

Write out the exact amount of money you need on the paper. Specificity is the key to this spell. Fold the paper three times towards you, flipping it clockwise at a ninety-degree angle and folding it three times again towards yourself. Take your candle and, using the shiny dime, carve the planetary symbol of Jupiter. Anoint this candle in peppermint oil, starting at the center of the candle and pulling the oil down towards you. Flip the candle and do this again, bringing the oil toward you. Light the candle and say:

Jupiterian power! Hear this plea!
Money I want, money I need, money come
So Mote It Be!

Use the melting wax to create a wax seal on the paper fold to keep it closed shut. Set the candle on top of the petition and allow it to burn down completely. Put the envelope in a place where you may forget about it. This spell has worked in a matter of days for me, usually in the form of strange coincidences: receiving a raise, bonus pay, or finding extra cash lying around.

SELF-COMPASSION SPELL

When you are casting any love spell, you are primarily working on yourself so that you become a magnet to attract the right people. If there is somebody specific in mind you wish to attract, this can be done but with greater risk of natural consequences. You may not end up wanting that person, and the last thing we need is to feel stuck in a relationship. By using love spells on yourself, you are nudging to communicate to the world that you are open to giving and receiving love freely.

Self-love is different from self-esteem, and self-esteem is different from self-compassion. Self-esteem is tied into our work, it's what we *do*. Self-compassion, on the other hand, is the proactive practice of creating a haven for ourselves that dissolves self-judgment, which tends to distort our thoughts and perspectives. Self-compassion is how we achieve the state of self-love. It is the core building block of healthy emotional regulation, starting with the recognition that we are worthy to accept our internal suffering, but can release the self-criticism that comes with that.

Begin by making a jasmine tea infusion. Allow your kettle to come to a boil while you bless your tea blend:

By the power I cast, that stirs the blood
I infuse compassion in this jasmine bud.
Quenched by the water brought to a boil
May this tea soothe and clear the toil!
Relax and fill with thoughts pure and good
For I adore my personhood.
I charge this tea to serve me well
In the Goddess's name, I cast my spell!
So Be it!

Stir in honey to taste while reciting:

In the name of Diana's lunar crest
May this potion now be blessed!
May I sip this brew, with honey-sweet
The chaff now divides from wheat!

Stir your tea, invoking compassionate thoughts for yourself. See if you can manage to say three nice things that you like about yourself. Is difficult to do? This can be a helpful inspection of the shadow self to find the blocks you may need to work through. Sip your tea at your altar and feel the infusion work its spell.

LOVERS TALISMAN FOR ROMANCE AND PARTNERSHIP

Find the reddest apple you can find without any blemishes on the skin. Take it to your peyton or hearthstone and cut the apple in half horizontally, revealing the five-seed core in the shape of a star. Do this while enchanting it with the following spell:

> *By my will, I make a swift slice*
> *This apple brings me a lover to entice!*
> *Work for me! Fruit of the Venus's Eye*
> *This spell of love I now apply!*

Take a square of parchment paper and inscribe the talisman as pictured:

Fold the talisman three times and place it between the two apple halves, using a skewer to keep the two halves together and drive your intent into the apple. Bury on your property, and in three moon cycles, your love will find you.

SEXY NIGHT SPELL

Find a place like a busy street or sidewalk with a lot of foot traffic and throw a handful of lust powder. Ideally, the person we would find most desirable would be influenced by stepping on this powder we have cast. We can also cast powders in the cardinal directions by calling on the winds to blow where an attractive target is. As you make this powder, make a mental list of all of the features and qualities you find attractive. Talk to the powder as if it was your matchmaker! Give them all the specifics with no shame.

To make the lust powder, crush all of the following ingredients to the same consistency, as finely as possible, with your mortar and pestle.

- 3 parts damiana
- 2 parts red sandalwood powder
- 2 parts Dragon's blood resin
- 2 parts star anise
- 2 parts lily of the valley
- 1 part clove
- 1 part cinnamon
- 1 part fenugreek

MALEFICA

There are bullies, liars, and abusers in the world. Some people will stop at nothing to damage our sense of self-worth and actively cause us harm. When our society and our legal systems fail the people, we as magical people have always turned to the powers of banishment, binding, and blasting. *Karma* is an interesting buzzword that has popped up in metaphysical and Witchcraft spaces in this manner. However, it's borrowed from an Eastern philosophy that has absolutely nothing to do with the older forms of Witchcraft.

It just isn't true that there is a complete absence of curses and hexes in Witchcraft, especially when you look at the vast amount of history and folklore that says otherwise. Practitioners who know their history are pragmatic with this. Most of these New Age concepts have never been part of the Traditional Witch's worldview. This can be partially due to what's known as *the rede*. The rede itself is simply "harm none do what ye will."[272] It was written by Doreen Valiente, and later adapted by Lady Gwen Thompson.[273] As a rede, it's just advice, not a law. Things like the rede and the threefold law don't speak universally for Witches, and the rede is not a part of several traditions that have been around a lot longer than even Crowley's original poetic verse: "Do What Ye Will Be the Whole of the Law."[274]

Spells of this nature are predominant in marginalized, enslaved, and oppressed communities for obvious reasons. This is a way to fight back, protest, and get shit done. In this way, malefica is just another side of protection magic and a form of self-defense. It has been a conversation for a long time in magical spaces, and it still needs to be a conversation because it's *important* and part of our history as Witches. There is a difference between magical self-defense and actively laying a trick on someone because we have an ego problem.

I have organized the following set of spells in the order of situational emphasis. The last few are extreme and are rarely ever used. If the circumstance justifies getting the spirit's attention to point them in the direction of an enemy, then so be it! Consult your oracles and have at it, but only if you are willing to take the risks of cause and effect. Here are just a few rules to keep in mind.

You must cleanse your space thoroughly before *and* after. You must have personal protections and shields up while doing these kinds of workings, not just around you but also in your immediate space. You should never discuss or make it known that you do these kinds of spells, as it's still not entirely safe to be a Witch today with this affiliation. Even today, the public may accuse modern-day practitioners over circumstances people can have no real control or effect over. I've been accused of spells

---

272 Valiente, Doreen. "The Wiccan Rede: A Historical Journey." *Witchcraft for Tomorrow*. Robert Hale. 1978, pp. 72–74.

273 Mathiesen, Robert. *Rede of the Wiccae*. Witches' Almanac Limited, 2006.

274 Crowley, Aleister and Rose Edith. *The book of the law, Liber al vel Legis, with a facsimile of the manuscript as received by Aleister and Rose Edith Crowley on April 8, 9, 10, 1904*. Weiser Books, 2004. See Chapter One, verse 40.

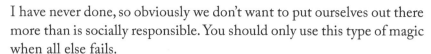

I have never done, so obviously we don't want to put ourselves out there more than is socially responsible. You should only use this type of magic when all else fails.

You should also keep in mind to never cast out of uncontrolled emotions, like unhealthy anger, for instance. This work is only effective if you approach it calmly, focused, and fully in control. Think of this like dealing with big corporations (that's very much how this operates from my perspective). Lastly, any spell remains must be removed and placed off your property. I have a friend who has a dark altar in the woodland swap far behind his house for this reason. You just don't want that negative frequency around you longer than it has to be. This is *dirty* work, after all.

BELL, BOOK, AND CANDLE

This is a rite of banishment. Interestingly enough, the saying "bell, book, and candle" originates with the Catholic Church as a form of excommunication. The association with heretics is what lent it to be known as a witchy phrase an even better film from 1958.[275] It's best to call upon the land spirits before this, as they tend to be responsive to these requests in times of need, especially if the situation or enemy threatens the land.

You will need the following:

- A bell or chime that has a good tone
- A piece of parchment paper cut into a square
- A black taper candle
- Salt
- Dried rue wrapped into a saining bundle

Start by creating a mental image of who or what you are banishing. As you hold this image, create a ring of salt and place the black candle

---

275 *Bell, Book and Candle*. Directed by Richard Quine and George Duning. Columbia Pictures, 1958.

in the middle of it. Once the candle is charged as the representation, the salt around any representation is an immediate neutralizer of ill will coming from that person, place, or thing. You can inscribe the candle with an X, a zero with a line through it, or a small arrow that points the power into the ground, so it becomes one with the Earth again, back to the sublunar realm. Some Witches will collect water from thunderstorms and use it to wash the candle with this high frequency of power. The water, of course, brings in a storm to keep away the target.

Write the following words on the parchment:

Expel, exile, eject!
Repel, remove, repulse!
Relego in nomine inferno!

Allow the words of power to be your guide as you send the mental image of your situation dissolving and being removed. Focus on the final result of the banishment: not how it will happen, but that it *will* happen. Recite the words from the parchment while fixating your focus on the candle flame once lit. Take up your rue bundle and hold it to the flame, allowing it to fumigate. Allow the smoke to be added to the banishment work. As you burn the herb, the plant ally is released into the air to go off into the world and do your bidding.

Once there is very little candle left, recite the chant once more, but this time, intone each word as strongly and slowly as possible. Before and after each word, ring the bell three times. The sound not only forces the influences away but can also act as a vibration used to torment. Repeating bell ringing can be very interrupting and annoying and that is exactly the point.

Conclude the banishment with the following verse while tracing a banishing pentagram with your athame. Start from the bottom left point of the star, stating:

Banishment! Spirits of the Inferno!
Catch wickedness and evil of this land
Take away (the target) by this command!
Cast in the power of the Will by my hand.
Away it is and banished shall it be
Granting a life of peace and serenity!

"PIN 'EM DOWN"

Binding is considered a type of curse because, even though you are protecting a person or situation from harming themselves (and, more importantly, others), you are still taking away their free will and exerting control over the person. To take on the role of the target, you will need a picture, a physical link, or a black figure candle. It's also necessary to have black-headed pins, black thread or ribbon, and a good amount of sulfur. If you want to incorporate a magical root to add, find yourself some calamus root. This plant has been long held in tradition for commanding and compelling everything to the Witch's willpower. Take up your link and consecrate it with your athame as that person or situation. Place your blade on the object and say:

This which harms, that will hurt,
Upon ye I catch, I bind, I assert!
Pinned to the station, that I direct
My spell upon thee I intersect!

Sprinkle the sulfur on the link while saying:

Flesh to bone! Encased in brimstone! May the truth be shown!

If you are using the calamus root, take this up next. Silently tap the root three times and whisper the name of your target while saying:

Bind…bind…bind!

Take up your black pins and stick nine pins into your artifact at every point you can find. This keeps them stuck. Take up your black ribbon and wind it around the link tightly with aggressive force. Create as many knots as possible and wrap it until the artifact is covered completely. When this is done, make a statement of separation to the object that you will no longer engage with them for as long as they are bound. Express out loud any unresolved feelings, and don't hold anything back.

Keep this concealed in a small box if you plan to reverse the binding at some point. It's best to keep it in a low-profile location. If you've set a time limit on how long the binding will last, then you can dispose of the spell artifacts at a crossroads or off your property.

HEXENSCHALE OR WITCH BOWL

This method levels up from binding to a hex.

Take a clay terracotta pot or a clay bowl. Using black ink, write your enemy's name backwards and forwards. Add any appropriate symbols or specifics of what exactly you want the effect to be to the writing. For example, you can destroy someone's finances by writing a negative sum of money, or you can break up a relationship with the symbol of a broken heart. Once this is done, find a dark and secret place at night. The best locations are a three-way crossroads, cliff tops, and swamps. Speak the spell, and then break the bowl with all of your force and intent.

Spirits hidden, full of woe!
Attend the bowl
By this hex, I throw!

THE TWISTED TREE SPELL

This hex not only removes an enemy, but also ensures the scales of justice have been balanced in your favor. You will need to acquire either clothing or fabric your target has made physical contact with. If you can't get access to a link, then take a square of fabric and consecrate it as your target with charged water and oil.

Take this artifact and dip it in bleach or urine. Go to a tree with large, twisted roots that get lots of Sun exposure facing the East. Approach the tree and ask permission if it will take on your enemy. After it permits (in feeling or divination), tack or staple the artifact to the tree stretching out the artifact tight and taut. Make sure that the artifact will get as much light exposure from the rising Sun as possible, fading the fabric over time. Speak the spell and then leave, never looking back:

As this tree twists and turns
The Sun upon it burns and burns!
Fade and fade, disintegrate!
By this hex, I create!

PLAGUED MIND SPELL

Cursing is the last resort. Use these spells with the utmost caution.

Carve a small hole out of an onion. This needs to be big enough for a small slip of paper to be placed inside. Write out a specific intrusive thought for your target to suffer with and bury the onion, saying:

As this onion rots
So do your dreams, hopes, and desires!

THE MALLUM

Go to your local butcher and purchase a cow heart. Go to the woods in a location where you will have access to a fire, taking a flask of vinegar, two large rusty nails, and the following cursing blend with you:

Valerian root
Cat's claw
Cayenne pepper
Sulfur

Start a fire and begin muttering as many curse words as possible under your breath as the flames grow to a flickering dance. Allow the swearing to build the energy as you roll the heart in the cursing blend mixture, while fixating upon the mental image of your target.

Take the two nails and drive them into the heart. Cover the heart in vinegar while thinking in your head over and over again:

"I sour you, you evil (expletive of your choice)!"

Say the person's name and declare them as the target. Be specific and deliberate with your words. Once completed, build up energy by walking and pacing widdershins until the momentum feels right to propel the heart into the fire. Watch the heart burn in the flames and don't leave until the heart burns completely. Leave no traces you were ever there and thank the land spirits for their allowance of such a rite on their land. Leave and never look back or return to this place ever again.

BIBLIOGRAPHY

Adler, Margot. *Drawing Down the Moon: Witches, Druids, Goddess-Worshippers, and Other Pagans in America Today.* Beacon Press, 1986.

Aitchison, N.B. "Kingship, Society, and Sacrality: Rank, Power, and Ideology in Early Medieval Ireland." *Traditio*, vol. 49, 1994, pp. 45–75. doi:10.1017/S036215290001299X.

Albright, *William F. Yahweh and the Gods of Canaan: A Historical Analysis of Two Contrasting Faiths.* Athlone Press, 1968.

Aldred, Cyril. *The Egyptians.* Thames and Hudson, 1988.

Ankarloo, Bengt and Stuart Clark. *Witchcraft and Magic in Europe: Ancient Greece and Rome.* University of Pennsylvania Press, 1999.

Aristotle and H. Rackham. *The Nicomachean Ethics.* Harvard University Press, 2003.

Athanasakēs, Apostolos N. and Benjamin M. Wolkow. *The Orphic Hymns.* Johns Hopkins University Press, 2013.

Baigent, Michael. *From the Omens of Babylon: Astrology and Ancient Mesopotamia.* Arkana, 1994.

Barret, Francis. *The Magus.* 1801.

Bates, Douglas C. "The Forgotten Delphic Maxim." Medium, 24 Mar, 2021, pyrrhonism.medium.com/the-forgotten-delphic-maxim-e4f-b640cc4e5. Accessed 28 Feb. 2024.

Beaulieu, Paul-Alain. The Pantheon of Uruk During the Neo-Babylonian Period. Brill, 2003.

Bede the Venerable Saint. *Ecclesiastical History of the English People; with Bede's Letter to Egbert.* Penguin, 1990.

"Bell, Book and Candle." Directed by Richard Quine, performances by James Steward and Kim Novak, Columbia Pictures, 1958.

Berlin, Andrea. "The Archaeology of Ritual: The Sanctuary of Pan at Banias/Caesarea Philippi." *Bulletin of the American Schools of Oriental Research*, no. 315, 1999, pp. 27–45. doi:10.2307/1357531.

Best, Kenneth and Mitchell S. Green. *Know Thyself: The Philosophy of Self-Knowledge*. UConn Today, 2018.

Boccaccini, Gabriele and John Joseph Collins. *The Early Enoch Literature*. Brill, 2007.

"Book of Shadows." *Salem*. Written by Brannon Braga, Adam Simon, and Joe Menosky, created by Adam Simon, Fox 21 Television Studios, 2015.

Brannen, Cyndi. "Hekate Enodia: Goddess of the Road (Recorded Class)." Keeping Her Keys, 6 Aug. 2022, keepingherkeys.com/home/f/hekate-enodia-goddess-of-the-road-recorded-class. Accessed 28 Feb. 2024.

Brink, Nicholas E. *The Power of Ecstatic Trance: Practices for Healing, Spiritual Growth, and Accessing the Universal Mind*. Bear & Co, 2013.

Burkert, Walter. *Greek Religion*. Harvard University Press, 1985.

Burns, William E. *They Believed That? A Cultural Encyclopedia of Superstitions and the Supernatural Around the World*. Bloomsbury Publishing, 2022.

Burrows, Millar. *The Dead Sea Scrolls*. Gramercy Pub. Co., 1986

Charles, R.H. (trans.) *The Book of Enoch*. The Society for Promoting Christian Knowledge, 1917.

Christ, Rachel. "The 17th Century World of Witchcraft." Salem Witch Museum, 23 Aug. 2022, salemwitchmuseum.com/2021/12/17/the-17th-century-world-of-witchcraft/. Accessed 28 Feb. 2024.

Chumbley, Andrew D. *The Azoetia: A Grimoire of the Sabbatic Craft*. Xoanon Publishers, 1992.

Clarke, David and Andy Roberts. *Twilight of the Celtic Gods: An Exploration of Britain's Hidden Pagan Traditions*. Blanford Press, 1996.

Collins, Andrew. *From the Ashes of Angels: The Forbidden Legacy of a Fallen Race*. Inner Traditions, 2007.

Crowley, Aleister and Rose Edith. *The Book of the Law, Liber al vel Legis*. Weiser Books, 2004.

Crowley, Aleister. *Liber XV. (Liber 15) The Gnostic Mass*. Universal, 1919. https://www.sacred-texts.com/oto/lib15.htm. Accessed 28 Feb. 2024.

—. *Magic in Theory and Practice*. Dover Publications, 1929.

Davies, Owen. *America Bewitched: The Story of Witchcraft After Salem*. Oxford University Press, 2013.

Davies, Owen and Ceri Houlbrook. *Building Magic: Ritual and Re-enchantment in Post-Medieval Structures*. Springer International Publishing, 2021.

Day, John. *Yahweh and the Gods and Goddesses of Canaan*. Sheffield Academic Press, 2002.

Deerman, Dixie and Steve Rasmussen. *The Goodly Spellbook: Olde Spells for Modern Problems*. Sterling Publishing Co., 2008.

De Laurence, L.W. *The Lesser Key of Solomon, Goetia: The Book of Evil Spirits*. Scott & Co., 1916.

De Vries, Eric. *Hedge-Rider: Witches and the Underworld*. Pendraig Publishing, 2008.

Dieter Betz, Hans (ed.). *The Greek Magical Papyri in Translation, Including the Demotic Spells, Volume 1*. University of Chicago Press, 1986.

Dronke, Ursula. *The Poetic Edda*. Oxford University Press, 2011.

Durrant, Jonathan and Michael D. Bailey. *Historical Dictionary of Witchcraft*. Scarecrow Press, 2012.

Earth Magic Video. Alexandrian Witchcraft Timeline and Archive, 1988. https://alexandrianwitchcraft.org/earth-magic-video/.

Eberle, Gary and John Layman. *Haunted Houses of Grand Rapids*. Silver Fox Publishing, 1994.

Edmonds, R. G. *Drawing Down the Moon: Magic in the Ancient Greco-Roman World*. Princeton University Press, 2019.

Faerywolf, Storm. *Betwixt & Between: Exploring the Faery Tradition of Witchcraft*. Llewellyn Publications, 2017.

Fort, Charles. *Wild Talents*. Baen Books, 1932.

Foxwell Albright, William. *Yahweh and the Gods of Canaan: A Historical Analysis of Two Contrasting Faiths*. Athlone Press, 1968.

Frazer, J. G. *The Golden Bough*. Macmillan, 1966.

Farrar, Janet and Stewart. *Eight Sabbats for Witches, Revised Edition*. Phoenix Publishing, 1988.

Gardner, Gerald. *The Meaning of Witchcraft*. Red Wheel/Weiser, 2004.

—. *Witchcraft Today*. Citadel Press, 2004.

Gary, Gemma, and Jane Cox. *Traditional Witchcraft: A Cornish Book of Ways*. Troy Books, 2008.

Gilmore, David D. *The Trotula: A Medieval Compendium of Women's Medicine*. University of Pennsylvania Press, 2001.

Ginzburg, Carlo. *The Night Battles: Witchcraft & Agrarian Cults in The Sixteenth & Seventeenth Centuries*. Routledge, 2015.

Goodman, Felicitas D. and Gerhard Binder. *Where the Spirits Ride the Wind: Trance Journeys and Other Ecstatic Experiences.* Indiana Univ. Press, 1989.

Goswami, H. D. "The Etymology of the Word 'God.'" H. D. Goswami, 16 Aug. 2011, hdgoswami.com/the-etymology-of-the-word-god/. Accessed 28 Feb. 2024.

Graves, Robert. *The White Goddess: A Historical Grammar of Poetic Myth.* Straus and Giroux, 1948.

Grey, Peter. *Lucifer: Princeps.* Scarlet Imprint, 2015.

Grimassi, Raven. *Hereditary Witchcraft: Secrets of the Old Religion.* Llewellyn, 1999.

Guiley, Rosemary. *The Encyclopedia of Witches, Witchcraft and Wicca.* Facts On File, 2010.

Gwynn, Edward (trans.). *The Metrical Dindshenchas.* School of Celtic Studies, 1991.

Harper, Douglas. "Etymology of *dyeu-." Online Etymology Dictionary, https://www.etymonline.com/word/*dyeu-. Accessed 28 Feb. 2024.

Heide, Eldar. "Spinning Seidr." *Old Norse Religion in Long-Term Perspectives: Origins, Changes, and Interactions.* Nordic Academic Press, 2004.

—. *Gand, Seid og åndevind.* University of Bergen, 2006.

Henningsen, Gustav. "The Witches' Flying and the Spanish Inquisitors, or How to Explain (Away) the Impossible." *Folklore*, vol. 120, no. 1, 2009, pp. 57–74. doi:10.1080/00155870802647833.

Hirschman, Jack (trans.) and Johann Maier. T*he Book of Noah: Also Called the Book of the Mystery from the Book of Raziel.* Tree Books, 1975.

Hodgart, John and Martin Clarke. *Bessie Dunlop: Witch of Dalry.* Hodder & Stoughton, 1995.

Howard, Michael. *By Moonlight and Spirit Flight: The Praxis of the Other-worldly Journey to the Witches' Sabbath.* Three Hands Press, 2019.

—. *Children of Cain: A Study of Modern Traditional Witches.* Three Hands Press, 2011.

—. *Modern Wicca: A History from Gerald Gardner to the Present.* Llewellyn Worldwide, 2010.

—. *Liber Nox: A Traditional Witch's Gramarye.* Skylight Press, 2014.

Howard, Michael and D. A. Schulke. *The Luminous Stone: Lucifer in Western Esotericism.* Three Hands Press, 2016.

Hughes, Sarah. "American Monsters: Tabloid Media and the Satanic Panic, 1970–2000." *Journal of American Studies*, vol. 51, no. 3, 2016. doi:10.1017/s0021875816001298.

Huson, Paul. *Mastering Witchcraft: A Practical Guide for Witches, Warlocks, and Covens.* G.P. Putnams, 1970.

Hutcheson, Corey Thomas. *New World Witchery: A Trove of North American Folk Magic.* Llewellyn, 2021.

Hutton, Ronald. "Finding a Language." *The Triumph of the Moon.* Oxford University Press, 2019, pp.1–34.

—. *Pagan Britain.* Yale University Press, 2022.

—. *The Triumph of the Moon.* Oxford University Press, 2019.

"Inana's Descent to the Nether World: Translation." Electronic Text Corpus of Sumerian Literature, 2000, http://etcsl.orinst.ox.ac.uk/section1/tr141.htm. Accessed 28 Feb. 2024.

IndyBabalon. "Faces of the Holly King." Crossroads Coven, 4 Dec. 2011, crossroadscoven.wordpress.com/2011/12/04/faces-of-the-holly-king/. Accessed 28 Feb. 2024.

Jackson, Nigel and Michael Howard. *The Pillars of Tubal-Cain.* Capall Bann Publishing, 2000.

Johnston, Sarah Iles. *Ancient Religions.* Belknap Press of Harvard University Press, 2004.

Jones, Evan John and Doreen Valiente. *Witchcraft: A Tradition Renewed.* Robert Hale, 1999.

Jones, Prudence and Nigel Pennick. *A History of Pagan Europe.* Routledge, 1997.

Jordan, Michael. The Historical Mary: Revealing the Pagan Identity of the Virgin Mother. Ulysses Press, 2003.

Jung, Carl. *Memories, Dreams, Reflections.* Vintage Books, 1989.

Kelly, Henry. "Hebrew Backgrounds." *Satan: A Biography.* Cambridge University Press, 2007.

King, Graham. The British Book of Spells & Charms: A Compilation of Traditional Folk Magic. Llewellyn Worldwide, 2020.

King, Kimball, and Brett Rogers. *Western Drama Through the Ages.* Greenwood Press, 2007.

Laycock, Donald C. *The Complete Enochian Dictionary: A Dictionary of the Angelic Language as Revealed to Dr. John Dee and Edward Kelley.* Red Wheel/Weiser, 2023.

Lecouteux, Claude. *Phantom Armies of the Night: The Wild Hunt and Ghostly Processions of the Undead.* Inner Traditions, 2011.

—. *Witches, Werewolves, and Fairies: Shapeshifters and Astral Doubles in the Middle Ages.* Inner Traditions, 2003.

Leland, Charles Godfrey. *Aradia or the Gospel of the Witches*. Samuel Weiser, 1974.

—. *Legends of Florence*. MacMillan and Co., 1895.

—. *Etruscan Roman Remains*. Routledge, 2002.

Levack, Brian. *The Witchcraft Sourcebook*. Routledge, 2015.

—. The Witch-Hunt in Early Modern Europe. Taylor and Francis, 2013.

Lewis, C.S. *Prince Caspian*. HarperCollins, 1951.

Levack, Brian. *Demonology, Religion, and Witchcraft: New Perspectives on Witchcraft, Magic, and Demonology*. Taylor and Francis, 2001.

Long, Natalie (Glaux). "Hecate." *American Folkloric Witchcraft*, 29 Mar. 2013, afwcraft.blogspot.com/2013/03/hecate.html. Accessed 28 Feb. 2024.

Lumpkin, Joseph B. *The Books of Enoch: The Angels, the Watchers, and the Nephilim, with Extensive Commentary on the Three Books of Enoch, The Fallen Angels, the Calendar of Enoch, and Daniel's Prophecy*. Fifth Estate Publishers, 2015.

Luppius, A. Arbatel: De Magia Veterum. 1575.

Macalister, Stewart, Robert Alexander, and John Carey. *Lebor Gabála Érenn: The Book of the Taking of Ireland*. Irish Texts Society, 2009.

MacGregor Mathers, S.L et. al. *The Greater Key of Solomon: The Grimoire of Solomon*. 1888.

Macquire, Kelly. "The Minoans & Mycenaeans: Comparison of Two Bronze Age Civilisations." *World History Encyclopedia*, 4 Sept. 2020. www.worldhistory.org/article/1610/the-minoans--mycenaeans-comparison-of-two-bronze-a. Accessed 28 Feb. 2024.

Magliocco, Sabina. *Who Was Aradia? The History and Development of a Legend.* Pomegranate, 2001.

Magliocco, Sabina and Ronald Hutton. "Aradia in Sardinia: The Archaeology of a Folk Character." In Dave Evans and Dave Green (eds.), *Ten Years of Triumph of the Moon*. Hidden Publishing, 2009.

Mankey, Jason. *The Horned God of the Witches*. Llewellyn Publications, 2021.

—. *Transformative Witchcraft*. Llewellyn Publications, 2019.

Mathiesen, Robert. *Rede of the Wiccae*. Witches' Almanac Limited, 2006.

Mayani, Z. *The Etruscans Begin to Speak*. Simon & Schuster, 1963.

"Meeting the Goddess of Consciousness, Sally Kempton." YouTube, YouTube, 11 Feb. 2016, www.youtube.com/watch?v=MPYhEyIjFrM. Accessed 28 Feb. 2024.

Meisner, Dwayne A. *Orphic Traditions and the Birth of the Gods*. Oxford University Press, 2018.

Mengoni, L. (ed.) *Aradia, il Vangelo delle streghe di Charles Leland.* Firenze: Olschki, 1999.

Michelet, Jules. *Légendes démocratiques du Nord; La sorcière.* Ernest Flammarion, 1895.

Murray, Margaret Alice. *Witch-Cult in Western Europe: A Study in Anthropology (Classic Reprint).* Forgotten Books, 2022.

Nethersole, Scott. *Art and Violence in Early Renaissance Florence.* Yale University, 2018.

Newman, Sharan. *The Real History Behind the Templars.* Berkley Books, 2007.

Nissinen, Martti and Risto Uro. *Sacred Marriages the Divine-Human Sexual Metaphor from Sumer to Early Christianity.* Eisenbrauns, 2008.

Ó hÓgáin, Dáithí. *Myth, Legend & Romance: An Encyclopedia of the Irish Folk Tradition.* Prentice Hall Press, 1991.

Oates, Shani and Evan John Jones. *The Star Crossed Serpent.* Mandrake of Oxford, 2012.

O'Donnell, James Joseph. *Pagans: The End of Traditional Religion and the Rise of Christianity.* HarperCollins Publishers, 2016.

Pausanias, *Description of Greece.*

Paxson, Diana L. *The Way of the Oracle: Recovering the Practices of the Past to Find the Answers Today.* Red Wheel/Weiser, 2012.

Pearson, Nigel G. *Treading the Mill: Workings in Traditional Witchcraft.* Troy Books, 2017.

Penczak, Christopher. *The Gates of Witchcraft: Twelve Paths of Power, Trance & Gnosis.* Copper Cauldron Publishing, 2012.

—. *The Inner Temple of Witchcraft.* Llewellyn, 2021.

Pennell, Elizabeth Robins. *Charles Godfrey Leland: A Biography.* Houghton Mifflin, 1906.

Pepper, Elizabeth. *Witches All: A Treasury from Past Editions of the Witches' Almanac.* Grosset & Dunlap, 1977.

Perry, Laura. *Labrys & Horns: An Introduction to Modern Minoan Paganism.* Potnia Press, 2020.

Peters, Edward and Alan Charles Kors (eds.). *Witchcraft in Europe, 400-1700: A Documentary History.* University of Pennsylvania Press, 2000.

Prabhu, Mahesh. "Understanding Deva and Devi." *Vedic Management Center,* 3 July 2023, www.vedic-management.com/understanding-deva-and-devi/. Accessed 28 Feb. 2024.

Rabinovitch, Shelley and James Lewis. *The Encyclopedia of Modern Witchcraft and Neo-Paganism.* Kensington Publishing Corporation, 2004.

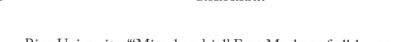

Rice University. "'Mitochondrial' Eve: Mother of all humans lived 200,000 years ago." ScienceDaily, 17 Aug. 2010. www.sciencedaily.com/releases/2010/08/100817122405.htm. Accessed 28 Feb. 2024.

Richardson, Alan and Marcus Claridge. *The Old Sod: The Odd Life and Inner Work of William G. Gray*. Skylight Press, 2011.

Robichaud, Paul. *Pan: The Great God's Modern Return*. Reaktion Books, 2023.

Roper, Lyndal. "Evil Imaginings and Fantasies: Child-Witches and the End of the Witch Craze." Past & Present. 2000 Volume 167, Issue 1, May 2000, Pages 107–139, doi:10.1093/past/167.1.107.

Rouget, Gilbert. *Music and Trance. A Theory of the Relations Between Music and Possession*. University of Chicago Press, 1985.

Ruck, Carl A. P. and Mark Alwin Hoffman. *Entheogens, Myth, and Human Consciousness*. Ronin Publishing, 2012.

Salo, Unto. *The Gundestrup Cauldron: Cultural-Historical and Social-Historical Perspectives: An Essay. Institute for the Study of Man*, 2018.

Scot, Reginald. *The Discoverie of Witchcraft*. Dover Publications, 1989.

Seymour, John. *Irish Witchcraft and Demonology*. Humphrey Milford, 1913.

Shakespeare, William. *Macbeth*. Edited by Samuel Thurber, Allyn and Bacon, 1806.

Sledge, Justin. "Witchcraft - the Witch Flight to the Sabbat - from Inquisitional Myth to Psychedelic Flying Ointment." *Esoterica*, YouTube, 22 Oct. 2021, www.youtube.com/watch?v=1CaLMJgYVuk. Accessed 28 Feb. 2024.

Sousa, Johnathan. *Reflections in Diana's Mirror*. Self-published by Rev. Jonathan Sousa, 2015.

—. *A Star From Heaven: An Introduction to Angelic Magic*. Self-published by Rev. Jonathan Sousa, 2018.

Spencer, Craig. *Aradia: A Modern Guide to Charles Godfrey Leland's Gospel of the Witches*. Llewellyn Worldwide, 2020.

Starhawk. *Dreaming the Dark: Magic, Sex, and Politics*. Beacon Press, 1997.

Stewart, Macalister et. al. *Lebor Gabála Érenn: The Book of the Taking of Ireland*. Irish Texts Society, 2009.

Stewart-Sykes, Alistair. *The Gnomai of the Council of Nicea (CC 0021): Critical Text with Translation, Introduction and Commentary*. Gorgias Press, 2015.

Strube, Julian. "The 'Baphomet' of Eliphas Lévi: Its Meaning and Historical Context." *Correspondences*, vol. 4, pp. 37–79, 2017.

Studebaker, Jeri. *Breaking the Mother Goose Code: How a Fairy-Tale Character Fooled the World for 300 Years*. Collective Ink, 2015.

Taylor, Bron. *Encyclopedia of Religion and Nature.* Bloomsbury Publishing, 2008.

Taylor-Perry, Rosemarie. *The God Who Comes Dionysian Mysteries Revisited.* Algora Pub, 2003.

The Bible. Authorized King James Version, Oxford University Press, 1998.

"The House That Jack Built." People of Goda, the Clan of Tubal Cain, June 24, 2019. clantubalcain.com/2013/06/30/the-house-that-jack-built/. Accessed 28 Feb. 2024.

"The Linear B Word A-Ke-Ro." Palaeolexicon, www.palaeolexicon.com/Word/Show/16647. Accessed 28 Feb. 2024.

The Occult Experience. Directed by Frank Heiman and Nevill Drury, Cinetel Productions and J.C. Williamson, 1985.

Thomson de Grummond, Nancy. *Etruscan Myth, Sacred History, and Legend.* University of Pennsylvania Museum of Archaeology and Anthropology, 2006.

Turner, Robert. *Elizabethan Magic.* Element Books, Ltd., 1989.

Von Spee, Friedrich, and Marcus Hellyer. *Cautio Criminalis, or a Book on Witch Trials.* University of Virginia Press, 2003.

Valiente, Doreen. *An ABC of Witchcraft: Past and Present.* Phoenix Pub, 1986.

—. *The Rebirth of Witchcraft.* Robert Hale, 1989.

—. *Witchcraft for Tomorrow.* Robert Hale, 1978.

Walter, Philippe and Jon E. Graham. *Christian Mythology: Revelations of Pagan Origins.* Inner Traditions, 2014.

Watkins, Calvert (ed.). *The American Heritage Dictionary of Indo-European Roots.* 2nd ed., Houghton Mifflin, 2000.

"The Wickerman." Directed by Robin Hardy, performances by Christopher Lee, Edward Woodward, and Britt Ekland. British Lion Films, 1973.

Wilby, Emma. *The Visions of Isobel Gowdie: Magic, Witchcraft and Dark Shamanism in Seventeenth-Century Scotland.* Sussex Academic Press, 2013.

Wilde, Oscar. *Salome.* H.M. Caldwell Co., 1907.

Worthen, Hannah. "Early Modern Witch Trials." The National Archives, The National Archives, 4 Aug. 2022, www.nationalarchives.gov.uk/education/resources/early-modern-witch-trials/. Accessed 28 Feb. 2024.

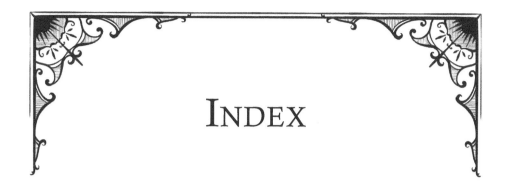

INDEX

F

G

H

I

J

K

L

M